I0453392

from GUILT *to* Grace

Hope and Healing for Christian Moms of Addicted Children

by

— Dawn R. Ward —

©2024 by Dawn R. Ward

Published by hope*books
2217 Matthews Township Pkwy
Suite D302
Matthews, NC 28105
www.hopebooks.com

hope*books is a division of hope*media
Printed in the United States of America

First Edition

First paperback edition.
Paperback ISBN: 979-8-89185-089-7
Hardcover ISBN: 979-8-89185-090-3
Ebook ISBN: 979-8-89185-091-0
Library of Congress Number: 2024941756

hope*books
hopebooks.com
Because the world needs your hope filled
words now more than ever

I dedicate this book to my Lord and Savior, Jesus Christ, who has faithfully held me every step of the way.

And to my mother, Gloria, who always believed the best in her children and inspired me to do the same.

"Let us then with confidence draw near to the throne of grace, that we may receive mercy and find grace to help in time of need."

Hebrews 4:16 ESV

Endorsements

"Dawn's writing is compelling and authentic with a refreshingly raw honesty. In *From Guilt to Grace*, she creates an intimate portrayal of the struggles related to addiction and openly shares the grace she discovered through her faith in Christ. Dawn offers a message of hope and shines the light on the power of trusting God when facing the pain and loss associated with addiction."

—**Mary Rooney Armand**, Author of *Identity, Understanding, and Accepting Who I am in Christ, Life Changing Stories*, Life Coach, and Creator of ButterflyLiving.org.

"In *From Guilt to Grace*, Dawn Ward offers hope and practical wisdom for mothers fighting their child's addiction. With empathy and biblical insights, Dawn addresses the pain and guilt, providing strategies for spiritual warfare and setting healthy boundaries. This compassionate guide empowers moms to move from guilt to grace and find peace. Don't miss this life-changing resource—grab your copy today and start your journey to healing and hope."

—**Laine Lawson Craft**, Bestselling author, Host of Warfare Parenting Podcast, and Speaker

"From Guilt to Grace takes readers on a very personal journey from the darkness of despair to the light of God's glory. This powerful book will encourage you to pray like never before, to meditate on God's word, and to seek first the One who offers the rescuing, life-giving, transforming grace we all so desperately need."

—**Kathryn Inman**, Author of *Counting Spoons*

"God has entrusted a unique and powerful message to Dawn Ward, as she writes to the hearts of Christian mothers of addicted children. If you are looking for biblical and practical advice on how to navigate the difficult and painful journey of parenting a struggling adult child, Dawn's book, *From Guilt to Grace: Hope and Healing for Christian Moms of Addicted Children,* will guide you on your path to freedom. After watching Dawn navigate others through guilt and into grace for years, I am thrilled to see individuals able to benefit from all she offers in this beautiful and powerful book."

—**Niccie Kliegl**, CEO of Fulfill Your Legacy, 5-Time Best-Seller and Life & Business Coach

"Sharing our struggle with our loved one's addiction for the sake of fellow sufferers requires bravery. Dawn blazed a trail and generously held a lantern, inviting other mamas to follow her as she followed Christ from guilt to the broad places of His grace!"

—**Ashley Moore**, Host of *Be the Two* Podcast

"As a pastor who has worked with addicts, it has been a great pleasure to connect with Dawn Ward. She has a powerful ministry to moms of addicted children and does so much to strengthen, uplift, and guide them. In *From Guilt to Grace: Hope and Healing for Christian Moms of Addicted Children*, Dawn continues in her role of trustworthy guide. She vulnerably shares her own story and her knowledge of the Lord's deep concern for families struggling with addiction in their midst. It is full of spiritual wisdom and practical tips."

—**Dr. Pam Morrison**, Author of *Jesus and the Addict*

"As a pastor of a church in Las Vegas, I regularly encounter moms desperately battling the challenges of raising addicted children. For this reason, I am grateful that Dawn Ward has courageously and transparently used her journey and extensive knowledge of Scripture to provide a bright light to bring real hope and healing to hurting hearts. *From Guilt to Grace* is a guide to help moms with addicted children as well as a resource for church leaders to shepherd the flock God has entrusted to them well."

—**Derek Neider**, Lead Pastor of Awaken Las Vegas

"When my friend Dawn shared this resource with me, I was amazed and encouraged by the words and the hope that is freely flowing throughout the pages. Filled with stories, life experiences, wisdom, thought-provoking questions, and biblical guidance, I highly recommend this book to any mom who is dealing with family addiction issues. Honestly, I think it could also prove helpful to anyone who is living through the challenges of addiction. Get a copy; it's time to move from guilt to grace!"

—**Melanie Redd**, Best-selling Author of *Live in Light: 5-Minute Devotions for Teen Girls,* Speaker, Podcaster, Mentor, Wife, and Mom

"Dawn Ward has written a breakthrough resource for parents of children battling addiction. After reading it, I would say that this is a reality for everyone who loves someone going through that struggle. Dawn writes with a wisdom gleaned only from traveling through her own valleys of trouble. In this book, she freely shares the lessons she has learned along the way. There is a fear that tries to invade one's heart when your child seems unreachable, but God provides everything needed to fight for a loved one's healing. Dawn teaches proven practices such as boundaries, prayer, and trusting God while at the same time encouraging the reader that they can find a place of peace and hope in the midst of chaos. She reminds us that God watches over these wayward ones, and He remains faithful. She inspires us to hold on to Jesus, who has all of the answers we seek. This book is like an arrow shooting straight to the heart of God. It is a clarion call to the One who can do the impossible. Her words help us shift our focus from the wind and the waves to the gaze of Jesus. This book will change your mindset, your heart, and your life!"

—**Amanda Schaefer**, Author, Speaker, and Global Podcast Host of "A Cup of Gratitude"

"From Guilt to Grace offers a compelling and heartfelt exploration of a mother's journey through her son's addiction, providing solace and guidance for others facing similar challenges. Dawn skillfully intertwines her emotional narrative with insightful perspectives, offering a beacon of hope rooted in faith. This poignant book resonates with mothers who may be grappling with feelings of guilt or helplessness while witnessing their children struggle with addiction. Drawing on the wisdom in God's word, the book offers strength and comfort for those on this challenging path. Dawn's personal experiences are a powerful reminder that hope and healing are possible, even amid profound challenges. *From Guilt to Grace* emerges as a vital resource for any mother seeking guidance and support while navigating the turbulent waters of addiction within their family. Dawn's skillful writing and engaging storytelling will keep you reading from page one. This book is necessary for mothers on a similar journey, offering a glimmer of hope and a reminder that they are not alone."

—**Valerie Silveira**, Award-Winning author,
Founder of Warriors in Hope®

"My opportunity to meet Dawn came about twenty years ago as she pioneered her family's journey through the many wiles of addiction challenges. She was a typical Christian mother struggling to understand how such oppression could infiltrate her family. Determined to save herself and her loved ones, Dawn learned to lean on Jesus, the Great Physician, and the comfort and power of the Holy Spirit to carry her through. Her book "*From Guilt to Grace: Hope and Healing for Christian*

Moms of Addicted Children" gives insight to her daily challenges, the path she traveled, where she found comfort and hope, and the many victories she experienced along the way. It is not just a good read, but a powerful deliverer of hope to others still struggling." Dawn Ward is a strong and clear voice of hope for moms of addicted children.

—**Robert T. Tucker**, PhD, DBAC, LAADC, ICAADC, founder of New Life Spirit Recovery Treatment Center, Tucker Counseling Services, and author of *Christian Families in Recovery*

"Addiction is not an easy topic to cover, but Dawn does it so well. In *From Guilt to Grace*, Dawn has pulled back the covers of her life to give hope to all who live in and through the brokenness that comes with addiction. She willingly shares the difficult parts of her story to shine light on the truth of God so we can experience God's grace. This book will minister to every heart that is willing to deal honestly with the shattered pieces of their not-so-perfect lives and allow God's sweet Spirit to heal, humble, and transform them even if circumstances don't change."

—**Lea Turner**, Speaker, Coach, and Author of *The Freedom to Feel: Finding God in the Midst of Grief and Trauma*

"In *From Guilt to Grace*, Dawn touches the reader's heart, relating mom-to-mom with her personal stories of heartache and triumph. Her descriptions are raw and vulnerable, depicting how moms mirror the well-being of their children, losing themselves in the pain and trauma of a hurting child.

But rather than sitting in the guilt or shame, Dawn challenges moms to find their identity in Christ and bask in His unfailing love and grace."

—**Barb Winters**, Author of *Sexpectations: Helping the Next Generation Navigate Healthy Relationships* and Founder of Hopeful Mom

"Dawn Ward's authenticity and vulnerability will draw you in as she takes you on a healing journey from guilt to grace. Every brokenhearted mom or dad whose child struggles with an addiction or some other challenging situation needs to discover this path of transformation. I love how Dawn shares her heart, valuable lessons learned, and insightful reflection questions at the end of each chapter. If you are a hurting parent in need of help, this book can be your travel companion. You're not alone anymore. *From Guilt to Grace* offers the kind of practical and spiritual guidance I wish I'd had on my painful journey."

—**Dena Yohe**, Co-founder of Hope for Hurting Parents, Speaker, and Award-Winning Author of *You Are Not Alone: Hope for Hurting Parents of Troubled Kids*

Disclaimer

*P*lease note that I am not a licensed professional in the fields of addiction medicine or mental health counseling. This book is not intended to replace a medical diagnosis or treatment, professional mental health counseling, or spiritual guidance for your individual circumstances.

Personally, I have equipped myself to grow in wisdom, knowledge, and understanding of what the Bible teaches about addiction by studying its truths and receiving education in biblical addiction and mental health counseling and coaching from accredited programs. The purpose of this book is to minister to the hearts of hurting moms and to offer them hope and healing through faith in Jesus Christ.

*To protect the privacy of those mentioned in this book, names have been changed or certain story details excluded when necessary.

Table of Contents

Introduction

"My joy is gone; grief is upon me;
my heart is sick within me."
Jeremiah 8:18 (ESV)

*D*ear Mom,

It shouldn't be this way. No mother should have to admit that her son or daughter is addicted to drugs, alcohol, or self-harming behaviors. Your child may be struggling with mental health issues, causing them to feel the need to self-medicate. They are engaging in an unsafe lifestyle, putting themselves or others at risk. Sadly, some have turned their backs on God and their families to pursue substances and habits that promise them pleasure but, ultimately, lead to pain and suffering. What happened to the sweet babies we held in our arms not so long ago? Where have they gone?

Like you, I felt heartbroken as I watched my children abandon their dreams and aspirations to chase after a temporary high. If only I could wave a magic wand, turn back the hands of time, and start over. I would place our children on a different path, one that didn't lead to addiction, darkness, bondage, and potential death. Instead, this path would lead them to freedom, peace, and joy, one that we moms would walk upon as well.

For a few moments, let's take our eyes off our children and reflect inward. How are you holding up under the burden of stress brought on by your child's addiction? If you're like me, the toll it has taken on you is far worse than you ever could have imagined. While trying to save your child, you may have let your own health suffer. Emotionally, you're likely stressed out and feel you're headed towards a breakdown. Consider your physical health. Are you experiencing symptoms like stomach discomfort, headaches, or high blood pressure? Brain fog may be obscuring your thoughts and making it difficult to concentrate.

Sleepless nights…who needs sleep?

You're running on pure adrenaline as you try to fix this mess and get things back to normal. You've powered through this far on sheer will and determination and have the worn-out adrenals to prove it.

Perhaps your child is on the streets, and you haven't heard from them in months or even years. They are on their own path, doing their own thing, and you're home worrying and praying for their safe return. Even if they're in a good place right now, you're always on high alert, waiting for the next crisis to occur. Does any of this sound familiar?

It's likely your relationships with your family, friends, and colleagues have also suffered. Some marriages crumble under the intense stress brought on by their child's addiction. When you focus your attention on saving your wayward child, your other children may feel ignored and respond by acting out or isolating themselves. Sadly, you may be lacking the support you need from your family or close friends.

Are guilt, shame, and self-doubt your constant companions, driving wedges between you and the people who care about you? Every concerned comment, constructive criticism, or well-meaning suggestion serves only to create a deeper chasm in your already strained relationships.

The stress you're under could be negatively affecting your job performance. It's challenging to meet the demands of a career when you're fighting to keep your head in the game. Perhaps you're calling in sick or arriving late to work. It's understandable. When you can barely drag yourself out of bed in the morning, how are you supposed to focus on your work responsibilities? Even though you're trying to keep your family's issues private, your colleagues sense something is amiss. Why wouldn't they? After countless sleepless nights, there isn't enough concealer in the world to cover the dark circles under your eyes.

Next, consider your relationship with the Lord. Although you love and trust Him, your faith is being tested like never before. Prayerful moments in His presence become desperate pleas for help. "Lord, save my child! Keep him out of jail! Don't let him die!" Your relationship with Jesus may feel distant, but there is time to address that once your child is healthy, safe, and free from their self-destruction.

The scenario I just described might seem extreme to you. Perhaps addiction hasn't torn at your heart and soul to the depths it has mine. It may be early in your journey, and you're just beginning to feel the weight of the burden you're carrying. However, I suspect almost every word written resonates with your momma's heart. You know all too well the heartache that comes from watching your child destroy their own life.

While it's possible for some mothers to navigate these uncharted waters with unwavering faith and resilience, you may question if you're going to survive this storm. Unlike those who seem calm and composed amidst the chaos, you're convinced your life will always be consumed with watching, waiting, and worrying. If that's the case, I want to encourage you to keep reading.

This describes my life for many years as the mother of two sons who abused substances. I've felt intense fear, heartbreak, and guilt as I tried to help them but felt powerless to do so. Consumed with hopelessness and despair, I've wanted to give up more than once. But the Lord wouldn't let me. Through it all, He continually heard my desperate cries for help. Time and time again, He revealed His faithfulness to me. He wants to do the same for you. Why? Because He loves you and has a better plan for your life than to see it destroyed by addiction. Despite all this pain and suffering, God's plan and purpose for your life are good.

Let's pause for a second, close our eyes, and take a deep breath. Now, imagine what it would feel like to be at peace. Calm, light, rested, cared for. Feels incredible, huh? I missed that feeling. After years of living in chaos, I couldn't remember what it was like for my soul to be at rest. Honestly, I was tired of being anxious and depressed. I wanted my joy back.

Maybe you feel the same way. What if I told you that you can experience healing and peace even if your child continues to live recklessly? Would you be ready and willing to make the changes necessary to do so? Before answering, you may be wondering, "*How can I have peace in my life when my child is self-destructing?*" That's an important question I also asked as I was searching for answers. This is what I've discovered. *It begins by taking one step forward in faith and then changing our perspective.*

When we decide to no longer set our eyes solely on our painful circumstances, we can shift our gaze to the beauty surrounding us. Gratitude fills our hearts as we uncover the blessings hidden beneath years of darkness. We are refreshed and hopeful because we are no longer consumed with our child's addiction. Our hearts are steadfast and our faith strong because we live in the full assurance that God loves our children and is watching over them.

Are you ready to pursue this new life of peace even if it means you must leave the path you are on to find it? What if doing so requires you to think and respond differently than you have before? Finally, here's the tricky one. Are you ready to break free from all-consuming worry, fear, and shame even if your child isn't ready to change? As mothers, the last one is especially hard for us, isn't it?

As you prepare to embark on your journey, remember to keep your eyes on Jesus as He guides you each step of the way. Instead of leaning on your own understanding, you will learn to rely on the Holy Spirit to give you wisdom and discernment as you follow Him. Before taking this leap of faith, I want to offer you some words of encouragement.

Jesus knows you are heartbroken. He counts the pieces of your shattered heart. Not one goes unnoticed. He understands that chasing after your wayward child has left you feeling lost and alone. I get it. So many times, I lost my way while fighting to save my loved ones. Thankfully, the Lord was always there to guide me back in the right direction. Despite having much to learn, I am getting better at asking Him for guidance before straying too far off course.

I have also decided that my relationship with Jesus is far too precious to be sacrificed on the altar of my addicted and self-destructing child. This may sound harsh to you; however, that is not my intent. I have learned we can love and support our children, but not to the detriment of our relationship with Jesus, the rest of our family, our friends, our communities, or even our personal health and sanity. It is possible to have balance in our lives and relationships, even when our family members are in turmoil.

As you read my story, marked by small successes and frequent setbacks, I ask humbly for your grace. Like many of you, I knocked on almost every door out there in my quest to save my children. Through it all, I made more mistakes than I care to admit. I've had to face my own selfish motives, as though fixing my children would somehow fix me. In doing so, I learned to acknowledge my weaknesses, brokenness, sin, and shame. I've also discovered the power of surrendering my pain to Jesus, who is healing and restoring me.

This journey I have been on and am still on has forever transformed me, mostly for the better. While walking this path with Jesus, He revealed to me His tender mercies and loving kindness. Gratefully, He has transformed me from a guilt-ridden mom into a grace-filled daughter of the King.

When the Holy Spirit first prompted me to write this book, I questioned my ability to offer guidance to other mothers going through similar trials with their children. Jesus reminded me that it is He who qualifies me, not only to share our family's story, but to guide you on your journey as well. Although I'm not licensed as an addiction counselor, I have extensive personal experience living and caring for family members who have battled addiction. The Lord taught me countless lessons as we traveled this road together. He then equipped me to share His message of hope and healing with you.

Throughout the years, I've studied under biblical teachers who specialize in addiction, mental health, and trauma. I've also been privileged to minister to other mothers facing similar hardships. I appreciate their willingness to share their stories courageously with me. I pray my insights will renew your hope, refresh your soul, and strengthen your faith.

As I sat with pen in hand, resisting the call to share our family's story, but knowing the Holy Spirit prompted me to write it, I couldn't help but wrestle with the demons of transparency and vulnerability. Would I say too much? Would my well-intentioned words expose our nakedness and risk hurting my family? Perhaps you will sense the inward grappling with my conscience as I penned their names, only to delete them for vague descriptions like "our son" or "his brother." Still, sometimes revealing their names brought clarity to their stories.

The same held true with "sharing" versus "over-sharing" the details of our personal lives. It's almost as though you were standing over my shoulder whispering in my ear, "It's okay to leave that part out, my sister. I know your heart. Those words are best left unwritten. It's time to put it to rest and have a good cry." Thank you for your patience with me as I scribbled, erased, re-wrote, and dumped my words into the trash, only to panic and pull them back out for fear they would be lost forever. The space between faithful obedience and fearful disobedience is narrower than one might imagine.

I have learned many lessons on this journey. One of the most life-changing is that I don't need to have all the answers because Jesus does. He has blessed us with His Word to teach us and His Spirit to guide us. The Bible has much to say about addiction. The Lord promises to lead us if we will follow Him. I learned we can trust Him to do the impossible because He is able to do more than we can ever imagine. We can be hopeful in the most hopeless of circumstances because Jesus is with us.

Are you ready to live a guilt-free, grace-filled life? I hope so! I have personally experienced God's grace as He freed me from guilt and shame. He can do the same for you. The path you will walk upon won't be easy or pain-free, but if you stay on it, the transformation you will experience will be life-changing.

I pray you are feeling up to the challenge and are eager to step onto this road of renewal. If your answer is "Yes," then let the journey from guilt to grace begin. Remember, you are not walking it alone. Jesus will be with you every step of the way.

The transformed life you desire awaits, because with God all things are possible.

"But Jesus looked at them and said, 'With man this is impossible, but with God all things are possible.'" (Matthew 19:26 ESV)

Reflection Questions

1. Are you suffering because of your child's addiction? What are you hoping to receive by reading this book?

2. As you reflect on the thoughts and questions in the introduction, are you ready to begin your transformational journey, even if it is challenging and painful? Who or what is motivating you to seek this transformation in your life?

3. Do you ask questions that are hard or impossible to answer, such as, "Why did this happen to my child?" How does this affect your faith?

4. Are you willing to lay aside any preconceived beliefs about your child's addiction and your part in it to examine what the Bible says about these life-controlling behaviors? Why or why not?

PART ONE

Why Me? Why Us?

CHAPTER 1

Our Story

"Train up a child in the way he should go; even when
he is old he will not depart from it."
Proverbs 22:6 (ESV)

THE CALL

*A*n unexpected ringing of my cell phone in the middle
of the night interrupted the silence, waking us from
a dead sleep. Startled, I jumped out of bed as I noticed an
all-too-familiar sick feeling forming in the pit of my stomach. Rubbing my eyes, I squinted to read the caller I.D. "Kern
County" appeared on the screen. With a faint hope it was the
wrong number, I handed my phone to my husband, Steve.
Reluctantly, he answered, "Hello," only to be greeted with a
recorded message on the other end of the line.

"Please hold while I connect you to an inmate at the Kern County Jail. If you wish to accept this call, please stay on the line. If you do not wish to continue, please disconnect at this time. At the end of the call, you will receive a prompt to make payment arrangements for future calls from this inmate."

"Should I accept it?" Steve asked nervously. We both knew what the call meant. Kyle had been arrested again. What could have happened? We spoke with him only four or five hours earlier. He should have been home by now. We also knew he had Steve's truck. None of this was adding up to anything good.

"I guess we have no choice," I whispered through gritted teeth. I wasn't ready to go down this road again. Yet here we were. After placing the phone on speaker, Steve pressed "one" to accept the call. To both our relief and dismay, we heard the desperate cry of our firstborn pleading with us, "Dad, it's not my fault. Can you please come and get me?"

Car accidents and subsequent arrests had become our new normal, as had the calls from the jails begging us to bail him out. It was never his fault, always an innocent accident, and certainly not related to driving while under the influence. No matter how many times we had been down this road before, it never got easier. It was far from normal, but like it or not, we came to realize it was normal for us. Another family vehicle was destroyed. Our son was in custody, out of state this time. Thank God, nobody got hurt. The reality hit me like a sucker punch to the gut. Kyle was using drugs again.

I would like to believe I am a pro at this by now, that I have mastered the art of not panicking every time the phone rings or we receive an unexpected text in the middle of the night. After all, our family's story began several years earlier when our younger son's friends introduced him to drugs in high school. Actually, my journey with addiction began as a child growing up in a home where my father abused alcohol. As far back as I can remember, my father's drinking was a part of our lives. By the time I moved out at the ripe old age of eighteen, I was burned out and fed up with the whole thing. I guess I thought if I could escape addiction's toxicity and make a new life for myself, it would not follow me.

Once I married and had children of my own, like every mom, I wanted the best for them. I prayed they would be healthy and happy and that their lives would be as pain free as possible. Naively, I believed I could protect them from the evils of the world by teaching them about Jesus, saturating them in prayer, attending church as a family, sending them to Christian school, and carefully vetting the kids we allowed them to befriend. Being cautiously optimistic, I convinced myself that if I taught them to follow the rules and stay between the lines, they would avoid the dangers of the world. They wouldn't fall prey to the enemy's schemes and lies. Instead, they would grow up to love and serve God, have successful careers, marry Christian spouses, and give me lots of sweet grandbabies to spoil. If only it were that easy.

FAIRYTALE OR SHATTERED DREAMS?

Welcome to Fantasy Land, or at least, my idea of it. Doesn't every girl dream of being swept away by Prince Charming on a majestic white horse to his enchanting palace atop a hill, safe from any harm? There, she will live happily ever after. While I loved to play make-believe and imagined myself as a beautiful princess, my childhood was far from a Cinderella story. Like most children, it was a blend of happiness, pain, and sorrow. Before long, I would be exchanging fairy tales for life in the real world.

I was born in a small town in South Dakota, surrounded by corn crops and cattle. By my first birthday, my family had relocated to the bright lights of "Sin City" because my dad went to work for the local fire department. My sister was born two years after me, with my brother following five years later. During our early childhood, Mom stayed at home to take care of us. In my eyes, we were an ordinary family, like everyone else.

My father's excessive drinking was always part of our lives. Alcohol consumption was as normal for him as drinking from the garden hose was for us kids. Dad was a firefighter, as were two of his brothers, so drinking beer went with the territory. While my uncles also drank excessively, they were always fun to be around. Unlike them, when my dad drank too much, he became angry and verbally abusive. While my father never gave me more than a well-deserved swat, the sound of his deep, boisterous voice when he was drunk terrified me. I learned early on to retreat to my bedroom or go outside to play when he came home intoxicated.

Our family was not in the habit of attending church, but my mom would take us to our neighborhood Lutheran church during the holidays. It was there, at the tender age of four or five, I felt the first touch of God's love. I remember when Jesus reached down to me. It was as though I could almost feel Him pulling me close. He knew this fragile little girl was about to experience brokenness.

"Take my hand, Dawn. Never let it go. You will need Me to get through this life." Although I had never heard Him speak to me before, I somehow recognized His voice, and I knew I could trust Him. With childlike innocence, I obeyed Him and grasped His hand. That day, He gave me the gift of faith, a gift I would learn to appreciate more as I grew older.

I am grateful that Jesus never released his hold on me. He has been with me even when I've made poor choices or wandered away from Him. He held me close when the neighbor man my parents trusted to be alone with me turned out to be untrustworthy. Jesus was there when shame imprinted itself into my identity.

Thankfully, I've never let go of His hand either. I am awed by His grace towards me and His power that strengthens me when my faith is weak. His constant presence has comforted me during moments of brokenness and despair. No matter the calm or the chaos, we are in this together.

Growing up, I craved stability in my life, but for the most part, it was anything but drama-free. I was always uncomfortable with the chaos alcoholism brought into our family. One day, Dad would come home "normal" and in a good mood. The next day, he would stay out drinking and not arrive home until after midnight. Oblivious to the late hour and that we needed to arise early for school, he often woke us up, despite our mother's pleas to let us rest. Although we tried to pretend to be asleep, Dad was persistent. If my father was up, the entire house was up.

Dad was and still is a loving father, but he also has experienced hurt and brokenness. Alcohol was his escape from the rejection he felt as his father drove off in their only car, abandoning his family and leaving a confused boy staring at its taillights. As a child, I always empathized with my dad, but this also meant I carried the burden of responsibility for his happiness (and sobriety). I convinced myself that if I could keep the peace in our home by being well-behaved, my father wouldn't drink as much.

To do so, I developed coping mechanisms that helped me feel secure. I tried to foresee and prevent chaos by being hypervigilant and controlling my environment. If there was a problem, it was my job to solve it, or so I thought. I was overly opinionated and took personal responsibility for everything and everyone, which meant I was basically a bossy brat.

By age five, I was the Norma Rae of the neighborhood. One to always defend the underdog, I was quick to jump into a quarrel and take matters into my own hands. After witnessing my father in altercations with my mother or other people multiple times, I learned that giving up was not an option. If there was a fight to be had, I was in it to win it. That's exactly what happened when my childhood best friend ran into trouble on the playground. Observing the class bully throwing sand in her face and yanking her hair, I jumped off the monkey bars and ran to her rescue. Without hesitation, I punched him in the nose and shouted, "Leave my friend alone, you big bully!" It never crossed my mind that defending my friend might be wrong—at least, not until the playground attendant reprimanded me and sent me to the principal's office. As the years went on, I continued to carry this overwhelming sense of responsibility for others' safety into adulthood.

In response to childhood trauma, we each develop strategies to manage stressful situations. These skills help us cope with the high levels of fear, pain, and anxiety we are enduring. When substance or behavioral addiction is present in a family, each member has their own way of dealing with the chaos it causes. For me, I believed my dad when he said it was his family's fault he drank. I now realize that was not the case, but as a child, I played the role of family peacekeeper and did my best to ensure the house was in order. To this day, I can still remember the anxiety I felt as one of my parents walked through the door and gave me a dissatisfied look. I just wanted to make them happy, so we could be a "normal" family like those whose dads didn't drink and moms weren't miserable. Before long, the fear of their disapproval took over my every action and decision. Without my awareness, perfectionism and people-pleasing cut through my soul and wove themselves into the fabric of my DNA.

When I was about ten years old, my parents purchased a small business that supplied keg beer to their customers' homes, picnics, and parties. Mom ran the family business while Dad worked at the fire department. Most days, she would leave early for work and was gone for many hours. By the time I was twelve, my parents gave me the responsibility of looking after my siblings and maintaining the house after school and on weekends. As they grew older, so did their resentment towards me for always bossing them around. After all, my sister was only two years younger than me and certainly didn't need me telling her what to do. Jamie was both beautiful and charming. She was a classic middle child, always the life of the party and had our father wrapped around her finger. My little brother, Travis, was the baby of the family and the apple of his father's eye. Because I was his big "Sissy," I catered to his every need. We all loved him to pieces and spoiled him rotten. As siblings, we were and still are very close to each other. Sadly, because of the chaos in our home, my brother and sister both turned to food for comfort. I stuck with controlling, rescuing, and fixing.

Any signs of family unrest triggered "Little Miss Fix-It" to jump into action. I was skilled at the arts of negotiation and diversion, both tactics that could draw my parents' attention away from their current quarrel and onto me for a while. I was happy to shift their attention my way if it meant they would stop yelling at each other. Sadly, my best efforts weren't good enough. After seventeen years of marriage, my parents divorced. The trauma we endured as children because of our broken home was immeasurable. Thankfully, my parents worked hard to co-parent and eventually became lifelong friends after years of healing.

NO PICKET FENCES

Things weren't all bad growing up. When I was 16, I met the boy next door, Steve, and we fell in love. Not long after my parents divorced and my father remarried, I married my knight in shining armor, just three weeks after my eighteenth birthday. However, instead of riding a white horse, he drove a beige Dodge Dart. How's that for romantic? Unlike my family, his upbringing looked like it was straight out of a "Leave it to Beaver" episode. His parents treated one another respectfully and modeled it in front of their kids. As a result, Steve is calm and well-balanced, the yin to my yang.

You would think by the time our first child, Kyle, came along seven years later, some of his yin would have rubbed off on me. Instead, I was a nervous mother, and he was a colicky baby. I came to accept that a perfect family, living in a charming house that's surrounded by a white picket fence, doesn't exist in the real world. Life turned out to be hard and far from a fairy tale. With severe postpartum depression and a colicky baby, I was a hot mess of a mom to my firstborn. It was nine long months before I felt like myself again. It took about that long for my son to stop being fussy and start sleeping through the night. It was then I finally felt the joy of motherhood for the first time.

Kyle was a sweet baby, but he was also rambunctious and full of energy. By the time he was one and a half years old, we realized it would be good for him to have a sibling. I got pregnant right away and gave birth to his brother, Matthew, when Kyle was two and a half years old. They were fun, energetic, and adventurous little boys. Together, they were quite a handful. I likened them to a Tasmanian Devil setting off a bomb in the house. Left to their own devices, someone was going to get hurt or something destroyed. They were a handful, but also lots of fun.

Next came their little sister, Jadyn, trailing three years behind her older brother. She was the polar opposite of her brothers, always content and serene. My friends nicknamed her "Angel Baby" because she never made a peep. She was the sweetness to the saltiness of her two brothers. Together, they were a perfect fit. With each subsequent birth, I gained confidence in my skills as a mother. Still, I remained an insecure woman deep down inside. It was hard to trust my gut because the voice in my head always demanded perfectionism as a Christian, a wife, and a mother.

My insecure nature led me to compare myself to other mothers. They actually seemed to "enjoy" being moms and parented with confidence and ease. Their zeal for motherhood made me feel like something was seriously wrong with my head. Why couldn't I just loosen up a bit and enjoy being a mom? Instead, a dark cloud hung over me, making me doubt almost every decision I made. Gratefully, in the middle of my desperate prayers, a sea of tears, and an entire box of tissues, Jesus reminded me I was not doing this alone. I had Steve, an amazing father, who supported me in my role as their mom. I had a supportive family close by to help me. Best of all, the Lord was with me, holding my hand and guiding me in the uncharted waters of motherhood.

"When you pass through the waters, I will be with you; and when you pass through the rivers, they will not sweep over you." (Isaiah 43:2a NIV)

As I grew more experienced in the fine art of mothering, there were still times I felt intimidated by other moms who convinced me I should raise my kids like they did. But for the most part, I was growing in confidence and felt like I was doing a pretty good job raising our kids. Sadly, the day addiction knocked at our door, I was forced to question everything I knew and believed about parenting.

Reflection Questions

1. Describe yourself as a woman prior to becoming a mom. How did becoming a mother affirm or change how you saw yourself?

2. How did you first discover that your son or daughter was struggling with addiction or other life-destructive behaviors?

3. Describe how you felt as you learned what they were going through.

4. Were your previous life experiences helpful or hurtful in preparing you to face your child's battle with addiction? Explain.

CHAPTER 2

Our Broken Pieces

"He heals the brokenhearted and binds
up their wounds."
Psalm 147:3 (ESV)

ACHY-BREAKY HEARTS

"*O*ur son is using drugs," Steve spoke the words calmly, as though he was talking about someone else, not our son. I mean, we were the classic "All American" family. We loved our kids and were actively involved in their lives. We did all the things parents do to encourage their children's success and keep them out of trouble. We expected good grades, as well as their participation in church, sports, and extracurricular activities.

Our middle child, Matthew, was smart and talented. He was a senior in high school and planned to attend college after graduation. He had everything he needed for success in life, so why was he experimenting with drugs in the first place? We warned our children of the dangers of substances and how they could ruin their lives. Despite our warnings, he succumbed to peer pressure. Why didn't he listen to us? Our questions far outnumbered the answers, as we fought to make sense of the news we just received.

While I suspected something was up with our son, in my wildest dreams or worst nightmares, I never imagined it was this. Over the last few months, I had noticed a steady decline in his grades and appearance. He had started breaking curfew, and I even caught him smoking cigarettes, something I would not tolerate. But drugs? They weren't even on my radar.

To our relief, Matthew knew that if he continued on his current path, the hopes and dreams he had for his life would never come to fruition. That's when he came to us and asked for help. Recognizing his inability to "just say no," he knew this was a problem he should not try to tackle on his own. He needed our help and support. As we sat down to discuss his options, I was impressed to find that he had already researched the resources in our area and was eager to get started.

Because this was new to us, we were in a state of shock. We didn't share our dilemma with our family or friends. Maybe if we didn't talk about it, it wouldn't be real. Denial is a normal response for families who just learned about their child's substance abuse. Denial can manifest in ways other than pretending everything is alright. We can be in denial when we mistakenly believe we are handling our circumstances better than we actually are.

Steve internalized his feelings. He coped with the news by downplaying it and convincing himself it was an easy fix. "Let's get him cleaned up and back to school as soon as possible. He has learned his lesson. He won't make the same mistake twice."

My denial took on another form. Rather than downplaying the seriousness of our situation, I panicked and bought into the belief that once someone started using drugs, they could never truly break free. I lacked faith in the power of God to deliver our son and bring our family through this ordeal. I felt alone and abandoned by Him. While I knew in my heart that this wasn't true, everything in me shouted, "You got yourselves into this mess! You've got to get yourselves out of it."

Immediately, I switched into Super-Mom mode and put all my efforts into fixing the problem. By doing so, I could avoid facing my own brokenness and lack of faith. Besides, my spiritual condition was the least of my concerns at the moment. I was determined my son would not end up another statistic and did everything within my power to make sure of it.

Although we may never understand why our son got involved with substance use, we admire his courage in seeking help. Our boy became a man when, as a teenager, he decided drugs would not have control over his life and entered an outpatient program. We were cautiously optimistic and hopeful that because we had caught this early, we would soon have our son back as good as new. Still, letting go and trusting his care to the professionals was one of the hardest things I've ever had to do as a mother.

Once the initial shock wore off, our faith grew stronger. Sure, we had read the statistics and heard the negative reports. But, as people of faith, we believed, and still believe to this day, that we serve a God who is bigger than anything the devil can throw at us, and that includes addiction to substances or life-destructive behaviors.

Matthew's journey was not without its challenges. Like other kids his age, he wanted to hang out with the same friends he got in trouble with before. He had to realize that if he didn't want to end up back where he had started, he would need to avoid them and find a new group of friends. This meant eventually moving out of state after graduating from high school to make a fresh start. Because he was young and sought help early on, he was quick to turn his life around. He was determined to conquer his problem, and he succeeded. Jesus completely transformed his heart and life with the help of Christian counselors and a supportive community.

Matthew's compassion for individuals dealing with substance use disorders or mental health challenges led him to go to school to become a mental health counselor. After a few years, he opted to go to college and successfully earned his Master's Degree. He now has a professional career and is married to a lovely and supportive wife. He is a constant reminder to me of the faithfulness of God to restore the lives of his struggling children.

As a family, it took several years to heal and feel somewhat "normal" again. Little did we know our journey was about to take yet another unexpected turn. I mean, lightning couldn't possibly strike twice, could it? No longer reeling from the devastation caused by the previous storm we weathered, we settled back into our daily routine. But things are not always as they seem. Once again, our family was about to face another run-in with drugs. This time it was my oldest son who fell victim to their trap.

From infancy, digestive issues have plagued Kyle. Without a definitive diagnosis, the pain continued to worsen until finally, in his mid-twenties, he received the news that he had a congenital birth defect requiring surgery. The doctors, seeking to relieve his post-surgical pain, prescribed him strong narcotics. The medications also provided a break from the constant anxiety he experienced since childhood. Sadly, our recent college graduate, ready to take the world by storm, was now addicted to opiates and anti-anxiety medications.

Just like before, I rushed into fix-it mode. Certainly, the same approach that helped his brother would work for him, but this did not prove to be the case. First, Kyle would not ask for or receive help. He was no longer living at home, so maybe he thought he could handle it on his own. Because of his initial refusal to accept and face his problem, his journey took him longer, with more serious consequences, than those experienced by his brother.

Legal problems, car accidents, jail time, mental health crises, disastrous relationships, and family dissension took their toll on all of us. Plus, we were still reeling from our first go-round with a child using drugs. It was at this point I realized we never really healed. We were merely surviving. Like a priceless porcelain vase, shattered into hundreds of shards and glued back together with school paste, we were fragile. A mixture of naivety, denial, and fake optimism were all that held together the pieces of our broken family.

THE FIXER-UPPER MOM

With each passing crisis, I became more desperate. My prayers, no longer faith-filled, became more like pleading with God to save my child. The longer our battle raged, the more fragile my faith became. Many times, I felt like giving up. The book of James tells us to rejoice in our trials because they cultivate perseverance in us, but I was anything but joyful. Instead, I found living in a perpetual state of "fight or flight" was just plain exhausting.

An overwhelming sense of guilt held me hostage. I was Kyle's mother. Why couldn't I save him? Shame was my constant companion, causing me to isolate and pull away from the close relationships that should have brought me comfort and support. Even when he was doing well, or at least staying out of trouble, I was always in a state of "high alert." Fear held its grip tightly around my neck. Satan was not only winning the battle for my son's life, but mine as well. Addiction was his perfect weapon of mass destruction.

The enemy, with his insatiable appetite, sought to not only destroy our children's lives but also those of the entire family. While I was focusing on saving my son, Steve became his next target. Because of back injuries he sustained in a major car accident and the multiple surgeries that followed, Steve became dependent on pain medication, a problem he kept hidden from me for years. How could I have been so blind as not to see it? While we were both battling for the lives of our children, he was also suffering. I needed him to co-parent with me through this journey. Instead, I felt all alone.

I will share more of Steve's redemptive story as we go on, but for now, remember we all have blind spots, those areas we cannot or will not see. So, while I was obsessing over my son, the news of Steve's substance abuse completely blindsided me from the opposite direction. That is what denial looks like. It's not necessarily a character flaw or pride that keeps us from seeing the situation clearly. We desire to know the truth, and though it is right in front of us, it is still like a big pink elephant in the room, obvious to everyone but us.

Denial was no longer an option. Addiction had enslaved our family in one form or another. For me, my drug of choice is control. I feed it by trying to fix everyone else. If something breaks, it needs to be fixed…right now. I get fixated on fixing everything from broken objects to broken people. I can be deeply empathetic towards others who are hurting and take matters into my own hands to expedite a solution.

But God is not like that. He does not rush in right away and set everything back in its place. He understands that our healing and transformation take time. Like that shattered vase, our brokenness is never a simple, cheap, or quick fix.

Surrendering my family to Jesus and trusting Him to take care of them has never been easy. I would rather swoop in and get to work than be stuck in a holding pattern of waiting and watching. After all, fixing comes naturally to me. My faith feels stronger and more authentic when it is actively involved in doing something that at least appears productive. Waiting doesn't feel like an exercise of my faith. It feels like abandonment. It feels like I'm smashing that cherished vase on the ground all over again, only to watch its pieces turn to dust beneath my feet. Still, God would not settle for my meddling in His work or plan. Faith required that I let go of the things I could not control, including my loved ones' choices.

Through this trial, I have discovered that I was in a prison of my own. Not one made with human hands, but one made with the bars of false beliefs and unrealistic expectations I had placed on myself and our family. Perfectionism, people-pleasing, shame, fear, controlling, rescuing, and enabling had all enslaved me.

If I wanted God to transform my troubled son, I was going to need to take a hands-off approach. But first, the Lord would have to pry him out of my cold, dead hands. I am not kidding. One day, in his wisdom, Steve spoke these words to me.

"You're going to worry yourself to death."

"I know. You're right," I sighed heavily. "You have my permission to write those words on my tombstone, 'She worried herself to death.'"

Just then, I had an "Aha" moment. What had become of me? What about that little girl who vowed to never let go of Jesus' hand as he spoke to her so many years before?

Shivers ran down my spine as I heard the voice of the Lord speak to me again, *"No, Dawn. I want it to read, 'She trusted God.'"*

From that day forward, I have fought desperately to put my relationship with Jesus first, no matter the cost. Despite a trial so big it brought everything I believed into question, I still hold on to that little mustard seed of faith God planted in my heart when I first followed Him as a child. And when I am tempted to give up and run to a deserted island, I remember the vow I made to never let go of His hand. Then I squeeze it a bit tighter.

RESTORER OF THE BROKEN

After all these years of motherhood, I am still willing to do almost anything to protect my children from pain and suffering. However, I've finally accepted that brokenness is a part of life. Individuals break. Families break. Hearts break. Jesus has taught me that healing from our brokenness is a restorative process. He doesn't use temporary repairs to mend intensely damaged souls. Restoring us to our previous condition is not God's goal for our lives. His plan is to complete the work He began in us. True transformation is only possible when our Great Physician reveals and heals our deeply buried wounds.

I'm far from being perfect, but thankfully, I'm on the mend. Because I will always be a work in progress, I'm trying to be more patient with the process. No longer the "Fixer-Upper Mom," I'm learning to focus on the transformation God is doing in my life instead of obsessing over my kids. Although tempted, I now resist the urge to force my agenda on them. Instead, I strive to trust in the Lord's infinite wisdom and timing.

We may not always receive immediate answers to our prayers or the questions we have about our child's addiction, mental health issues, or life-destructive behaviors. If I had my way, Kyle would be free from the struggles he continues to face as he fights to rebuild his life. I would give him a pass from all his pain and turmoil. Instead, God continually reminds me that none of His children are beyond repair. He is the Healer of the broken and is working to restore each member of our family. My role is to love, encourage, and pray for them.

At this point you might be thinking, *"That's great for you, but what about me? What about my kid? I thought this was going to be a book about getting help for my child."* Well, it is—sort of—but please hear me out first.

As mothers of addicted children, we've neglected ourselves and failed to recognize our own brokenness. While experiencing the pain, shame, and guilt of parenting hurting children, we didn't realize that we also needed healing. It is tempting to believe that if our children are healthy, happy, and whole, we will be just fine. *"No need to look any closer, Lord! I am A-Okay!"* If only that were the case, but truthfully, if we slow down long enough to remove our Super-Mom capes, we might find out we need to be rescued as well.

In the upcoming chapters, I will reveal the valuable lessons I learned while dealing with addiction in our family. We will explore biblical truths and insights to help equip you to stay strong in your faith while facing your child's battle with substances or life-destructive behaviors. But first, I would like you to do a quick mindfulness exercise with me.

If you can, take a few moments to find a quiet place to sit and reflect. Remember the shattered porcelain vase I wrote about earlier? Close your eyes and picture that vase crushed into thousands of fragments that sift through your fingers like sand. Those fragments represent your broken heart. Helplessly, you try to sweep them up, only to have them slip through your fingers again. Like that priceless vase shattered into pieces, you're certain your heart is broken beyond repair. That's what it feels like to be the mother of a son or daughter whose life is consumed by addiction. The pain is almost unbearable.

Keeping your eyes closed, allow yourself to grieve for your child, for your family, and for yourself. Mourn the lost hopes and dreams you once had for your child. Take time to process the pain of losing the relationship you once shared with them. Weep for the days when you could answer the phone without feeling your heart race. Allow yourself to grieve what once was. Now, open your fingers and let go of any remaining pieces you are holding onto. That's right. Just let them go. Let it all go.

Before opening your eyes, ask Jesus to reveal Himself to you in your brokenness. See, He is right there with you, gathering up each speck of dust as it falls. Not one slips away unnoticed. His nearness is beautifully conveyed in these verses.

"Are not two sparrows sold for a penny? And not one of them will fall to the ground apart from your Father. But even the hairs of your head are all numbered. Fear not, therefore; you are of more value than many sparrows." (Matthew 10:29-31 ESV)

This is how precious you and your child are to our Lord. As you release the shattered pieces of your life, He will gently pick them up and lovingly restore you to wholeness. As you proceed on this transformative journey, I encourage you to embrace Jesus and hold on tightly to His hand. Like me, you're going to need Him to get through this life.

Reflection Questions

1. Do you feel responsible or blame yourself for your child's drug use? Why or why not?

2. Do you ever find yourself in denial about your child's addiction? How has denial played out in your life?

3. Are you feeling broken because of this ongoing battle? Explain why you feel this way.

4. Are you ready to hand over the pieces of your broken heart and life to Jesus? If so, take a few moments to say a prayer of surrender now.

CHAPTER 3

Mistaken Identity

"For if anyone is a hearer of the word and not a doer,
he is like a man who looks intently at his natural face
in a mirror. For he looks at himself and goes away
and at once forgets what he was like."
James 1:23-24 (ESV)

LOSING ME

Losing myself began gradually, dating back to my child-hood. In those days, children were to be seen and not heard. There was no "me" in the equation. Other people whose opinions mattered more, like my parents and teachers, decided what I liked to do and what I would become when I grew up. It's natural for our loved ones, who care for us and are responsible for our welfare, to have their own opinions about what's best for us. Their guidance is priceless as we make decisions that will shape the course of our lives. But when their voices grow louder and their opinions overshadow the still-small voice of the Holy Spirit, we will struggle to comprehend God's will and purpose for our lives. Ultimately, we will lose sight of the unique person He created us to be.

Like many little girls who dreamed of growing up to become figure skaters or ballerinas, my dreams were crushed when my parents told me I had two left feet and no rhythm. My aspirations of becoming a famous writer ended when I learned that writing books wasn't financially rewarding and could only be a hobby. Ultimately, I did the responsible thing. I honed my secretarial skills and went to work for our local utility company as an administrative assistant. Although I was proficient at the job, I loathed it.

This was just one of many times that I ignored the Lord's voice in favor of doing what others believed was best for me. All too often, I did the "right thing" instead of asking Him the right questions. Rather than seeking the Lord's guidance, I presumed I understood what He wanted for my life. Sometimes, this led to decisions I later regretted.

When Steve and I started a family of our own, I loved being able to stay home with them for several years. Eventually, when he became disabled because of his injuries and had to take an early retirement, I made the tough decision to return to work. I trained for a new career as a Licensed Aesthetician and re-entered the workplace about the same time our youngest entered kindergarten. I was employed in the medical field and worked with Plastic Surgeons and Dermatologists as their

Skin Care Director. I have always enjoyed working with people, so this career was a perfect fit for me.

However, working outside the home meant that I couldn't be as hands-on with my children as I once was. I had to rely on others to help me raise them. Steve and my mother-in-law kept watch over the kids after school until I got off work. The situation seemed ideal because it meant they didn't have to go to after-school childcare. Steve was a wonderful father, and we worked together well as a team. Still, I longed to be home with my children. Throughout the years, I did my best to stay involved in every aspect of their lives. But because my job was demanding and consumed my time, I often missed important events like their games and club activities. Plagued with guilt and self-doubt, I couldn't ignore the gnawing feeling I had somehow missed the mark in my role as a mother.

Once the boys were in high school and busy with their studies, jobs, and extracurricular activities, we breathed a sigh of relief. Because they had avoided getting into any serious trouble, I felt that even though I was no longer staying at home with them, I must be doing something right as their mother. When I received the shocking news that my son was using drugs, I felt like a total failure. Even though I knew any mom could have a child who gets in trouble, the news sent me on the worst guilt trip ever. Because I didn't understand that my identity is found in Jesus, not in whether I received a passing or failing score as a mother, I found myself smack dab in the middle of an identity crisis. As his mom, why didn't I see this coming? Worse yet, what had I done to deserve this?

While it broke my heart to find out my son was involved with drugs, it was nothing new. Addiction and alcoholism have been a part of many of my relationships as a daughter, wife, sister, and mother. Throughout the years, I have worn several hats to adapt to the many roles necessary to live with a person who basically controls the homeostasis of the entire family. I couldn't grasp my identity or who God created me to be because I was too busy playing the roles of parent, provider, caretaker, rescuer, enabler, first responder, peacemaker, counselor, and advocate, just to name a few.

Through all the chaos and added stress of living with addiction, I lost sight of Dawn somewhere along the way. The hobbies and relationships that once brought me joy, I now found uninteresting. Worse yet, I stopped looking at myself through the grace-filled eyes of my Savior. I could no longer see His image in me. Instead, when I looked in the mirror, a condemning glare stared back.

Right now, you might feel lost yourself. You miss the care-free, confident woman you once were. You may even long for the days when you felt "normal" like the other moms. And while there's no such thing as normal, you still long for the routine, even mundane, duties of motherhood. Boring is desirable for a mother whose son or daughter lives life on the edge. How can it be possible to worry this much?

While I love being a mom, I never thought I would find such immense worth in my role as one. When I gave birth to my first child, all my self-assurance flew right out the window. *"Was he warm enough? Was he hungry? Was he sleepy? Would I drop him on his head?"* I had plenty of experience taking care of babies, but now I had one of my own. This was a whole new ballgame. I wondered if I was the right woman for the job. Maybe God had made a mistake. It was too late to give him back. We were in this together.

As moms, it's tough to admit our weaknesses and insecurities. Our families depend on us. We can't fall apart. It is important that we keep it together for our children. We save them. They don't save us. We kiss boo-boos. We put towels on feverish heads and wrap shivering little bodies in warm blankets. When they are afraid of the dark, we chase away the Boogie-Man. Mommies do this stuff naturally. We are nurturers and healers. Moms are fearless protectors. No one messes with our kids. We are a force to be reckoned with, no matter how powerful the opposing enemy might be. We must be. Their lives are at stake, and so are our identities as their moms.

THE WOMAN IN THE MIRROR

When you look in the mirror, who do you see looking back at you? Do you look fine by all outward appearances, or have the pressures of life taken a toll on you? We each respond to stress differently. Certain factors, such as personality traits, family dynamics, physical well-being, mental health, learned behaviors, and faith influence how we react in a crisis. Some people have more stoic and reserved personalities, while others are highly emotional and volatile. One is not better than the other. It is just our make-up. Some have boundless energy, while others exhaust easily. It's wise to understand that just because our friend, Sally, is a super-mom and gets by on caffeine and three hours sleep doesn't mean we can do the same.

Doing so might land us in the hospital. The stress put on us when our children are self-destructing is intense, and if we aren't careful, our bodies will suffer under its weight. There is no way around it.

Addiction certainly took its toll on me. Although outwardly I appeared to be fine, on the inside I was falling apart. I was all tied up in knots, easily overwhelmed, and found it hard to focus. By the grace of God, I made it to work every day and could perform my job responsibilities. But addiction hijacked my mind, my peace, and my sense of purpose. It felt as though I had been taken hostage and replaced by a stranger. I had imposter syndrome, feeling like a big phony in all areas of my life. Perhaps you are feeling this way as well.

One area hardest hit was my faith. I wrestled with God, demanding answers to questions like, *"Where are You in this mess?"* I was born with an amazing resilience to withstand very difficult circumstances. My faith kept me going because I always believed things were going to get better. Addiction stole that from me. I was no longer empowered by my faith. Instead, I lived with an ongoing sense of doubt and unbelief.

I finally accepted my hopelessness when I reached the point of believing I would never be happy again unless my children were happy. They say a mother is only as happy as her most unhappy child. That was my motto, for sure. Stubbornly, I decided God could not work on me unless He first saved my son. The way I performed as his mother shaped my sense of identity and self-worth. I can trace this longing in my heart back to my childhood. My feelings of worth were based on my performance. While my dad often referred to my sister as "Miss America," he reinforced my need to perform well in school, as I was the "brains" of the family. However, while I embraced the challenges of earning good grades, I longed to be wearing the diamond tiara. Like my dad who knew his daughters were both attractive and smart, it's easy for us as parents to see our children in certain roles.

Once I had kids of my own, I still measured my self-worth based on my performance. Whether it was their public behavior, grades in school, or how they treated their friends, I saw every action and attitude on their part as a reflection of my job performance in the mothering department. When drugs entered the equation, well, that was when I knew for sure I was failing miserably. It was bad enough I allowed this to happen right under my nose. The least I should have been able to do was fix it. I lived by the mantra, "Fail your child, disappoint God. Save your child, earn God's favor."

A crushing sense of personal responsibility, shame, and guilt had stolen the truth from me, the truth that the Lord's favor is not something to be earned. Because I didn't understand His grace, I lost sight of who I was. This beloved daughter of the Most-High King forgot her identity and that He created her in His image. I was fragile, broken, and powerless to save myself. I convinced myself I would be this way forever.

It was years into our journey before I began to see myself through Christ's eyes. I didn't understand that my identity is found in Jesus, not on whether I receive a passing or failing score as a mother. I knew in my head that my child's behavior did not define my identity, but my heart was slow to follow. Something had to give if I was going to get rid of the guilt and shame I was carrying once and for all. I immersed myself in the scriptures and discovered the truth of who God says I am. When I forgot my identity, I clung to His Word and reminded myself that I am His because He loves me. I am His daughter because He redeemed me and calls me by name.

> "Fear not, for I have redeemed you; I have called you by name, you are mine." (Isaiah 43:1b ESV)

Likewise, when Jesus looks at you, He sees His daughter. He calls you by your name, not by your job title. Your worth is not based on who you are or what you do, but on "Whose" you are. And you, dear sister, are a daughter of the Creator of the Universe. There is nothing you have to do to earn God's favor. Because of His grace, you no longer have to strive to earn His acceptance. That's the beauty of grace. It's not what we do, but what God does, that restores us from our state of brokenness.

BEYOND RECOGNITION

As you look back on your life before addiction, or even motherhood, entered your world, consider who you were as a woman. How would you describe yourself and your personality? Maybe you were outgoing and confident. You may have been shy and reserved. Perhaps you were a thrill seeker and loved adventure. Or, like me, you may have preferred to play it safe.

Let's go back even further. As a teenager and young adult, what were your dreams and aspirations? Maybe your ambition was to go to college to become a teacher, an accountant, a nurse, or even a doctor. It's possible that fashion was your fancy, and you envisioned yourself as a famous clothing designer. Maybe you had your heart set on marrying and starting a family. Every little girl dreams of who she wants to be when she grows up. It's normal to change our minds as we try to figure it out. But when our dreams fail to come to fruition, it's tempting to feel like we somehow missed out on God's best for our lives, right?

From the time you were in your mother's womb, God had a plan and purpose for your life. From birth, He creatively wove together your unique character traits, talents, and abilities to equip you to fulfill your calling, including that of being a mother. But long before you were a mother, you were first a woman, wonderfully created in the image of your Creator. This truth is important to hold on to as you move forward on your transformational journey.

"So God created man in his own image, in the image of God he created him; male and female he created them." (Genesis 1:27 ESV)

When we became mothers, we did not throw our womanhood out the window. We are still women with needs. Our bodies have needs, as do our souls. There are many reasons we put our own needs on the back burner for someone else, and occasionally, it may be necessary to do so. But self-sacrifice to the detriment of our well-being is not healthy, nor does Jesus expect it of us. Look at these verses in 1 Corinthians.

"Or do you not know that your body is a temple of the Holy Spirit within you, whom you have from God? You are not your own, for you were bought with a price. So glorify God in your body." (1 Corinthians 6:19-20 ESV)

Entering the world of motherhood is a game-changer. Once we give birth to our children, their needs automatically outweigh ours. But prioritizing their needs is no excuse for neglecting ours altogether. To see if this is happening, it is helpful to examine your life before addiction rocked your world. By doing so, you'll gain insight into how it has affected your mental, emotional, physical, and spiritual health.

Consider the person you were before you had children. Next, think about the person you are today. Start by considering the impact of stress on your overall well-being. Ask the Lord to help you answer these questions as honestly as possible.

- How is your **mental** health? Are you experiencing brain fatigue or fog? Consider how stress has affected your ability to make decisions, remember daily tasks, and remain focused throughout the day.

- How is your **emotional** health? Are you handling the stress well, or are your emotions all over the place? Note if you are experiencing anxiety, depression, angry outbursts, uncontrollable crying, constant worry, or feeling overwhelmed.

- How is your **physical** health? Is your body bearing the weight of all the tension you are carrying? Consider if you have recently developed headaches, high blood pressure, heart disease, adrenal fatigue, autoimmune disorders, digestive issues, chronic pain, or other health conditions. Note if your sleeping and eating habits have changed or if you have experienced sudden fluctuations in your weight.

- How is your **spiritual** health? Do you sense God's presence in your life? Contemplate how the stress you are under has affected your faith. Take a moment to consider if you are still actively involved in spiritual disciplines such as reading the Bible, worshiping, praying, attending church, and fellowshipping with other believers.

As you reflect on your spiritual condition, allow me to ask you the most important question of all. "Do you know Jesus as your personal Lord and Savior? Have you asked Him to come into your heart, forgive your sins, and give you eternal life?" Maybe you have asked Him into your heart, but you still feel far from Him. I want to reassure you that we all sin. We all make wrong choices. We rebel against God, and we all need a Savior. The book of Romans tells us, *"for all have sinned and fall short of the glory of God" (Romans 3:23 ESV).*

Jesus came to pay the penalty for our sins. He suffered and died, and on the third day, He rose from the grave. He conquered sin and death so we can be with Him in Heaven. He did this because of His great love for us, because of His love for you.

"For God so loved the world, that he gave his only Son, that whoever believes in him should not perish but have eternal life. For God did not send his Son into the world to condemn the world, but in order that the world might be saved through him." (John 3:16-17 ESV)

Before moving forward in this book, if you would like to ask Jesus to be your Lord and Savior, please stop and pray this prayer of salvation.

Dear Jesus,
I come to You knowing I am a sinner. I repent of my sins and ask for your forgiveness. I believe You died for my sins and rose from the grave. Please come into my heart and take control of my life. I receive You as my Lord and Savior and choose to follow You from this day forward. Thank you for saving me. In Jesus' name, I pray.
Amen.

Welcome to the family of God. As you continue your transformational journey, I would like to encourage you to carry a journal with you throughout the day. Use it to pen your thoughts, prayers, and any revelations given to you by the Holy Spirit. Re-visit the questions above several times while reading this book. Ask Jesus to search your heart and reveal the areas in your life where you are struggling. We don't know ourselves the way He knows us. We can become skilled at faking fine, convincing ourselves and others that because we still have a heartbeat, we must be okay. It will take some honest reflection to understand the true condition of our hearts. We will need to do some deep soul-searching as we examine who we were before our child's addiction shattered our world, who we are now, and who God wants us to be.

For starters, that hole you most likely have in your heart and that knot in your gut may be good indicators that something is seriously broken and needs to be mended. That something is actually someone, and that someone is you—and me. Remember, we are in this together.

Begin by contemplating how your health has declined due to the intense suffering you have endured. Take a good long look at the woman in the mirror. Is she beyond recognition? If so, ask God to dig deep under the layers of self-neglect to reveal any wounded places in need of healing. Standing (or kneeling) in the middle of your crushed dreams, hopes, and expectations may seem overwhelming. It can be, and it is okay to grieve your losses. But this is also a place of new beginnings and new vision. In the middle of the rubble, God is here, and He is willing and able to restore the hearts and lives of His broken children.

Reflection Questions

1. Did you have to lay aside any of your dreams once you became a mother? Which ones?

2. After reviewing the questions in the paragraph above, in what ways has your health suffered because of your child's addiction?

3. In what ways has dealing with your child's addiction affected how you understand or view your identity?

4. How does understanding that your identity is based on "whose you are" instead of "what you do" affect how you see yourself? Does it help you have more reasonable expectations of yourself as a mother moving forward?

PART TWO

Making Sense of the Senseless

CHAPTER 4

The Heart of the Matter

"Search me O God, and know my heart! Try me and
know my thoughts! And see if there be any grievous
way in me, and lead me in the way everlasting!"
Psalm 139:23-24 (ESV)

SEARCH ME, OH GOD

In the previous chapter, we looked at how the stress caused
by our loved one's substance use affects us personally. Early in our family's journey, I had countless questions about why
my child struggled with drugs and what to do about it, so I
joined a few support groups to learn from other parents going

through similar experiences. It was eye-opening to hear the stories shared by the moms within our group and realize I was not alone in my pain. Without my saying a word, they knew by my body language I was feeling hopeless and overwhelmed. All the shame, guilt, and blame I carried into those meetings needed no explanation. I appreciated having the support of other parents who were going through a similar situation.

Although there were numerous advantages to attending these meetings, the hardest part for me was leaving with a sense of impending doom. Most of the parents shared the opinion that our children had a brain disease that could only be managed, but never cured. The old-timers quoted statistics off the top of their heads without giving a second thought to the impact on us newbies in the group. Being a facts girl, the numbers whirled in my mind like food in the garbage disposal. My brain was mush from my constant overthinking. I just couldn't shake the thought that our family would be one of those statistics.

One message repeated in each meeting I attended was called "The Three Cs."[1] While I didn't agree with everything taught in the 12-step programs, this one resonated with me because it provided three simple declarations I needed to remember regarding my child's addiction: "I didn't **cause** it. I can't **control** it. I can't **cure** it." Like music to my ears, these affirmations reassured me I was not responsible for my loved one's addiction. They also emphasized my need to be in "recovery" myself, since addiction is a "family disease." They challenged me to consider my own spiritual condition rather than focusing on saving my child. If I ever wanted to be free from constant self-blaming, fear, and anxiety, I was going to have to work on helping myself rather than waiting for him to be drug free.

If you're hearing this for the first time, you might be thinking, *"How can I work on myself when my child is in crisis?"* I agree that a child's addiction is one of the most stressful trials a parent can face, but they made a good point in those meetings. We can only control ourselves—our beliefs, choices, and behaviors. We aren't supposed to hold our children responsible for our mental, emotional, and physical well-being. Instead, we need to go deeper into the spiritual issues of our hearts. Do we trust Jesus with our lives...and with theirs?

I found this easier said than done. Desperately, I pleaded with the Lord to search my heart and show me why I was trapped in a continuous cycle of laying my prodigal at His feet, only to pick him up again. Although it's true that when our children hurt, we hurt, this was not healthy for me or my son.

I began searching for groups of Christian parents who believed Jesus could set our children free from their addictions, heal us of our brokenness, and restore our families. With much anticipation, I attended my first faith-based support group, but alas, I found it to be similar to the secular ones I attended previously. I loved that the meetings included worship, prayer, and testimonials. However, their beliefs and teachings concerning addiction were based more on the philosophies of the 12-step programs than on the truths of the Bible. Although the attendees could freely proclaim Jesus' name, their focus remained on discussing their substance use disorder or life-destructive behavior rather than on Christ's power to save, heal, and deliver. While I was grateful for their support and encouragement, I hoped to receive more from these meetings.

Allow me to explain my rationale. I realize these support programs have helped many people become and remain sober and drug-free. They have also been a tremendous source of encouragement for the families of those caught in addiction's snare. Many lives have been saved because of the support found within these communities. But I believe Jesus wants more for our loved ones than just their sobriety. He wants them to be set free in Him. As their moms, He wants us to experience that same freedom in our lives. Sadly, I was feeling anything but free. And so my search continued.

In the book of Luke, we read the following words spoken by Jesus as He started his public ministry. *"The Spirit of the Lord God is upon me, because the Lord has anointed me to proclaim good news to the poor. He has sent me to proclaim liberty to the captives and recovering of sight to the blind, to set at liberty those who are oppressed, to proclaim the year of the Lord's favor"* (Luke 4:18-19 ESV).

Jesus came to bring good news to the poor in spirit, to bind the wounds of those in despair, and to proclaim freedom to the captives. The freedom He offers us is not limited solely to deliverance from our sins. He also came to set us free from our misery, pain, and bondage. I truly believed these words and knew God wanted more for me than to drown in my sorrow, waiting for my son to be free from his addiction. But why was I so miserable? It was time for me to make a major change in my attitude and in my life. I had been self-focused for way too long. If I wanted to stay miserable, there was no better way than to wallow in self-pity. Instead, Jesus had a different plan for me. Not only did He want me to believe these words He had spoken, it was time for me to share His message of hope with others.

It was about that same time I felt the Holy Spirit nudging me to start a ministry. While in prayer, He gave me a vision of a green pasture with fat sheep grazing on its sweet grass. Shepherds were keeping watch over them and tending to their every need. It was a place where people could come for healing and restoration. I loved the idea of caring for the Lord's sheep, so I was all in except for one caveat. With no thought to the matter, the words flippantly rolled off my tongue, *"Anything but addiction, Lord."* I couldn't grasp the idea of living with the stress of addiction all day, every day, and also being responsible for a ministry aimed at supporting women devastated by it. What was Jesus up to? I was still struggling myself and felt underqualified for the job! We would shelve that idea for a while.

Fast forward to 2017. By then, I was in a much better place myself and had a desire to share what I had learned with other mothers of addicted children. Together with my friend Valerie, I co-wrote a faith-based version of her workbook, designed to aid women facing challenges due to their child's substance or behavioral addiction. We also started a Facebook group to offer the moms a supportive community. The group was thriving when I heard the Holy Spirit speak to my heart, *"Start one for Christian mothers of addicted children."* Now, I was certain I must be losing it. There was no way Facebook needed another parents' addiction support group. I knew of several good ones started by amazing women of faith who had their books and resources already in place to help their members. Valerie had tremendous resources in addition to our workbook to help moms on their journey to freedom. It made little sense to me why God was leading me to start another group on social media. I was about ready to brush off the idea and blame it on my overly active imagination when the Spirit pressed me harder. *"Do it anyway."*

Not needing to be told again, I logged on and formed the group, Christian Moms of Addicted Children, with no idea what it would look like. As I stepped out in obedience, I suddenly knew what would make us unique. Quietly, I heard the Lord speak to my heart. *"Encourage the moms, pray for their children, glorify Me."* It was then I knew I didn't need to be an expert or have all the answers. Why? Because Jesus did. I merely was called to set the stage and watch God do His work. Over the years, I have witnessed moms who came into our group weary and broken, some even suicidal, grow into women of unwavering faith. Many who were on the verge of giving up stuck with us. They are now encouraging others with the hope they found in Jesus.

Some have amazing testimonies of children set free from their bondages after many years of addiction. Others have been with us as their children have continued their cycle between sobriety and relapse. Sadly, others have watched as their children spiraled deeper into their addiction, ultimately losing their lives to it. While some of our members decided the group wasn't the right fit for them, most have been with us since the beginning. I believe this is because the group's foremost mission is to glorify Jesus as we place our children's lives in His hands.

Over time, I have come to know and respect the women in our group as they share their wisdom, compassion, and encouragement with each other. Mostly, I find our group to be a safe and judgment-free zone, one where each member can share her heart and beliefs without feeling rejection or condemnation. By attentively listening to our members as they shared their stories, I have grown significantly as a mother and woman of faith.

As I prepared to write this book, I wanted to gain insight from our members' personal experiences with addiction. I ran several polls covering various topics concerning their child's drug use and how it affected their lives. As you review the polls, check any boxes indicating your responses.

Poll #1 asked, *"In what way has your child's addiction negatively affected you?"*
With over 700 participants responding, the group's unanimous answer was:

☐ It has caused my mental health to suffer.

Other top responses included:

☐ It has negatively affected other family members.

☐ It has caused us financial problems.

☐ It has caused me physical illness because of stress.

☐ It has caused me to put my personal needs and goals on hold.

One poll result I found enlightening was that few members answered that their child's addiction had a negative effect on them spiritually.

Poll #2 asked, *"What do you want or need to better equip you to handle your child's addiction?"*

In a landslide, two answers stood out among the rest.

☐ I would like to learn how to live peacefully, even if my child never changes.

☐ I want to draw closer to the Lord and be equipped to fight addiction spiritually.

Poll #3 asked, *"If you had one book you could read this year to help in your current situation with your addicted child, what would it be?"*

The members' answers were quite revealing.

☐ I need a book that will teach me how to engage in my addicted child's life, but disengage from their negative behaviors by learning to discern God's voice and will. (41 percent offered this response.)

☐ I need a book that will show me how to draw closer to the Lord and have peace in my life regardless of how my addicted child is doing. (25 percent offered this response).

In contrast to the initial poll, which suggested that the moms' spiritual lives remained unaffected by their child's addiction, this poll yielded different results. While our moms knew they were suffering in their minds and bodies, they couldn't see how they were also hurting spiritually. Our moms were struggling with their faith. They felt unseen and unheard by God, isolated in their suffering. Sadly, most didn't realize it. As moms whose kids are in crisis, we can barely keep our heads above water, much less take a deep dive into the spiritual issues of our hearts.

Our group polls, along with continual input from our members, helped me to better understand why we, as mothers, struggle so much and hurt so deeply. We each have trauma, fears, and false beliefs we have kept buried until the stress of our child's addiction brought them to the surface all these years later. We were simply too busy trying to save our children to notice or address our own spiritual needs and longings.

We may be stressed out and worn out. We may be worrying ourselves sick. We may feel as though we are on the verge of a mental breakdown, which might very well be the case. Understandably, we are heartbroken for our children. If instead of searching within, we blame our misery solely on our children's behaviors, we may miss the opportunity for God to reveal our painful places and heal us from our deepest wounds.

Because we are spiritual beings living in physical bodies, perhaps our brokenness stems from something deeper than the stress addiction has brought into our lives. Suddenly, I realized what was missing when I attended those meetings several years earlier. The Lord revealed to me that this was a spiritual battle, and to be set free, I would need to get to the heart of the matter.

THE BLAME GAME

As I asked the Lord to search my heart and examine my thought life, I discovered the first things that had to go were finger-pointing and fault-finding. Satan is the accuser of God's children (Revelation 12:10). One of his most destructive weapons is to accuse us before our God day and night. What better way to wreak havoc on our families, communities, and world than to lure us into this same destructive behavior?

Like I mentioned before, my upbringing was chaotic. My parents were angry or frustrated much of the time. They both were in the habit of blaming either each other or the kids for their inability to cope with stressful situations. Naturally, we mirrored what we observed, so rather than admitting when we did something wrong, we got into the habit of blame-shifting. When our finger-pointing failed to reveal the kid at fault, Mom, in her frustration, would sarcastically remark, "Oh, let me guess. The ghost did it!"

The Merriam-Webster Dictionary defines the term "the blame game" as "a situation in which different individuals or groups attempt to assign blame to each other for some problem or failure."[2]

This was the story of my life. There was always someone to blame for my parents' bad moods, and it was usually one of their kids. In their defense, we could be a handful. Still, it was not our fault our father drank in excess or that our mother was miserable because of her unhealthy marriage. Sadly, in those days, instead of working on their issues and seeking professional help, it was easier to finger-point.

Likewise, we live in a society that shirks any personal responsibility. All it takes is looking around us or listening to the news to find someone blaming someone else for whatever awful thing is happening in their lives. Politicians accuse each other, world leaders point their fingers, and convicted criminals cry out, "It wasn't me! You got the wrong guy!" Blame is a game, and we play it well.

Addiction and alcoholism perpetuate a cycle of blame in our families and our society. While our country faces an addiction epidemic with hundreds overdosing and dying daily, we look for who is at fault. We blame the pharmaceutical companies, the government, or plain bad parenting for a crisis that should have been avoided. Fathers and mothers point their fingers at each other when their children go astray. More often than we care to admit, we may even blame God for not protecting our children from the evils of this world.

Because both of my sons got involved with drugs, there was no getting out of the blame game for me. Maybe if it was only one, I'd have a good excuse to pass the buck onto someone else: Peers, social media, public school, anyone but me. If only it was that simple, but my upbringing instilled in me a deeply rooted sense of self-blame. Truthfully, I did not force my children to use drugs. Nor did I abuse or traumatize them by my actions. However, I still blamed myself. For what? I am not sure exactly. I likely felt I should have had enough influence to keep them from experimenting with drugs in the first place.

Even if we do not hold ourselves responsible for our child's addiction or self-destructive behaviors, we blame ourselves for not being able to save them. "I should have used tough love." "I shouldn't have kicked him out of the house." "I should have prayed more." Our lists of "shoulds" and "should nots" grow longer every day. As all-knowing moms, we "should" be able to see into the future, foresee dangerous situations, and steer our children out of harm's way, but alas, we really are only human.

If our love was enough to save our loved ones from the evils of the world, no one would ever get sick, suffer, or die. But regardless of how close we keep them, we can't protect them entirely from physical pain, suffering, or emotional trauma. No amount of prayer can keep hardship from entering their lives. It is part of living in a fallen world.

Truthfully, another person may be responsible for the pain that led to your child's drug use. Someone may have hurt or abused your son or daughter during their childhood. They may have become dependent on pain medications following an injury or surgery. Perhaps they have undiagnosed or improperly treated mental health issues, causing them to feel the need to self-medicate. Maybe your child's friends convinced them to give drugs a try.

I looked for someone to be the fall guy but found no comfort in blaming myself or anyone else. Regardless of who or what was to blame for our child's addiction, we need to recognize that the act of blaming will keep us stuck in a place of guilt, shame, and bitterness. It is not healthy to blame ourselves, make excuses, or blame-shift. While self-deprecation or shifting blame may be understandable, it is toxic to ourselves and those we are around. Who hasn't met someone knee-deep in past regrets or resentments? When people have a victim mindset, they can be challenging to be around.

I know the feeling. Too often, my mind has been the devil's playground. Rather than holding my adult child responsible for his addiction, I kept returning to his childhood to see where I went wrong in raising him. The answers never came, and repeatedly asking the same questions kept me focused on the problem, not the solution. Seriously, how could placing blame change anything? What's done is done. It was time to move on.

As the Apostle Paul taught that finger-pointing is never the right way to handle a situation. *"You, therefore, have no excuse, you who pass judgment on someone else, for at whatever point you judge another, you are condemning yourself, because you who pass judgment do the same things" (Romans 2:1 NIV)*. To experience lasting freedom and healing, let's challenge ourselves to move beyond the blame game.

WHOSE FAULT IS IT THEN?

As mothers of hurting children, we struggle to find answers, don't we? Apart from blame-shifting, the question remains, "What caused my child's addiction?" As we explore the reasons behind our children's substance use and self-destructive behaviors, we must resist the urge to get stuck there. Theirs is a personal and complex journey, one we may never fully understand. It is an oversimplified explanation to say addiction is solely a brain disease or disorder, thus removing from the equation any responsibility on our child's part. On the other hand, blaming it on their moral failure ignores the complex physiological, mental, emotional, and spiritual factors contributing to their addiction.

Addiction specialists, scientists, researchers, and medical experts, while well-studied, fall short when they fail to consider the spiritual roots of addiction. The Bible is not silent on the matter, instead revealing within its pages the selfish desires, deep longings, and sinful nature of the human heart. Unlike other species, God created human beings with the ability to make choices; He gave us free will.

God created every person with a free will so they can choose whether to obey or disobey Him. They can choose to subdue their fleshly desires and obey the Holy Spirit, or they can ignore His promptings and rebel against God. This is a privilege given to us by our Creator and should not be taken lightly.

This is also the case for our children. They are not animals who live by primal instincts. They are human beings. Even when they're caught in their addiction's chokehold, God doesn't take away their free will. Sadly, the longer they abuse drugs or take part in life-destructive behaviors, the harder it becomes for them to exercise their freedom to choose right from wrong.

Although we pray that if and when our children cry out to Jesus for freedom, they will never return to their addiction, realistically, most will need the ongoing support of their family, friends, church, and community to gain complete victory in their lives.

Likewise, the roots of our brokenness are buried deeply, making them difficult for us or others to recognize. We may settle on the belief that if our child is whole, we will be whole as well. If we can fix them, we will no longer be broken ourselves. If only it were that simple. Truthfully, the matters of our hearts are every bit as complex as those belonging to our children. We will explore this more as we move forward on our transformational journey.

> "If our minds and hearts are not filled with God's truth, something else will take His place: cynicism, occultism, false religions and philosophies, drugs—the list is endless." ~ Billy Graham[3]

Reflection Questions

1. Have you attended family or parent support groups for education and encouragement in dealing with your child's addiction? In what ways were they helpful? Were there any times you left feeling more discouraged? Why or why not?

2. Have you engaged in the blame-game, either blaming yourself or someone else for your son or daughter's addiction? How has this affected you personally and in your relationship with others? Have you forgiven or asked them for forgiveness?

3. In what ways has your child's addiction affected your faith? Do you see areas where your faith is weak? In what way is Jesus strengthening you for this difficult journey?

4. As we close our study today, ask the Lord to reveal to you any lingering questions, doubts, or concerns that are robbing you of your peace and joy. Pray for His peace that passes all understanding to guard your heart and mind, even when you don't have all the answers.

CHAPTER 5

Sin, Soul, or Sickness

"And do not get drunk with wine, for that is
debauchery, but be filled with the Spirit."
Ephesians 5:18 (ESV)

TIME FOR "THE TALK"

When you dreamed about being a mother, I bet you never thought you were signing up for this, right? I always said I signed up for the eighteen-year plan. You know, the one where our children graduate from high school, go to college, start their careers, get married, and have 2.5 kids? Ya. That one. But things don't always go according to our plans. Honestly, even in our worst nightmares, few of us could have imagined that our children's lives would turn out like this.

Raising children who ultimately turned to substances or self-destructive behaviors to cover their pain or pursue pleasure wasn't on my radar. I imagine it wasn't on yours, either. If your child is not abusing substances, but is self-harming or has a behavioral addiction, they are still bound by something that will ultimately lead to their destruction if continued. These lessons for moms of addicted children will be enlightening to your situation as well.

Our children are hurting. We ask ourselves, "Why?" We have come to the place in this book where we need to address the reasons for their addictions and what we can do to help them. Is sin, soul (mind, will, emotions), or sickness at the root of their addiction? Is the root cause one or all three? This is a challenging topic to discuss, but together let's ask the Lord to give us open minds and hearts as we search for answers in the pages of the scriptures.

First, let's make up our minds to let go of any preconceived beliefs surrounding addiction and its origins. Disagreements over addiction's causes and cures have been around for many years. Originally, there were two fundamental theories on its cause: disease or moral failure. However, experts now believe external and internal influences such as trauma, environment, genetics, peer or social influences, mental illness, emotional issues, and brain disorders may play a role in addiction's origins. As we move through this chapter, you will find it heavily weighted with research from addiction experts, quotes from Christian scholars and teachers, and scriptures. I included this information to clarify how I reached my conclusions and to help you as you seek answers of your own. During my research, I concluded it is not unusual to find varying views and conflicting information within the addiction community itself. Here are some fascinating quotes from some articles I reviewed.

1) *"Addiction is defined as a chronic, relapsing disorder characterized by compulsive drug seeking and use despite adverse consequences. It is considered a brain disorder, because it involves functional changes to brain circuits involved in reward, stress, and self-control. Those changes may last a long time after a person has stopped taking drugs."*[4] National Institute of Drug Abuse, *Drug Use and Addiction*

2) *"Research shows that "changes to the brain do not necessarily indicate a disease process. Nor does the disease model alone seem to be an accurate depiction of the phenomenology/first-person accounts of addiction." We are left with the possibility that addiction, although a choice, is a condition where there is diminished responsibility to some extent. Taking responsibility for one's actions is a path to freedom. Freedom from guilt and shame with the learned ability to do things differently."*[5] Anjali Talcherkar, *The 5 Reasons Addicts Tend to Lie*

3) *"In the past two decades, research has increasingly supported the view that addiction is a disease of the brain. Although the brain disease model of addiction has yielded effective preventive measures, treatment interventions, and public health policies to address substance-use disorders, the underlying concept of substance abuse as a brain disease continues to be questioned, perhaps because the aberrant, impulsive, and compulsive behaviors that are characteristic of addiction have not been clearly*

tied to neurobiology.[6] Nora D. Volkow, et. al., *Neu-robiologic Advances from the Brain Disease Model of Addiction*

A current leading expert in the study of substance use dis-order, Dr. Gabor Maté, in his book, *The Myth of Normal,* of-fers a definition of addiction that shuns the term disease:

> "Addiction is a complex psychological, emotional, physiological, neurobiological, social, and spiritual process. It manifests through any behavior in which a person finds temporary relief or pleasure, and there-fore craves, but that in the long term causes them or others negative consequences, and yet the person re-fuses or is unable to give it up."[7]

Although opinions vary widely, I'll leave these discussions to the addiction experts, medical professionals, and research-ers. As I searched for answers, their views were sometimes helpful, but other times left me perplexed. Our responsibility as Christian parents is to observe the research and education available to us through the lens of God's perspective and then draw our own conclusions. To do so, we will need to explore the deeper spiritual reasons why our children turn to drugs, alcohol, and destructive behaviors to cope with or escape life. The Bible can offer us valuable insights about addiction if we are open to the lessons found within its pages. If not, we risk embracing a belief system that is exclusive of, rather than in-clusive of, these scriptural truths. We will dig deep into these biblical views as we move on in this chapter.

Scientific research widely supports the view that drug ad-diction is a chronic, progressive, and incurable disease. The suggestion that the person abusing substances might have any personal responsibility for their addiction is unsettling to many who hold this viewpoint. Consequently, discussions about weaknesses of the flesh, moral failure, and sin are often excluded from the conversation.

As people of faith, let's determine to explore the possibility that addiction may have deeper spiritual roots, carrying with it mental, emotional, and physical implications. Perhaps if the Bible can answer our questions about the roots of addiction, it can also teach us how to better help our loved ones find the lasting freedom they long for.

THE WORLD OR THE WORD?

For the most part, historically, the Church has remained silent or pointed a judging finger at people trapped in the bondage of addiction. Christian clergy and counselors, while desiring to help, often felt ill-equipped or under-trained to minister to those struggling with addiction. Rather, they guided the substance user towards a secular rehab, licensed addiction therapist, or twelve-step meeting. Although well-intentioned, they left the deeper, spiritual needs of the hurting unmet. Instead, what if the Church could serve as a source of godly counsel and support to those who are struggling? Gratefully, over the years, the Church has come a long way in how they approach and care for people enslaved by addiction.

In our case, our family attended a Bible teaching church for many years prior to our run-in with addiction. Since our children also attended the church's school, everyone knew them. As you well know, like small-town living, it can be a blessing and a curse to have your neighbors all up in your business! Our kids were good kids, not perfect by any means, but good. However, unlike the large public schools, where students often fly under the radar, my children were always under the watchful eye of the school's administrators and staff.

The issue was that our church's leadership started leaning towards legalism, where a "saved by grace" theology intersected with a "prove it by your works" doctrine. On a few occasions, we were called into the church or school office because one of our children did something that caused their teachers or youth group pastors to "question" their salvation or spiritual condition. I am not exaggerating. The "something" I am referring to was usually a video game they played, a movie they watched, a song they listened to, or the way they talked to their classmates.

We left most of these meetings feeling hurt and embarrassed by these allegations. Sometimes, we even felt angry. While we understood they were only trying to help, it left our children feeling hurt and confused. As time went on, we realized it was no longer the best environment for our children. After prayer and careful consideration, we decided to leave the church and change schools. We soon settled into a new church, but found it lacked the resources to support us when addiction became part of our lives.

Our primary source of guidance came from an excellent, but pricey, Christian counselor. While his advice was worth its weight in gold, insurance did not cover his fees. We could only pay for his services occasionally, as we needed to reserve most of our finances for providing care and counseling for our sons. How I longed to find the biblical guidance and support

I needed within the church walls. While I was grateful for their support groups, their teachings were usually based on the disease model. I longed to explore the deeper scriptural teachings concerning addiction and somehow knew the Bible would provide the answers I sought.

I share this with you not to criticize the Church, but to emphasize that as the body of Christ, we can do better. We can begin by educating ourselves in both the biblical and secular worldviews of addiction in order to engage in open and honest conversations with those whose lives it controls. In doing so, we can reverse the stigma often found within the walls of the Church that labels those addicted as "less than," and instead embrace their intrinsic worth as human beings, created in God's image.

While it may appear as though I am over-spiritualizing the causes and effects of addiction, that is not my intent. Addiction is a multi-faceted and complex issue. Regardless of why our loved ones started using in the first place, drugs and alcohol are extremely risky and harmful to the person abusing them. It is imperative they seek medical attention when detoxing from most substances and alcohol to ensure their safety. It is also important for our family members to receive professional treatment if they are suffering from mental health issues. I highly recommend therapy with a Christian counselor who specializes in substance abuse. We should also seek professional therapy for ourselves if the burden of supporting our children has taken a toll on us. But we only scratch the surface if we stop there.

Personally, I wanted to believe my sons had a disease due to no fault of their own. It had to be the family genes or chem-

FROM GUILT TO GRACE

ical imbalances in their brains that predestined them to become chemically dependent. No person in their right mind would choose to use, much less abuse, drugs. I longed to believe it was the luck of the draw that sentenced my children to a life of addiction and suffering. However, while addiction and alcoholism ran in our family, no one forced my sons to experiment with drugs. They had a choice to make, and regretfully, they made the wrong one.

Ultimately, abusing substances and self-harming behaviors can lead to sickness and possibly death if continued. Because our children are spiritual beings living in physical bodies, their suffering is more than simply physical, mental, and emotional. Their souls are being tormented as well. As their moms, it tears us apart to watch them suffer. We will stop at nothing to ease their pain and save their lives. But to do so, we first need to know who to call for help. Do we need a psychologist, a physician, or a pastor? Maybe all three?

We've already spent countless hours educating ourselves on what the experts and professionals say about addiction, alcoholism, and self-destructive behaviors. We have gained insight and understanding of the psychological and physiological reasons for addiction. Now, let's look at the Word of God to learn its perspective on these issues.

BACK TO THE BEGINNING

The Bible is clear on most controversial topics. When it comes to addiction and alcoholism, why do we overcomplicate the matter? Over the last fifty-plus years, while society has embraced the disease model, the Church has allowed the discussion of free will, sin, and rebellion to take a back seat for fear of sounding judgmental and contributing to the shame of those who are bound within addiction's grip. While the Bible doesn't use the words *alcoholism or addiction* specifically, it always refers to drunkenness as a sin. For an example, read the following verses:

> "Who has woe? Who has sorrow? Who has strife? Who has complaining? Who has wounds without cause? Who has redness of eyes? Those who tarry long over wine; those who go to try mixed wine. Do not look at wine when it is red, when it sparkles in the cup and goes down smoothly. In the end it bites like a serpent and stings like an adder. Your eyes will see strange things, your heart utter perverse things. You will be like one who lies down in the midst of the sea, like one who lies on the top of a mast. 'They struck me,' you will say, 'but I was not hurt; they beat me, but I did not feel it. When shall I awake? I must have another drink.'" (Proverbs 23:29-35 ESV)

The New Testament also teaches that drunkenness is against God's commands.

> "Now the works of the flesh are evident: sexual immorality, impurity, sensuality, idolatry, sorcery, enmity, strife, jealousy, fits of anger, rivalries, dissensions, divisions, envy, drunkenness, orgies, and things like these. I warn you, as I warned you before, that those who do such things will not inherit the kingdom of God." (Galatians 5:19-21 ESV)

(For more examples, see Genesis 9:18-27; 1 Kings 16:9; 1 Corinthians 5:11; 6:9-10)

Even though God does not forbid alcohol consumption, these verses express His stand on drunkenness. Most Christ followers agree with the Bible's warning against getting drunk; however, the dispute arises when we lump substance dependence into the same "sin" category as drunkenness. So what exactly does the Bible teach on the subject? Because addiction is not limited to substances, let's start by looking more closely at its definition.

In his book, *The Heart of Addiction: A Biblical Perspective,* Mark Shaw describes addiction as:

> "The persistent, habitual thoughts, words, and actions associated with excessive pleasure-seeking which are known to the user to be harmful and physically enslaving, sinful and willful choices to disobey God (whether one acknowledges it or not)."[8]

As we read this definition, we see that addiction is not limited to chemical dependency. Instead, it includes *any habitual thoughts, words, or actions that are harmful and enslaving for us and disobedient to God.* So before proceeding, allow me to offer a word of caution for those who are **not** bound by a substance or life-dominating behavior. It can be tempting to play judge and jury. Please resist the urge. For those controlled by substances or addictive behaviors, any choice they once had to say, "No" was hijacked the moment their addiction took the reins. Addictions like nicotine, television, social media, pornography, exercise, shopping, work, gambling, sex, caffeine, people, food, or countless other behaviors can enslave any of us. We are all sinners who have fallen short of the glory of God (see Romans 3:23).

Because we are born into sin, we are naturally driven by our fleshly passions and desires. The struggle is real! Who hasn't run into a battle between their willpower and their desire for a piece of chocolate cake or an extra bowl of ice cream? Or, perhaps your weakness is turning off your device so you can get to bed at a decent hour. Our minds are willing and want to do the right thing, but our flesh is weak, always tempted by its cravings. Jesus understood and addressed temptation when he spoke these words: *"Watch and pray so that you will not fall into temptation. The spirit is willing, but the flesh is weak"* (Matthew 26:41 NIV).

To better understand our propensity towards temptation and sin, let's observe the first couple in the Bible, Adam and Eve (see Genesis 2-3). As the story goes, they lived in a perfect utopia, the Garden of Eden. While there, the two encountered a serpent who was bent on their destruction. This cunning tempter deceitfully hissed that God was withholding his best by refusing to allow them to partake of the fruit of the tree of the knowledge of good and evil. With her husband by her side, the serpent challenged the naïve woman to doubt God's word, as though obedience to it was optional. As he wove his web of lies, he tempted the couple with the lust of the flesh, the lust of the eyes, and the pride of life. We all know the outcome of the story. Both took the bait, disobeyed God, and as a result, all humanity fell into a state of perpetual sin, resulting in spiritual and physical death and separation from God.

Since that fateful day, sin has held its chokehold tightly around our necks. The lust of the flesh tempts us to do what we want. The lust of the eyes entices us to have what we want. And the pride of life convinces us we can be what we want. There are those who believe that excessive drinking or substance abuse is an inherent illness, not a matter of disobedience to God, but the Bible contradicts this. When we allow our fleshly desires to control us for any reason, we are sinning against God. And while I understand many people unintentionally began their self-destructive behaviors, this does not nullify the spiritual root causes of addiction. What began as a wrong choice soon became a snare that entrapped their minds and bodies in a life of suffering. Once someone begins abusing substances or engaging in self-destructive behaviors, they can quickly become enslaved to them.

In his book, *Addictions: A Banquet in the Grave*, Ed Welch states:

> "The biblical view of drunkenness – the prototype of all addictions – is that it is always called sin, never sickness. Drunkenness is against God and his law. Scripture is unwavering in this teaching and relentless in its illustrations."[9]

It is important for us to realize that many people did not start using, much less abusing, substances intentionally. As I mentioned earlier in the book, some became addicted to prescribed pain medications. Others have mental health issues that were not properly treated, so they turned to drugs or alcohol for relief. Sadly, there are also people who were abused and traumatized by others and turned to drugs as a source of comfort. How can we accuse them of sinning against God? It's hard to feel as though we are judging someone else when we have not walked in their shoes, isn't it? I need to warn you about debating with your loved one over why they began using drugs. The main purpose for understanding the spiritual causes of addiction is for us to extend grace and hope to those caught in its grip.

The good news is that spiritual problems have spiritual answers. The grace of God abounds towards all of us. As we examine the spiritual roots of addiction, let's remember that our children are hurting. Many have experienced deep pain and trauma in their lives. We are called to come alongside them and encourage them in their battle, offering hope, love, and support. When we speak to our children about their emotional, mental, and physical struggles, let's not stop short of discussing these important spiritual matters with them as well.

"Hear, my son, and be wise, and direct your heart in the way. Be not among drunkards or among gluttonous eaters of meat, for the drunkard and glutton will come to poverty, and slumber will clothe them with rags." (Proverbs 23:19–21 ESV)

What are some practical ways we can open the discussion with a loved one who is battling addiction and believes a chemical imbalance, poor genes, or a brain disorder caused it? First, it's important for you to humble yourself and approach them with open ears and an equally open heart. Listen more than you speak. Ask them questions without jumping in to share your opinion. What has been their experience with drugs or alcohol? Where do they hurt? What relief do substances offer them? What are their thoughts on why they became addicted to drugs or alcohol?

When I first learned what the Bible says about alcohol and other addictions, I didn't like it either. I didn't want to be the one to speak the truth into someone else's life, much less write a book about it. I would much rather have left this sensitive topic to the pastors and theologians to tackle. But after slowing down and taking a deep breath, I realized the Bible is written with redemption in mind. It contains a message of hope for those lost and separated from God. What if someone had been afraid to talk to me about sin? What if they refused to point out the error of my ways for fear of offending me? Where would I be today? Well, not saved, that's for sure.

When we address sin in the context of addiction with someone, it should always be with their personal well-being in mind. We should first ask ourselves, "How does having this conversation help or hurt my loved one? By encouraging them to share their story, we create an opportunity for honest and open communication. For me, it's much more helpful to talk to them about what addiction has done to their relationship with Jesus. Do they feel loved by Him? Do they blame God for their addiction or for not being able to break free from it? Have they committed sins because of their addiction for which they need forgiveness? When we get to this place, I remind them that God loves them very much, and as a good Father, He puts nothing on His children (including a disease) that would cause them to sin against Him. This is clearly stated in these verses from the book of James.

"Let no one say when he is tempted, 'I am being tempted by God,' for God cannot be tempted with evil, and he himself tempts no one. But each person is tempted when he is lured and enticed by his own desire. Then desire when it has been conceived gives birth to sin, and sin when it is fully grown brings forth death." (James 1:13-15 ESV)

I remember a time when I had the "talk" with my son. I asked him about his view on addiction. Because he attended secular 12-step programs and rehabs, he believed he had inherited a disease brought on by bad genes and a chemical imbalance that caused him to misuse drugs and alcohol. He confessed he was powerless over his cravings for these substances. He couldn't understand why God would put something like this on him. Not only did he feel helpless, he also felt hopeless. He was convinced he would live the rest of his life fighting to resist relapsing, yet would never feel "normal" like everyone else. Sad, right? When he finished sharing his feelings, I asked him about his thoughts regarding sin and addiction. He shared with me his belief that he was sinning against God by using drugs. Interesting, huh? This shows me that there is a genuine need to reckon spiritual truths with the false teachings that our loved ones have received. Many have embraced a victim mindset, while still bearing the guilt and shame of feeling they did something wrong to cause it. This is where we can share the hope God's grace offers them.

CAN'T WE ALL JUST GET ALONG?

I realize some of this may be hard to digest, so I thank you for sticking with me this far. I wrote this book to offer spiritual support and encouragement to you as the mother of a wayward and struggling child. I pray that what I've learned will help you better understand and prepare for the spiritual battle you are engaged in as you fight for your child's freedom from life-controlling bondages. I do not have the space in this book to go into a lengthy discussion about addiction's origins. Instead, I am sharing my conclusions after thoroughly researching both the science and scriptures. I encourage you to do the same.

Although scientific research points to addiction being a brain disease, one that predisposes people to abuse substances or engage in habitual self-destructive behaviors, the Bible clearly reveals that at its root, addiction is a heart problem, one only God can heal. Are our loved ones physically sick as a result of abusing drugs? Yes! Might some people be more susceptible to addiction than others? Absolutely. Neurobiology and physiology play a significant role in understanding why our loved ones abuse substances. But, as Christ's followers, we must hold to the Bible as the final authority on every matter, including addiction. Thus, when science and the scriptures collide, the scriptures trump science every time. I encourage you to keep this in mind as you do your own research.

Satan, God's enemy, is divisive and seeks to keep us at odds with each other. His mission is to destroy our addicted loved ones, their families, and our communities. What better way than to conquer and divide? He is relentless in his efforts to prevent God's people from coming together to bring healing to those who are suffering. It is imperative we take a united front against addiction and the toll it is taking on our families, our communities, and our country.

It is my prayer that after conducting your own research, your findings will give you a renewed sense of hope, not simply for your child's recovery, but for complete transformation and freedom from their bondage to addiction. They are not a lost cause. They do not have to live their lives believing the lie that they will never experience freedom from their addiction. Their hope is in Jesus who sets the prisoners free. Amen!

"So if the Son sets you free, you will be free indeed."
(John 8:36 ESV)

Reflection Questions

1. What are your beliefs about addiction's origins? Has anything in this chapter changed your point of view? Why or why not?

2. Pick one quote from this chapter and note your thoughts on their perspective on addiction.

3. Have you ever felt judged by the church for your child's addiction? Describe.

4. How will what you've learned in this chapter affect how you view your struggling child moving forward?

CHAPTER 6

Sink or Swim?

"We have this hope as an anchor for the soul,
firm and secure."
Hebrews 6:19a (NIV)

FALSE ANCHORS

Several years ago, our family made our way to beautiful Northern California. As part of our family vacation, we visited the lake for an afternoon of boating. The day was clear and beautiful, the water smooth and pristine. About halfway through our adventure, we found a quiet lagoon to take a break, grab a snack, and cool off in the water.

As Steve brought the boat to a halt, he shouted to me, "Drop anchor!" Hastily, I grabbed the anchor and cast it into the blue waters below. Proud of myself for a job well done, I watched as the shiny anchor plunged quickly into the darkness. Suddenly, I realized I had made a big mistake. Trailing just seconds behind the anchor, its unhitched line followed without restraint. I had failed to notice that the line wasn't properly secured to the boat's cleat. Although I attempted to grab hold of the sinking line, to my dismay, it was too late. The anchor was lost forever.

My error cost us a pretty penny, but it also taught me something about anchors. While boat anchors are a safety device when properly secured, when not, they are useless and can even put us in danger. The same thing holds true for the anchors of our lives.

It would have been foolish for us to put our trust in that unsecured anchor to keep our boat from drifting away from shore or crashing into unseen rocks below the water's surface. The boat required a secure anchor to keep us safe. Likewise, as we navigate the waters of life, we should consider the anchors we hold on to. Are they trustworthy and secure? Or are they unreliable or false anchors?

As mothers, we crave security and stability, not only for ourselves, but also for our children. While we encourage them to put their trust in Jesus, we often wrestle with the same insecurities as they do. Just as anchors are to be a source of stability for vessels in rough seas, we are to rely on Him to be our stability in the storms in our lives.

Sadly, our children have anchored themselves to substances and behaviors that falsely promised them peace and safety, but instead pulled them out into rough and perilous waters. Our first instinct and most natural response is to jump in after them, isn't it? But what if we can't swim or are unable to pull them safely back into the boat? What if we are in over our heads?

Since we lived in the desert, our family routinely escaped the summer heat by heading to the lake. Each year, my mother enrolled us in swimming lessons to ensure we could splash and play safely in its deep waters. She also insisted we wear a life vest while the boat was in motion. In full disclosure, our mom was terrified of water because she couldn't swim, something we often poked fun at her over. She was powerless to come to our aid if one of us was in trouble. But the good news was that our father was a skilled swimmer and a trained first responder. Because he was in the boat, she could relax knowing he could fully handle an emergency, should one occur.

In retrospect, I gained a valuable lesson from my mother. Mom knew her limitations around water and understood her inability to save us in the event we were in trouble. Instead, she put her confidence in a strong anchor, one she could trust with the lives of her children.

Mom also knew how dangerous our lake could be if an unforeseen storm caught us off-guard. Out of nowhere, ominous clouds would appear, a sign we should head for the safety of dry land. If my father did not heed the warning and get us ashore quickly, we would find ourselves in danger during a tumultuous storm.

As moms of wayward children, we will do just about anything to help them. While they are anchoring themselves to self-destructive habits, we anchor ourselves to them as we attempt to save them. The problem is, like my mother who couldn't swim, if we dive in after them, we could be at risk of being pulled under and drowning ourselves.

When facing uncharted waters and raging seas, we should cling to the only anchor in which we can trust, Jesus. In our deepest pain and darkest moments, we can rest secure knowing He is with us. In return, he requires us to let go of our false anchors and hold on to Him. As we go through these times of testing, we learn to rely on the Lord rather than ourselves to make it through.

If your faith seems to grow weaker as you pass through troubled waters, you are not alone. Fear and faith collided when Christ's disciples faced a storm that could have cost them their lives. As you read the passage below, remember these were experienced fishermen aboard this vessel, trained to navigate rough waters in inclement weather. Based on their reaction, this must have been one fierce storm!

> "One day he got into a boat with his disciples, and he said to them, 'Let us go across to the other side of the lake.' So they set out, and as they sailed he fell asleep. And a windstorm came down on the lake, and they were filling with water and were in danger. And they went and woke him, saying, 'Master, Master, we are perishing!' And he awoke and rebuked the wind and the raging waves, and they ceased, and there was a calm. He said to them, 'Where is your faith?' And they were afraid, and they marveled, saying to one another, 'Who then is this, that he commands even winds and water, and they obey him?'" (Luke 8:22-25 ESV)

I wonder if there was a cloud in the sky as Jesus and His disciples embarked on their journey. By the looks of it, no one suspected trouble was coming. Once aboard, I picture Jesus, weary from His work, lying down to take a nap. Suddenly, the sailors found themselves in dangerous waters as the wind and waves pummeled their boat. Despite their valiant efforts, the storm had them beat. Sensing their impending doom, the disciples cried out to Jesus, "Master! We are perishing!"

This is where the story gets intriguing. In their panic, these weary travelers failed to remember who was with them in the boat. They forgot Jesus was no ordinary man. They had witnessed His miracle-working power to heal the sick, raise the dead, and cast out demons. But when the storm arose, they went back to what they knew. They trusted in their own knowledge, skills, and instincts until they could rely on them no longer. It was then, and only then, they finally cried out to Jesus for help.

Isn't that just like us? We are sailing along smoothly when out of nowhere a tsunami strikes. Like His disciples, we forget Jesus is with us, not only during the calm periods of our lives, but also during the storms. We rely on our own capabilities to keep ourselves afloat, only crying out for His help when we are at the end of our rope. Instead, what if we find encouragement in the presence of the Lord, our refuge and anchor of hope in the storm? (see Hebrews 6:18).

We must understand our weaknesses and limitations when trying to save our troubled children. We need a reliable anchor when we are in over our heads. Before plunging in to rescue our drowning loved ones, let's ask ourselves these challenging questions. *"In whom or what do I find my security?" "In whom do I hope?" "Where do I anchor my trust?"*

FORGETTING GOD

When we put our trust in anyone or anything other than Jesus, the person, object, or behavior becomes a false anchor in our life. The Bible calls these idols. We can make idols out of anyone (ourselves included) or anything in which we seek security, pleasure, acceptance, power, love, or relief from pain. While these are not the household idols forbidden in Deuteronomy 5:8-9, the Bible warns us against lusting after idols of the heart (see Ezekiel 14:3-6).

> "Son of man, these men have taken their idols into their hearts, and set the stumbling block of their iniquity before their faces." (Ezekiel 14:3a ESV)

The warning against the sin of idolatry was not solely for the Israelites of the Old Testament. In the New Testament, the Apostle John also instructed Christ's followers to keep themselves *"free from idols" (1 John 5:21 ESV)*. But is idolatry a problem in the church today? As believers, worshiping false idols may seem repulsive, as it should. However, before we deny practicing idolatry ourselves, let's examine our hearts by asking, *"Who or what do I worship?"*

> "They exchanged the truth about God for a lie, and worshiped and served created things rather than the Creator—who is forever praised. Amen." (Romans 1:25 NIV)

Our children have chased after idols in the form of substances to satisfy their desires and appease their flesh. In their attempt to outrun God, they endanger their lives by chasing after idols. Consequently, they have bound themselves to false anchors in extremely hazardous waters.

As for you, dear mom, to whom or what are you bound? Before answering, ponder these questions. *"Have I become obsessed with saving my child? Have I neglected my health, my family, and my relationship with God while trying to rescue him? Have I anchored myself to the lie that if I don't save my child, no one else will?"* If you answered, "Yes" to one or more of these questions, your child may be an idol in your life. Still not sure? Author Timothy Keller describes idolatry well in the following quote:

> "What is an idol? It is anything more important to you than God, anything that absorbs your heart and imagination more than God, anything you seek to give you what only God can give." ~Timothy Keller[10]

The author's definition of an idol perfectly described my relationship with my son when the Lord confronted me about the sin of idolatry. I never could have imagined that I was anchoring myself to anything or anyone instead of the Lord, but I eventually came to understand that I had made my son an idol in my life. I was familiar with the term "codependency," and admitting that our relationship was unhealthy was hard enough. But realizing that I had made him an idol? That was a hard pill to swallow.

Codependency is a widely used term in the addiction and recovery community. The dictionary defines "codependency" as "a psychological condition or a relationship in which a person manifesting low self-esteem and a strong desire for approval has an unhealthy attachment to another often controlling or manipulative person (such as a person with an addiction to alcohol or drugs)."[11]

The Bible does not use the word "codependency," but it does warn against unhealthy or sinful attachments to anyone or anything that might enslave us. This includes becoming consumed with rescuing and fixing our children. If we obsess over our children, rather than worshiping the Lord, we risk making them our idols.

Why is it we are so easily ensnared by the people and things we love but sometimes loathe? I believe it is because they satisfy something that is missing in our lives. They fill a void inside our souls—our wants, needs, and can't-live-without's.

This can be hard to take in. By now you might be thinking, *"I would never allow my child to become an idol in my life!"* I have wrestled with this thought as well. It's hard to imagine anything or anyone taking priority over our relationship with the Lord. As women who love Jesus with our whole hearts, there is no way we would ever put our children above Him. Or would we? Look at the following verses in Matthew.

> "And he said to him, 'You shall love the Lord your God with all your heart and with all your soul and with all your mind. This is the great and first commandment. And a second is like it: You shall love your neighbor as yourself.'" (Matthew 22:37-39 ESV)

God created us with the capacity to love both Him and people. We are to love Him first. Then the natural overflow will be to love other people. However, regarding worship, He has a hands-off policy. If we offer our worship to anyone or anything other than God alone, we are sinning against His commandments. Ouch!

"You shall have no other gods before me."
(Deuteronomy 5:7 ESV)

I understand that loving our children and being concerned about their welfare does not necessarily qualify as idolatry. After all, as their moms, we have a God-given responsibility to watch over them. But when doing so controls our every thought, feeling, and action, we may be playing too close to the fire.

Satan has been scheming since before he caused trouble in the Garden of Eden to see all creation groveling at his feet. It all began in Heaven when he, along with a third of the angels, formed a rebellion against God. No longer would he settle for being the worshiper. Instead, he demanded to be worshiped.

Next, he moved on to the first humans God created, Adam and Eve. Once they sinned, all humanity was free rein! He would no longer sit back passively and watch God steal his glory. There was work to be done! To carry on his attempted coup, Satan seduced God's chosen people, Israel, into following other gods through intermarriage with foreigners. He would stop at nothing to steal the hearts of these people away from God. Little did he know, the Lord had a plan to win back what His enemy had stolen.

Fast forward to the birth of God's one and only Son, Jesus, who came here on a holy mission to redeem His lost creation. Not one to give up easily, the devil waited to make his move until after Jesus had completed His 40-day fast in the wilderness. In his belief that Jesus was weak, he sought to tempt Him. If he could persuade the Son of God to worship him, it wouldn't be long before every man, woman, and child was bowing down at his feet.

There was one major flaw in the enemy's plan, however. He forgot his place as a created being. The Creator designed the "created" to worship Him, not vice versa. Jesus would not bow down to this created and fallen being. He understood that worship belonged solely to the Creator.

"Then Jesus said to him, 'Be gone, Satan! For it is written, "You shall worship the Lord your God and him only shall you serve."'" (Matthew 4:10 ESV)

Because of Satan's rebellion against God while he was in Heaven, the Lord sentenced him to spend eternity in hell (see Matthew 25:41). Driven by his arrogance, not only did he tempt Jesus in the wilderness, he continues to target humanity to satiate his appetite for worship. He would rather see us worshiping a piece of stone or wooden block than the Lord God. In order to accomplish his agenda, he attempts to deceive every man, woman, and child to accomplish his agenda.

But what does idolatry have to do with addiction? Certainly, no one addicted to harmful substances or behaviors set out to worship an idol. It seems more like slavery, if you ask me. Exactly! Once enslaved by addiction, our children's only desire is to get more drugs.

Likewise, when we become fixated on fixing our child, our feelings, thoughts, and desires rule over us. We are not in control. They are. Unless we are vigilant, they will lead us to act in ways we never imagined. Our child has now become our idol, demanding and receiving our full attention, and if we are not careful, our worship.

How can we keep ourselves free from idols? The Apostle Paul made it clear when he instructed the church at Corinth with these words, *"Therefore, my beloved, flee from idolatry"* (1 *Corinthians 10:14 ESV, emphasis mine).* We begin by acknowledging our weaknesses. Satan lures us by setting up traps of our heart, mind, and flesh. These are vulnerable areas where we are tempted by the lust of the eyes, the lust of the flesh, and the pride of life. These are what I call "sin traps" because if we're not careful, they will control us, rather than us having control over them.

What are these sin traps I am referring to? These are areas of weakness or temptation in our lives. They can vary from person to person. Satan uses them to entrap us as we pursue our own desires, rather than serving God whole-heartedly. Consider the following list and think about the areas of your life where you may be at risk of falling into a sin trap.

Sin Traps
- **Heart Traps**: Our *feelings* demand to be *pacified*.
- **Mind Traps**: Our *beliefs* demand to be *justified*.
- **Flesh Traps**: Our *desires* demand to be *satisfied*.

It's natural to be influenced by our feelings, beliefs, and desires. When we want what God wants, this is a good thing. But when we pridefully rebel against God's will to chase after what our heart, mind, or flesh demands, we will end up caught in a sin trap. If we continue in our rebellion, these sin traps will eventually become idols and have complete control over our lives. The same forces of evil seeking to destroy our children's lives are at work to destroy ours. If we're not careful, we might convince ourselves that having pure motives guarantees our actions will be good, or at least not harm anyone. This is not the case at all. Just because something feels right doesn't make it right. The same holds true for our relationship with our children. When saving them becomes a life-controlling obsession, our relationship has shifted from being a healthy parent-child one to an idolatrous one. But what can we do to transform our relationship into one that honors God? Let's begin by exploring the roots of our idolatry. Then we can work on the change that needs to take place.

FORSAKING OUR IDOLS

I have a confession to make. I am a control freak. This behavior most likely stems from a deep-seated insecurity, a sense that if I don't take care of myself, no one else will. Nothing could be further from the truth. I have a husband who loves me, family and friends who have always been there for me, and my Lord who promises to never leave me or forsake me (Hebrews 13:5).

Recently, it hit me that this root of insecurity has been the driving force behind most of my major life decisions. What others saw as a strong and independent personality was just my way of coping with the fear of being abandoned or rejected by the people I loved and trusted. Admitting I have lived most of my life controlled by unfounded fears is not something I am proud of. While I believed I trusted Jesus, when it came down to it, I was too scared to take the plunge and go all in.

As a result, I chased the idols of security and acceptance by others to flee my fears of scarcity and fear of rejection. I became a control freak, perfectionist, workaholic, and people-pleaser. While I knew Jesus loved me unconditionally, I carried my fears that I would never be enough, never have enough, and never be safe enough into motherhood.

When we become mothers for the first time, it's a brand-new experience for us. It's normal to feel insecure sometimes. Over time, we grow more confident in our parenting skills. But if we doubt ourselves and don't trust Jesus with our children, we will find those old mindsets and coping skills from our childhood creeping into our parenting.

That's what happened to me. Because I grew up in a volatile environment, I craved security. I wanted nothing more than for my kids to feel safe. Maybe if I slept with one eye open, I could ensure nothing bad would ever happen to them. While unrealistic, I believed their lives depended on me getting it right as their mother. These false beliefs became the root of my idolatry.

What beliefs have you brought into your mothering? Are they anchored in the promises of God or tethered to the lies of the enemy? If your beliefs are not founded on the Word of God, it's time to let them go. What does this mean for us as mothers of prodigals?

When we became believers in Jesus Christ, we were called to count the cost of following Him. The Lord distinguished between those who desired to be His disciples and those who merely paid lip service to the idea. Jesus addressed not only the crowd that followed Him, but also each of us personally in these verses.

> "Whoever loves father or mother more than me is not worthy of me, and whoever loves son or daughter more than me is not worthy of me. And whoever does not take his cross and follow me is not worthy of me. Whoever finds his life will lose it, and whoever loses his life for my sake will find it." (Matthew 10:37-39 ESV)

These are hard words to take in. However, if we desire to be Christ's disciples and follow Him, we will need to let go of the death grip we have on our children. This doesn't imply we should cut them off and refuse any contact until they get their act together. Jesus knows we love our children and desire to support them. It does mean we should not allow our concern for our children to hinder our complete and sacrificial devotion to Jesus. When we do so, they have become our idols.

But what does surrendering our children look like, especially if they are in crisis? Who will be there for them if we're not? How can we go on with our daily lives when they need our help? Letting go feels more selfish than sacrificial. But letting go doesn't mean we passively sit by and give up. Instead, we will need to cling to Jesus and trust Him with their lives like never before.

Over time, you will come to discern if a situation requires your involvement or if you should exercise faith while you pray and wait. I will guide you on how to handle these "what ifs" as we move forward.

First, be kind to yourself. Being a mother is hard...really hard! Our children pull at our heartstrings like none other. Mothers don't let go of their children easily. Releasing your child to the Lord will be one of the toughest things you ever do. This isn't a once-and-for-all, one-and-done deal, either. The daily sacrifice of surrendering our children requires what my friend calls "excruciatingly painful love." But where do we start? Let's start by untethering ourselves from any false anchors that are keeping us from surrendering completely to Jesus. Whether it's a person, a mindset, or a behavior holding you back, now is the time to let go and jump into the water, feet first. Are you ready to get your toes wet?

Reflection Questions

1. *Read over my story about dropping our boat's unsecured anchor into the water below. Can you remember a time when you trusted in something to keep you safe, only to find out it was unreliable? Share your thoughts.*

2. *What "false anchors" have you set up to help you cope with your fears and insecurities? Have they been reliable or unreliable?*

3. *Do you believe your child (or something or someone else) has become an idol in your life? In what way? How has this affected your relationship with them? How has it affected your relationship with Jesus?*

4. *As you read this chapter, has the Lord revealed the roots of your idolatry? If so, what are they? Take a few minutes to pray and ask the Holy Spirit to help you better understand why these false anchors offer you security. Pray for the faith you need to release them from your grip, so you can follow Jesus with your whole heart and life.*

PART THREE

Walk by Faith

CHAPTER 7

Bound by Love

"The more they were called, the more they went away;
they kept sacrificing to the Baals and burning
offerings to idols."
Hosea 11:2 (ESV)

WANDERING HEARTS

"How could this be happening again?" Julie cried. "I thought Adam finally had his drug problem under control once and for all. He has been clean and sober for three years. He has a great job, a wonderful wife, and a new baby. I don't understand!" Julie had shed countless tears and prayed thousands of prayers over the past ten years of her son's addiction. Now, when she finally felt she could breathe a sigh of relief, the news of his relapse hit her like a ton of bricks.

It's hard to find the right words to comfort a heartbroken mom who has just received the devastating news that her son or daughter has wandered off the path of sobriety and is once again abusing drugs. Besides discovering for the first time that her child is bound to addictive, life-threatening substances, learning they have relapsed is some of the hardest news she can receive. As I tried to sort out why this happened to Julie's son, I recalled the times addiction slithered in unnoticed and entangled my son back in its grip. Bewildered, I also wrestled with the question, "Why?" Why, when things seemed to be going so well, did he throw it all away for another high?

Relapse, a total return to previous substance use, is a possibility even after our loved ones have been sober for months or years. Cravings can come back unexpectedly after being dormant for extended periods of time. There are many reasons why someone returns to using the drugs that previously destroyed their lives. They may feel "off" as their brain readjusts and rebalances because of being altered by chemical abuse. Some people find trying to live "normal" lives more difficult than expected. Others buckle under the pressure and stress of daily responsibilities. What's important to remember is that relapses happen in stages and are not without their warning signs.

When someone returns to abusing drugs, it most often starts with an emotional relapse, then a mental, and finally, a physical relapse. This is because, like all people, their feelings strongly influence their decisions. When we are suffering, we will justify just about anything to feel better. Mentally, we grow weary of trying to resist temptation. Finally, a physical relapse happens when the person rationalizes that life with drugs is better than life without, so they resume using them.

God showed me that the reasons our loved ones go back to things they despise are similar to why we all wander after things that bring us more harm than good. Our flesh demands to be satisfied, and when we convince ourselves no harm will come, we fall easily back into temptation. Also, contrary to what some believe, temptation goes beyond the emotional, mental, and physical levels. This is a matter of the heart, one lost or won on a deeper spiritual level.

As I tried to wrap my mind around why not only our children, but each of us is prone to wandering away from God's goodness in our lives, the Lord led me to study the book of Hosea. This book portrays the fragmented relationship between a faithful husband, Hosea, and his promiscuous, wayward wife, Gomer. However, this story reveals much more than that. Within its narrative, we learn of God's steadfast love towards His wandering children, the rebellious and idolatrous nation of Israel. We watch in awe as the Lord relentlessly pursues, redeems, and restores His chosen people to Himself, only to have them reject His love and wander away again. As we observe their love story, we see ourselves within its pages.

It is impossible to conceive why the people God delivered out of Egypt over 500 years earlier would rebel against Him and follow foreign gods (see Hosea 11:1-3). But that is precisely what they did. Sadly, God's children are doing the same today.

"All we like sheep have gone astray; we have turned-ev-ery one—to his own way; and the Lord has laid on him the iniquity of us all." (Isaiah 53:6 ESV)

The Hebrew word for "gone astray or wander" is *taah*.[12] It means "to vacillate, reel, stray, or err (literally or figuratively)." It can also mean to "**cause** to go astray, wander, stagger; to deceive or seduce." Here, we learn a person can wander inten-tionally because of willful defiance or unintentionally, as the result of being deceived or seduced.

When I speak with moms of addicted children, I am al-ways drawn to their stories. The universal questions among them are, "Why did my child rebel and start using drugs? Why would they try them in the first place?" Whether their desire was to numb their pain or to have a great time partying, the choice was theirs alone. Still, we wonder what we could have done to keep them from straying onto a path that lured them with promises of freedom, but instead, led them into bondage. Perhaps you will find the answer to your questions of "why" your child wandered as our story continues.

One interesting part of the story of Hosea and Gomer is that it was God who commanded Hosea to, *"Go, marry a pro-miscuous woman and have children with her, for like an adulter-ous wife this land is guilty of unfaithfulness to the LORD" (Hosea 1:2 NIV)*. These verses reveal the rebelliousness of Gomer, a wayward woman who lived a life of promiscuity and idolatry prior to her marriage to Hosea. While the idea of marrying and settling down may have appealed to her momentarily, it was only a matter of time before her disquieted soul yearned to return to the arms of her lovers.

"...For she said, 'I will go after my lovers, who give me my bread and my water, my wool and my flax, my oil and my drink.'" (Hosea 2:5 ESV)

Gomer was restless, yielding to whatever temptation brought her temporary satisfaction. The faithfulness Hosea showed her wasn't enough to restrain her from chasing after her longings. The same was true for the nation of Israel. They always wanted more. While professing their love for the one true God, they continually wandered back to worshiping the gods of Baal who lured them with false promises of pleasure, security, and success. Sadly, they were too blind to see it was the Lord who was blessing them.

"And she did not know that it was I who gave her the grain, the wine, and the oil, and who lavished on her silver and gold, which they used for Baal." (Hosea 2:8 ESV)

As we contemplate the pull idolatry had on an entire nation of people, we can't help but consider its hold on the lives of our children. Today's influences are every bit as enticing as those experienced by people thousands of years ago. Our youth are being bombarded with the message, "If it feels good, do it. Why not? Everyone else does." Our efforts to warn our kids about the dangers in the real world are being overshadowed by external messages claiming "something they can do or have" will make them happy. Without addressing their deeper longing for a relationship with Jesus, they will always return to what they believe will satisfy them.

Frankly, it's human nature for people to go astray. From infancy, my children ran off if I didn't keep a constant eye on them. There is something adventurous about the call of the wild. Even those of us who prefer to stay between the lines like to do so on our own terms. For Christ's followers, it is no different. Look at these words of the Apostle Paul.

> "For I know that nothing good dwells in me, that is, in my flesh. For I have the desire to do what is right, but not the ability to carry it out. For I do not do the good I want, but the evil I do not want is what I keep doing. Now if I do what I do not want, it is no longer I who do it, but sin that dwells within me." (Romans 7:18-20 ESV)

Like our children, if we are not careful, we may also end up wandering away from the Lord because of our own foolish mistakes, selfish desires, or willful defiance. By following our instincts rather than being led by our Shepherd, we can deceive ourselves into thinking our wanderings aren't sinful or disobedient (see Isaiah 44:20; 2 Corinthians 11:3). Before chasing after our wayward children, we should first ask the Holy Spirit to search our hearts and reveal any weaknesses in our flesh or faith that need addressing.

As we continue to read through the book of Hosea, we observe Gomer's life unraveling. It might be tempting to judge her, as though it would be impossible for us to fall into the same sin as her. As women of faith, we do our best to be wholeheartedly committed to loving and serving Jesus. On the other hand, Gomer was bent towards a life of depravity, compulsion, and self-satisfaction. There is no way we would do the same. Or would we?

> "...(She) adorned herself with her ring and jewelry, and went after her lovers and forgot me, declares the LORD." (Hosea 2:13b ESV)

This verse reveals it all. Gomer *forgot* her husband. Israel *forgot* their God. And we *forget* the Lord when we chase after whoever or whatever pulls at our heartstrings. Like our children who wandered into dangerous territory to appease the yearning of their flesh, the craving for what's taboo has provoked each of us to make choices we later regretted. Sadly, there is probably a bit of Gomer in each of us.

If we are honest with ourselves, we should admit we all have wandering hearts. In our attempt to make sense of the senseless, we yearn to know why our kids behave so recklessly. By doing so, we compare our sins to theirs, as though somehow we are less "sinful" than them. In God's eyes, all sin is sin, separating us from Him, and causing each of us to need a Savior.

More than a love story, the book of Hosea is a heart story, revealing the condition of souls as they cry out for intimacy. We each crave acceptance. This desire for connection to whoever or whatever gives us a sense of belonging and leads us to wander away from God's best in pursuit of fleeting pleasures. Let's peer into the personalities of three types of wandering hearts—*the wanting, the wounded, and the wayward.* Each heart is motivated by a want, need, or desire they believe only their idol can fulfill.

> **Wandering Hearts**
> - **Wanting hearts** are *pleasure-seekers,* pursuing what **fulfills** them (see Hosea 2:13).
> - **Wounded hearts** are *pain-relievers,* seeking what **comforts** them (see Hosea 7:14).
> - **Wayward hearts** are *pride-builders,* driven by what **exalts** them (see Hosea 7:13).

Can you recognize any of these wandering hearts within yourself? When we get caught up in chasing after whatever satisfies us, trying to avoid pain at all costs, or living life as we please, we will ultimately sacrifice intimacy with Jesus on the throne of our personal idols. Whether we describe ourselves as a pleasure-seeker, pain-reliever, pride-builder, or a blend of all three, when left unchecked, each is a type of self-worship.

As you contemplate the dire heart condition of these wandering and wayward people, it's hard to take it all in. I wrestled with this as well. I agree these labels accurately describe the runaway Gomer, and even the nation of Israel. After all, they had a reputation for being stiff-necked people (see Exodus 32:9). But how does it apply to our lives and our children?

The thoughts whirling in your head right now may sound something like this. *"I agree that my prodigal child is most likely self-medicating because she has a wanting, wounded, or wayward heart. But what does this have to do with me? My child is self-destructing. My only motivation is to save her life!"*

I felt the same when I first learned about idolatry. I spent years trying to save my son from his addiction. I loved him fiercely and couldn't imagine life without him. No one could have persuaded me it wasn't the right thing for me to do. Then one day, while desperately seeking answers as to why he continued to battle his addiction, I felt challenged to examine my own heart. Had I placed the burden of responsibility for my happiness on my son's shoulders? Did I seek relief from my pain rather than seeking peace in God's presence? Was the overwhelming shame I felt rooted in a prideful attitude that cared more about the opinions of others than God's? You probably guessed my answers to all three questions. "Yes."

The disappointing reality was that there was little difference between the reasons my son used drugs and why I constantly obsessed over saving him. We both had a worship problem. So, while he was chasing after substances to fill the wants in his life, I was chasing after him to silence the anguished thoughts in my mind. We were both called to worship the one True God. Instead, we worshiped ourselves by prioritizing our own fleshly desires above our relationship with Him. As I continued soul-searching, I came to understand why we humans are prone to chasing after idols. The truth is, we all love to wander.

> "Thus says the LORD concerning this people: 'They have loved to wander thus; they have not restrained their feet.'" (Jeremiah 14:10a ESV)

From the beginning, people have chosen their own paths. In seeking to appease their flesh rather than obeying the Lord, like Gomer, they strayed from their beloved husband and wandered into dangerous territory. But because of His great love and mercy, God has always desired to be reunited with His rebellious children. The tale of Hosea and Gomer illustrates the lengths He will go to reclaim His wayward bride.

> "Therefore, I will hedge up her way with thorns, and I will build a wall against her, so that she cannot find her paths. She shall pursue her lovers, but not overtake them, and she shall seek them, but shall not find them. Then she shall say, 'I will go and return to my first husband, for it was better for me then than now.'" (Hosea 2:6-7 ESV)

God loves your children with the same steadfast love he has for Israel. Regardless of why they wander, whether because of ignorance or deliberate defiance, He wants a relationship with them. In our pain, we can feel unseen by God, as though He has forgotten us and our children. But that is not the case. He loves us so much that He has established boundaries to keep us from going astray or to draw us back to Himself when we wander off. We will refer to these as **biblical boundaries**. Keeping in mind that we all have our own ideas on when, why, and how boundaries should be implemented, let's start by learning more about them.

BOUNDARIES: BAD OR BIBLICAL?

It was early summer, and temperatures were rising in our desert valley. To escape the heat, Steve, Jadyn, and I traveled to our son's place in the lovely town of Prescott, Arizona. Relaxing on the outdoor patio at a local coffee shop, we enjoyed our favorite beverages while savoring the warm sun and cool breeze. To my delight, our conversation was relaxed and engaging.

"Hey, Mom. What are you writing about in your book?" Kyle asked inquisitively.

Without giving it much thought, I responded, "Well, right now, I am writing to moms about setting boundaries with their addicted children."

"Of course you are," he said with a grin. "Why wouldn't you be? You're the Queen of Boundaries. You could write an entire book on boundaries alone."

Giggling, I retorted, "Hmm, thanks for the compliment...I think."

Now, before you give me a Mother-of-the-Year award to go with my tiara, you should know I have not always been good at setting or keeping boundaries—quite the contrary. Boundaries were almost non-existent for most of my life. But before I delve into that story, let's explore the definition of a boundary.

Merriam-Webster's Dictionary defines a "boundary" as "something that indicates or fixes a limit or extent."[13] Here are a few examples of boundaries:

- A **physical boundary** establishes ownership such as the property line between houses or the place where the land begins and the ocean ends.

- A **personal boundary** is one we set for ourselves such as what we will eat, how much sleep we will get, or sticking to a budget. It also protects our personal body by determining how we will and will not allow others to treat it.

- A **relational boundary** sets the standard for proper conduct in personal or professional relationships. In relationships, boundaries are often defined as the line where one person ends and the other begins.

In their book, *Boundaries,* Drs. Henry Cloud and Dr. John Townsend write,

> "Boundaries are anything that helps to differentiate you from someone else, or shows where you begin and end." [14]

Before the publication of this best-selling book, we knew little about boundaries or how to implement them in our lives. With great wisdom and insight, Drs. Cloud and Townsend explained how to take control of our lives by teaching us the importance of discerning when to say "yes" or when to say "no" to others who encroach on our personal boundaries.

As I mentioned earlier, for most of my life, boundaries were virtually non-existent. This was especially the case during my childhood. In our home, we kids thought rules were optional. While my parents expected us to obey their rules, they did not lead by example. You know the saying "Do as I say, not as I do?" Well, that was the motto they lived by. To say it was confusing is an understatement.

One boundary they made but often disregarded was in administering discipline. The boundaries were gray, the consequences even grayer. Our parents, like many others, were prone to handing out punishment in the form of threats. One of my favorites was, "You're on restriction for a month." That was usually code for, "Wait until Mom calms down, and then remind her of the school dance this weekend."

The chaotic atmosphere in our household was not conducive to maintaining healthy boundaries. Without clear limits on how we spoke to each other or how we behaved, discussions quickly turned into shouting matches. Instead of being a safe place, our home was a hotbed for angry outbursts, tearful breakdowns, silent treatments, or faking fine to keep the peace.

In their defense, my parents likely had no experience with boundaries when they were raising us. In an era where children were best "seen and not heard," we weren't permitted to set limits or speak up for ourselves. We learned to keep our mouths shut and stay out of trouble. These coping mechanisms and communication skills established in our childhood naturally followed us into adulthood.

It wasn't until the late 1980s that the concept of "boundaries" came on the scene. Self-help authors, therapists, and psychologists suggested using boundaries to define appropriate and inappropriate behaviors in our relationships. Boundaries are to be set by the person who feels their time, resources, or emotional energy are being infringed upon. In a nutshell, boundaries protect what is good by keeping out the bad. If only things were that easy, right?

Growing up in a household with no respect for boundaries, I found it difficult to establish and enforce them, particularly with my own kids. When I did what was best and stuck to the boundary, it felt controlling and manipulative. When

I gave in and let them have their way, I felt guilty for allowing them to manipulate me. I made boundaries based on my feelings. If my kids were happy with me, I was probably doing something right. If they were upset with me, I was to blame and felt an urgent need to fix it.

Being the parent of an addicted adult child makes setting and enforcing boundaries more complicated. We were totally unprepared for the emotional and mental challenges that awaited us. Because there was no manual out when we got pregnant entitled, *What to Do When You're Expecting an Addicted Child*, we need to figure it out as we go. While it's difficult to establish boundaries with our substance-controlled children, without them, they will roll right over the top of us. Let me give you an example of attempting to set a boundary with my son while he was in active addiction. See if this conversation rings a bell.

"Mom, Can I borrow eighty dollars to make a credit card payment? It's due today."

"Didn't I just give you the money for that last week?" I asked suspiciously. In the past, eighty dollars was always code for drug money.

"Ya, but I forgot I had to put gas in my car and get a haircut. I was supposed to get paid today, but my dumb boss said there is a problem with payroll, so now we won't get paid until Monday. I promise I'll pay you back then."

"Well, that's your problem, not mine. I guess you will just have to figure it out. I told you the last time was the last time."

"Geez, Mom. You don't understand. I'm going to be delinquent on my credit card. If that happens, I won't have good enough credit to get a place of my own and move out. I've been doing great. Why don't you trust me?"

My internal dialog shifts as I think to myself, *"He is right. He has been doing great. He has been going to his meetings, keeping a job, and coming home on time. Why don't I trust him? I am a terrible mother."*

Overwhelmed by waves of guilt, I ignore the gnawing feeling in my gut that something doesn't add up. I must have been out of my mind to set such an unrealistic boundary, anyway. After all, what mom would vow to never lend her kid money again? Reluctantly, I opened my wallet and handed him the cash. "Alright, but this is the last time."

This is one example of the many times I set boundaries, only to give in when they became too difficult to enforce. Many parents, including me, have problems making and enforcing boundaries around money. Most addictions are very expensive, out-of-control habits. Drugs, alcohol, gambling, food, shopping, porn–all eventually break the bank. As with any addiction, if we continue to supply our kids with money, we are not only hurting them, but also ourselves.

Galatians 6:7 says, *"Whatever one sows, that will he also reap."* All behaviors have consequences. Parents do their kids no favors when we hinder what God is doing in their lives. Except in the most extreme circumstances, we should not interrupt the natural consequences our kids experience because of abusing substances or behaviors. Enabling them or rescuing them will provide a temporary bandage, but ultimately it will exacerbate and prolong their problem. The writers of the book, *Boundaries,* emphasize the importance of allowing for natural consequences in people's lives.

> "To rescue people from the natural consequences of their behavior is to render them powerless."[15]

Whether we choose to set boundaries with our children or not, there is no guarantee our relationship with them will improve. Without boundaries, they will view us as an *object,* someone who *gives them what they want.* With boundaries, they will see us as an *obstacle,* someone who *gets in the way of what they want.* When our kids see us as an object, we feel used and unappreciated. When they see us as an obstacle, they become angry, manipulative, or cut us out of their lives. Either way, it's painful to feel emotionally controlled, manipulated, and violated by them. The only way it's possible to have a healthy relationship with our children is by learning to set the same biblical boundaries with them as the Lord has for His children.

OUR BONDAGE BREAKER

Why all the fuss about boundaries? Why share the tale of the rebellious runaway bride, Gomer, who couldn't care less about God's boundaries or His consequences for breaking them? Why risk humiliation by revealing my own failed attempts at setting boundaries with my addicted children? Because we've gotten them wrong, that's why!

Everywhere we turn these days, we are inundated with books, articles, videos, and podcasts from experts teaching about boundaries. Even with their advice, it can be confusing as we try to understand the hows and whys of boundary setting. Is the boundary meant for our benefit, to protect us from further emotional or physical harm? Or, do we hope that by establishing it, our child will be motivated to make a change? Neither is wrong. But when setting boundaries, it is important to keep in mind realistic expectations for the desired outcome. Implemented properly, boundaries can bring about radical transformation in our children's lives. They can also help us personally to learn how to differentiate between our areas of responsibility and those where we should allow for natural consequences. Getting boundaries right is the tricky part. Let's eliminate any confusion by looking to the originator of the idea.

The Creator was the original boundary setter. He divided the land and the sea, distinguished light from darkness, and separated the seasons. He determined what is right and wrong, good and evil. The ultimate boundary God set was between His holiness and our sinfulness. The words of these verses draw a stark contrast between fearing God and respecting His boundaries versus stubbornly rejecting Him and going our own way.

"Do you not fear me? declares the LORD. Do you not tremble before me? I placed the sand as the boundary for the sea, a perpetual barrier that it cannot pass; though the waves toss, they cannot prevail; though they roar, they cannot pass over it. But this people has a stubborn and rebellious heart; they have turned aside and gone away. They do not say in their hearts, 'Let us fear the LORD our God.'" (Jeremiah 5:22-24a ESV)

When we feel the need to establish boundaries in a relationship, it's usually because another person's words or actions are detrimental to our physical, mental, or emotional well-being. For example, you've most likely never said to yourself, "Enough is enough! I need to set some boundaries around how I speak to my child. The way I talk down to him and berate him is uncalled for." Instead, we are usually licking our wounds after receiving yet another blow from our offender's lips.

But when God establishes a boundary, it is not to protect Himself from harm. Instead, He is looking out for our well-being. He knows we have an enemy determined to destroy our lives. The Lord's boundaries are never harsh or overbearing. When He sets a boundary, it's for our protection.

When it's time to set boundaries with our addicted children, it's important we check our motives for setting them. Prayerfully seek the Lord's will and guidance in this area. For the record, there is nothing wrong with establishing a much-needed boundary when our children are disrespecting us, lying to us, manipulating us, taking advantage of us, or threatening us. The issue is not the need for the boundary, but the heart behind setting it. When God sets boundaries, it is always with the intent of restoring His children. As we consider setting boundaries with our children, we should ask Jesus if the boundary will potentially hurt or help restore our children to a right relationship with Him and with us.

The book of Hosea was helpful for me as I learned to set boundaries. I love how it reveals the loving heart of God for His wandering and wayward children, something we as moms can identify with. As you read this verse, it's crucial to note that the nation of Israel had rejected the Lord God to worship other gods. While on their path of self-destruction, Israel refused to repent and would soon face intense consequences for their sins at the hands of their enemies. Still, the Lord did not use harsh manipulation or threats to lead His children. Instead, He graciously reminded them of how he led them with "cords of kindness and bands of love."

> "I led them with cords of kindness, with the bands of love, and I became to them as one who eases the yoke on their jaws, and I bent down to them and fed them." (Hosea 11:4 ESV)

Notice the word "cords" in the verse above. The Hebrew word for it is *chebel*.[16] *Chebel* is a *physical cord or rope* that is used for multiple purposes, one of which is to mark a *boundary or property line*. Figuratively, it represents *cords of affliction*, to express *pain or sorrow,* or the *suffering* experienced by the exiles of Israel. I recommend doing a word study to help you better understand its meaning and the variety of places it occurs in the Bible.

This cord or line can also describe the dire state of someone entrapped in their sin. We read in the book of Proverbs, *"The iniquities of the wicked ensnare him, and he is held fast in the cords of his sin. He dies for lack of discipline, and because of his great folly he is led astray" (Proverbs 5:22-23 ESV).*

Our finite minds wrestle to comprehend the loving kindness of God who allows His children to suffer intensely because of their rebellious behavior. But as with the Israelites, the Lord expects us to respect His boundaries for our own protection and will enforce consequences if we cross them. We may believe He is treating us harshly, but because of His grace, rather than punishing us for our rebellion, He allows us to experience natural consequences for our behavior.

Mom, your child may stray farther than you can imagine, to a place where they will be ensnared by the false idols that have replaced God in their life. When their idols don't deliver on their promises, only then will our wanderers regret trusting in them instead of Jesus. Because He desires a relationship with our children, He will allow their lives to unravel, so they become disillusioned by their false idols, repent of their sins, and return to Him.

Perhaps you're struggling with why God is allowing your child to experience such intense suffering. Perhaps you are contemplating the question you are too afraid to speak. *"How can a loving God be so cruel as to let my child suffer in addiction when he has no control over his actions? The drugs control him. He is bound to them with no hope of breaking free."*

This is not the case at all. When our fleshly desires hijack our minds and bodies, we feel powerless. We believe there is no way of escape. And ultimately, we act out of that false belief. But like the Apostle Paul, who shared his personal war against his own flesh, we each can cry out to the Lord for help. We are not alone in our battle. Jesus is our bondage breaker.

"For I delight in the law of God, in my inner being, but I see in my members another law waging war against the law of my mind and making me captive to the law of sin that dwells in my members. Wretched man that I am! Who will deliver me from this body of death? Thanks be to God through Jesus Christ our Lord!" (Romans 7:22-25a ESV)

As we seek to see our children free from their bondages, we should pray they will instead be bound to Christ. This means we put our faith into action by also binding ourselves to Jesus in absolute surrender. Only then will we be able to enforce healthy boundaries with our children.

How do we learn to set these boundaries? Before getting into the how-to's, let's examine our own attitudes. For starters, we must stop making excuses for our children's wrong behavior. If we believe they are incapable of reasoning and making wise decisions, we will react out of fear rather than responding in faith and trusting in the power of God to set them free. It's time we stop seeing our children as powerless to make appropriate choices. God has given our children free will, the ability to choose right from wrong. They may not see it this way, but they are more than able to admit their problem, cry out to Jesus, and choose to ask for help. Or they can make excuses, reject God, and choose to continue in their addiction. Ultimately, the choice is not ours to make for them.

Next, when setting boundaries, our priority is to honor God's holiness. If we excuse behaviors such as illegal drug use, lying and manipulating, stealing money, causing bodily harm, or destroying private property by labeling them as symptoms of their disease, we are enabling them to continue to sin against God without suffering the consequences of their actions. These consequences may include job loss, financial bankruptcy, homelessness, jail time, losing their parental rights, divorce, and the list goes on.

As mothers, we are willing to do almost anything to keep our kids from hitting rock bottom. Because our bottom is usually much higher than theirs, we believe they can't possibly sink any lower. We intervene repeatedly and keep lowering the safety net beneath them as we continue to catch them when they fall. Personally, I have never liked the term "rock bottom" because we are not in a position to know what that looks like for each individual. It is impossible for one person to decide for another when things must change. Therefore, it is important to be cautious when deciding whether to intervene or protect them from the consequences of their actions.

Like Hosea, who could have prohibited his wife from running off by tying her to the bedpost, we can try to protect our children by keeping them under our watchful eye. But God gave humans free will for a reason. That's what makes us different from animals. Our pastor recently delivered a thought-provoking message about this to our congregation. He said, "God gave you the gift of self-determination, the capacity to choose, so that you could first and foremost choose Christ and His gospel." Isn't that our goal for our children? When setting biblical boundaries, we should always respect our child's humanity and their ability to choose their own path, right or wrong.

When it comes down to it, we must consider how our loved one's actions affect not only them but us as well. We study the scriptures and reason how their sin separates them

BOUND BY LOVE

from God, but we often excuse the hurt they've caused us by their behavior. Because we are their moms, the thought doesn't cross our minds to set boundaries with our children, even when their actions are against us personally. Instead, our self-imposed guilt insists that any boundaries made on our part are selfish and controlling. Lysa TerKeurst addresses this in her book *Good Boundaries and Goodbyes.*

> "All the work you've done to draw boundaries was not about controlling someone else's behavior. It's about paying attention and being honest about how someone's poor behavior and lack of responsibility is possibly controlling you." [17]

When we are setting boundaries, it's wise to consider what's best, not only for our addicted child but for the entire family unit, ourselves included. Some examples of practical boundaries are:

- Not permitting our adult children to live at home if they are actively using drugs, are threatening, verbally abusive, destructive of our home and possessions, or stealing from us.

- Requiring our adult children in early sobriety and living with us to be employed, pay rent, respect curfew and house rules, attend church, and go to support meetings.

- Expecting our adult children to repay debt owed to courts, banks, attorneys, credit cards, and ex-drug dealers without asking us to help them financially.

These are only a few examples of practical boundaries you can set for your adult child. Each family's situation and dynamics are unique. I encourage you to seek biblical counseling

— 113 —

if you are unsure how to set boundaries in your circumstances. Setting boundaries with our adult children isn't about rewarding them for their good behavior. Nor is it beneficial if we rescue them from the consequences of their actions. Although we may desire to assist our children in getting back on track, we should not solve their problems for them. We should also avoid neglecting our own needs and financial stability in our efforts to help them.

Let me address one more important detail before we close. As I mentioned earlier, biblical boundaries should honor God. But they should also honor our individuality and identity as a child of God. We are not solely moms of addicted children. The Lord has chosen us to serve Him in many capacities with the gifts and talents He has given us. We are not to become so enmeshed in our child's life that we forget God has a plan and purpose for ours as well. When we set boundaries, we need to keep in mind our individual callings in other areas outside that of motherhood.

In closing, let's look back at the story of a romance gone bad. While Hosea was a faithful husband, his wife was determined to wander. Because God instructed Hosea to go after his thrill-seeking wife, he continued to do so. No matter how many times she betrayed, hurt, and rejected him, he faithfully obeyed God, no matter the cost. This may be what God asks of us as well. Right when we have our boundaries defined and ready to go, He may require us to do something that makes little sense to us or anyone else. We must not become so rigid that we refuse to bend if He instructs us to change our boundaries.

While this story is about God setting boundaries with His children and the painful consequences resulting from their disobedience, it's much more. It's a story of hope. In the middle of their mess, God had a plan to restore His children to Himself. In the middle of our mess, in the valley of our troubles, our Bondage Breaker is opening a door of hope and calling His wayward children to come home.

> "Therefore I am now going to allure her; I will lead her into the wilderness and speak tenderly to her. There I will give her back her vineyards, and will make the Valley of Achor (Trouble) a door of hope. There she will respond as in the days of her youth, as in the day she came up out of Egypt." (Hosea 2:14-15 NIV)

Reflection Questions

1. After reading the last few chapters, do you see your child's addiction as more than a physical, mental, or emotional problem? What has the Holy Spirit revealed to you about the deeper issues of the heart?

2. In the past, did you struggle with setting and maintaining boundaries with your child? In what ways?

3. How has what you've learned about biblical boundaries affected your beliefs about boundaries and implementing them in your child's life?

4. Do you plan to establish boundaries with your child moving forward? What boundaries will you set and why?

CHAPTER 8

The Truth Will Set You Free

"For whoever desires to love life and see good days,
let him keep his tongue from evil and his lips from
speaking deceit."
1 Peter 3:10 (ESV)

THE LIES WE BELIEVE

When was the last time you had a conversation with your addicted son or daughter where you felt free of suspicion? A conversation where you knew they were being one hundred percent honest? It's most likely been a while. When we catch our kids in yet another lie, if you're like me, you may feel like doing one of two things–chewing them out or ending the conversation immediately. Because our children believe they cannot survive without their addictive substance or behavior, they will stop at nothing to get it. Lying and deceitfulness become a means of survival for them.

I will never forget the day I had a conversation with someone that left me speechless. After relapsing and being kicked out of his sober-living house, Kyle called me to ask for a place to stay. Naturally, I demanded an explanation. He spilled out some story about how he got into a fight with one of the house residents who stole his belongings. Now he was on the streets with no place to live. Taking his word for it, I called the house manager to give him a piece of my mind. Much to my surprise, he laughed and retorted, "Why did you question him when you knew he would lie to you?" I felt dumbfounded, but you know what? He was right. Not only did I fall for Kyle's lie, I also inadvertently went along with it by not gathering the facts first. After that experience, I was not so easily conned.

One of the hardest lessons I learned from this experience is that we can no longer trust the children we love so dearly when drugs take over their minds and bodies. When my middle son was young, other than an occasional "small" white lie, he had always been an honest kid. When confronted with any wrongdoing, he was quick to come clean and confess to his offense. Once he started rebelling, that changed quickly. As his drug use progressed, so did his dishonesty. Soon, falsities flowed off his tongue like butter on warm bread. Without so much as a blink, he would lock eyes with me and lie through his teeth.

However, it didn't take long for me to figure out I was being duped. Doctors should hand new mothers a degree in Forensics in the delivery room. With the birth of our first baby, we become super sleuths, possessing the power to know when our kids are in trouble or causing it. We can sniff out a lie like a dog searching for a bone. With an uncanny ability to read minds, the CIA should employ us as intelligence agents. No lie on the planet can withstand the relentless interrogating of a mom.

When my oldest started using drugs, he was an adult and already skilled at the art of lying. Throughout his life, he always had a knack for painting a story with any color that suited him. He was natural at weaving tall tales, from blaming the dog for eating his homework to beating up his younger brother and insisting it was an accident. It took getting caught red-handed for him to admit his offense.

The ability of a mother to trust her gut instinct wanes as her child becomes deeply entrenched in their drug use and adept at the scheming it takes to keep their habit going. As one lie rolls into another, she grows weary, confused, and frustrated by the web of deceit her son or daughter weaves to satiate addiction's demands on their body. No longer can she easily recognize the truth from a lie or quickly discern good from evil. Instead, the lines are gray, just the way our enemy, Satan, the father of lies, intended.

> "...He (Satan) was a murderer from the beginning, and does not stand in the truth, because there is no truth in him. When he lies, he speaks out of his own character, for he is a liar and the father of lies." (John 8:44 ESV)

When warring against addiction in our families, turning the other cheek and pretending all is well is not the answer. We don't have to prove anything to know our kids are trying to deceive us. Addiction and lying go hand in hand. Why? Because their minds, bodies, and feelings are lying to them. The enemy of their souls has convinced them their addictions make them smarter, friendlier, funnier, happier, and more confident. As they continue in their addiction, he convinces them they can't live without the very thing that is destroying them. The authors of the book *Freedom from Addiction* assert that a person's actions are always consistent with their beliefs.

> "Our behavior will always be consistent with our beliefs. People will not always live what they profess, but they will always live what they believe. To the alcoholic or addict or anyone in bondage, it means their problem isn't their drinking alcohol or doing drugs or whatever. Their struggle is with misbeliefs or lies that cause their behavior."[18]

There are many reasons our addicted children lie. Some motives include denying their addiction, seeking financial support, avoiding confrontation or uncomfortable emotions, resisting change, avoiding guilt and shame, hiding their addiction, and self-preservation. Physiological changes within the brain can also exacerbate their lying behavior. Regardless of the reason, we should understand that lying is a serious offense to the Lord, as we read in the book of Leviticus, *"You shall not steal; you shall not deal falsely; you shall not lie to one another (Leviticus 19:11 ESV).*

Even though we can't control our children's lying, we can control our response by not enabling their dishonest behavior. We can gather the facts first instead of overreacting or panicking. Remember, the enemy's intention is to deceive us into enabling rather than helping our children. It's time we stop believing his lies about them and their addiction and start living in the truth, even if they refuse to do so. This doesn't mean we wage war against our kids. On the contrary, this war is against the enemy of their souls, Satan, who ensnares them with his lies.

In our battle to silence the confusion, win back our children, and gain back our sanity, we will first need to identify the lies we believe. Not only the lies we believe about our children, but the ones we believe about ourselves, our circumstances, and our relationship with God. How do we recognize these false beliefs? By paying attention to our thought-life. Our feelings, words, and actions most often start with a thought. If I were to ask you to make a list of the thoughts that go through your head during the day, what would you write? These might sound familiar:

- "My child will never be free from his addiction."

- "My son will end up dead or in prison."

- "I am so ashamed. I can't tell anyone about my child's addiction."

- "It's all my fault. I am a failure as a mom."

- "I tried praying for God to save my child, but He didn't answer my prayers."

To recognize the lies we believe, we first need to understand the negative mindsets and thought patterns that usually accompany them. Do you see yourself in any of the examples listed below?

Denial – Inability to accept facts because of limited thinking, blind spots, personal bias, or previous experiences.

Thought: *"My child isn't addicted to drugs. He just likes to party. Besides, all his friends are doing it."*

Deception – Blinded and unable to see the truth because of the lies of the enemy or manipulation of another person.

Thought: *"You're crazy, Mom. I did not come home drunk last night. I was just tired."*

Distorted Perceptions – False beliefs based on wrong assumptions, misunderstandings, or misinformation.

Thought: *"Addiction is a life sentence. My child will never be free."*

Double-Mindedness – Speaking the opposite of what the Bible says because of a lack of faith, fear, confusion, or doubt.

Thought: *"I know I should trust the Lord with my daughter's life, but if I don't protect her, she could get hurt...or worse."*

Defiance – Refusal to believe and obey God's Word because of pride, sin, hypocrisy, and stubbornness.

Thought: *"I know my son is lying, but it's not his fault. It is a symptom of his disease. Who am I to judge? Everyone lies sometimes."*

Once I identified the lies I believed, I still couldn't put my finger on why I accepted them as the truth. These lies had become strongholds in my mind, and I was being held hostage by them. I didn't challenge or question their validity. Yet, each contradicted the Word of God. I had always been a discerning person, especially with it being one of my spiritual gifts (see 1 Corinthians 12:4-11). But when addiction kicked down the front door, it's like my discernment escaped out the back window. Believing and acting on the lies floating around in my head had become a habitual way of life for me.

No wonder I was in torment! I was consumed by paralyzing feelings of confusion and self-doubt. Because I allowed the lies to go unchecked rather than confronting them, I couldn't decide on anything if my life depended on it. One reason I lacked discernment was because I wanted to believe my child was telling me the truth, that this time it would be different. I needed to believe he was being honest with me when he promised he had changed and was done with drugs. I hoped that circling the same mountain for the tenth time would lead to a different outcome than the many times before. Sadly, he was making promises he could not keep, and I was gullible and hopeful enough to believe them.

The hardest area hit was my faith. Remember that little girl who grabbed onto Jesus' hand all those years ago? She knew His voice. With simple childlike faith, she listened intently to His words. She felt joy when she heard Him say, "I love you." I wanted that intimacy back.

In the book of John, Jesus spoke these words, *"My sheep hear my voice, and I know them, and they follow me" (John 10:27 ESV).* But when addiction hijacked our lives, it took my mind hostage as well. I was like a deer in the headlights, dazed and paralyzed with fear. These intense emotions caused me to doubt my ability to recognize God's voice and understand His will. In a sea of conflicting opinions, I wanted my Shepherd to guide me. I needed to hear Him above all the noise and clatter as I navigated uncharted territory. Because Jesus had promised me wisdom to overcome any trial, I would need to learn to recognize His voice, reject the enemy's lies, and respond in obedience.

The first thing I had to do was work on my discernment. Who was I listening to? I came to the realization that I spent more time researching addiction and its treatments that I spent studying the scriptures. While doing my homework was good, it was taking its toll on me emotionally, mentally, and spiritually. For me to recognize my Shepherd's voice, I needed to press into His presence. I love this familiar Psalm, *"As a deer pants for flowing streams, so pants my soul for you, O God" (Psalm 42:1 ESV)*. As I drank from the refreshing and renewing water of the Word of God, I soon tuned into His voice as He spoke sweetly to me.

Next, I had to face the reality that accepting and living by any lie is not okay with God. Here is what He has to say about it. *"Lying lips are an abomination to the LORD, but those who act faithfully are his delight" (Proverbs 12:22 ESV)*.

God never makes exceptions for dishonesty. While we can conjure up all kinds of excuses for lying, none of them is acceptable. The act of lying has serious ramifications. To understand how serious, let's return to the birthplace of original sin, the Garden of Eden. Do you remember what the first sin was based on? That's right...a lie. Spoken over 6,000 years ago by a crafty serpent to an unsuspecting woman, this lie changed the course of history.

As we learned earlier, Satan wanted the worship that was rightfully God's alone. Because he knew God gave Adam and Eve free will to make decisions for themselves, he would have to be crafty. If he could convince them to believe his lie and doubt God's words, he would have them right where he wanted them (see Genesis 3:1-5). He succeeded in his mission by distorting the truth just enough to make it convincing to the couple. His deceitful scheme introduced sin into the world, and since that fatal day, lying and sinning go hand in hand.

Discerning truth from deception is a challenge we moms of wayward children face regularly. Our minds operate in a state of heightened alert as we try to stay one step ahead of the stories they conjure up. As you well know, our children are experts at creating chaos. They are masters at making demands on us at the absolute worst times imaginable. Whether it is the middle of our workday or while we are stuck in traffic, they will push us to react in a moment of panic. It's when we are caught off-guard and in crisis-mode, we cave in and give them what they want.

But God is not a God of confusion. He is a God of peace (see 1 Corinthians 14:33). While addiction makes us question our sanity, God has given us a sound mind and judgment. To remind myself of this truth, I repeated this verse often. *"For God has not given us a spirit of fear, but of power and of love and of a sound mind" (2 Timothy 1:7 NKJV).*

Do you need more truth? Well, here is one for you. You're not losing it, Mom! What you think is happening is most likely happening. You're praying. You're asking God for wisdom, and He is giving it to you. Don't doubt yourself. Knowing and walking in the truth is a powerful weapon against addiction's destructive forces in our families. If we are going to gain victory over the darkness in our lives and those of our children, we must choose to operate in the truth. Earlier in the chapter, I asked you to identify your thoughts. These thoughts whirling around in your head have everything to say about what you believe. It's time to expose the hidden lies we believe.

NO LONGER HIDDEN

I would like to share a personal account of how I lived with a lie for many years because it was a blind spot in my life. When the Lord revealed it to me, he did so through a recurring dream. If it had only been a dream, it would have been quite entertaining. But when the Lord sends me a dream more than once, I sit up and pay attention. This was just that type of dream.

To better understand its context, let's revisit my childhood. From the time I was about seven years old, we lived in a yellow house on Flower Street. A small block wall surrounded the grassy front yard. Within its borders, there were mulberry trees, a planter full of daffodils, and a fountain resembling a little boy relieving himself. (Yes, you read that correctly!) Hold on…it gets better.

Our front room, also known as "The Blue Room," was the first place our guests entered. When I say blue, I mean BLUE! This room was arrayed with almost every shade of blue imaginable. For starters, my parents painted the walls teal blue, while the carpet was more of an aquamarine color. Next, Mom added a faux-leather coach in a turquoise shade. To liven things up, she picked pampas grass from our neighbor's yard, spray painted it baby blue, and put it in a midnight blue vase. My favorite chair in the house, a Tiffany blue Naugahyde rocker, sat in the corner in all its glory.

The only pieces of furniture not painted blue were the end tables and my century old classic upright piano. Because I was the only one in the house taking piano lessons, I spent countless hours in that room. Blue, with a few shade exceptions, is now my least favorite color. Can you blame me? With this picture in mind, I will explain my dream.

In my dream, I had just finished redecorating my house. Sparing no expense, I poured myself into selecting the perfect pieces for each room. I carefully chose each design element to reflect my taste and personality. Once finished, I invited a few close friends and family over to an open house. Upon arrival, each guest marveled at the beautiful furnishings and décor of my home. I was quite impressed with it myself. One key point I failed to mention is that I had arrayed the entire living room and dining room in fifty shades of blue. Seriously. Except for the chandeliers and silverware, everything else was blue.

The dream continues. As my friends and family oohed and awed over my exquisite taste, one brave soul dared to question me on an unusual piece of living room furniture. Without hesitation, she pointed to an old chair awkwardly placed smack dab in the middle of the room. The once beautiful, overstuffed chair was in such poor condition, it was beyond repair. Broken springs and stuffing stuck out from beneath its tattered and stained formerly white fabric. The chair was fit only for the garbage heap.

"What are your plans for that old chair, Dawn?" she asked inquisitively.

"What chair?" I replied, unsure of what she was talking about.

With a bewildered look in her eye, she pointed to the tattered chair and answered emphatically, "Well, that one right there, of course!"

I had to adjust my focus a few times before the chair finally came into view. The oddest part of the dream wasn't that I decorated the room in a kaleidoscope of blue. It was my inability to see the dilapidated chair until my friend pointed it out. At this point in my dream, I woke up with no clue what it meant. I attributed it to having spicy Mexican food too close to bedtime. But when God wants to make His point, He repeats Himself. Over the next few years, the dream persisted until I finally asked Him to reveal what it meant.

As I prayed, I asked the Lord about the symbolism of the old chair. Before He answered, He prodded me to question the significance of the color blue, one I most definitely would not have chosen for myself. Assuming its meaning was unimportant to the relevance of the dream, I hadn't given the color of the room a second thought.

While not speaking audibly, I clearly heard the Holy Spirit speak to my heart, *"The color blue represents your childhood."* Because I was an adult and it was my house in the dream, I hadn't made the connection.

"And the old chair, Lord. What does it represent?" I asked.

"That chair represents the false beliefs you've held onto since your childhood. While they make you feel secure and safe, they are not true," He gently whispered.

Startled, I persisted, "Lord. I don't understand. What beliefs are you talking about?"

"The beliefs you've accepted because they felt and seemed normal to you. These are lies spoken to you, about you, and ones you spoke about yourself," Jesus answered as He drew me closer. "You are also holding onto false beliefs about Me."

With tears welling up in my eyes, I cried, "I am confused. Why are you showing all this to me now, Lord?"

"Because these wrong beliefs are holding you back. Just because you believe something is true doesn't make it true. You may feel comfortable in that old chair, but you don't belong in it. It's time to see it for what it is, throw it out, and move on," Jesus responded tenderly and with the certainty of a Father who knows what's best for his daughter.

The dream was a pivotal point in my life and faith. For the first time, God exposed the lies I believed and had kept hidden, even from myself. I thought I had victory over my past hurts and insecurities, but they still had a negative influence on how I perceived myself, related to others, and understood my faith. Because of the trauma I experienced as a child, I blamed myself for circumstances beyond my control. As a result, I carried with me feelings of guilt (I did bad) and shame (I am bad) into adulthood. Because I felt unworthy of God's blessings in my life, I never experienced the peace and security He promises His children.

In His wisdom, the Lord waited until just the right time to begin the restoration process. It wouldn't be easy. I would have to trust Him to reveal to me what I could not see on my own. I had so many blind spots, it would take a while for me to see the truth hidden behind them. Like the painstaking process of removing layer upon layer of wallpaper, God's work in my life would be done with patience and in His perfect timing.

I share this story with you because, while we are in a fight to save our children's lives, we must not disregard the restorative work God is doing in ours. All too often, we ignore the Holy Spirit as He convicts us of our sins in our attempt to save our children from theirs.

Like the old worn-out chair, we cannot see the deteriorating condition of our own heart because we are too busy gussying up everything and everyone else around it. Then one day, like my friend in the dream, Jesus pays us a visit, points to our tattered treasure, and asks, "What about that?"

While my dream revealed I was believing lies most of my life, I still needed to learn to recognize them and reject them. Since I was unaware of these false beliefs, I began by asking the Lord to expose them to me. I encourage you to do this as well.

"For nothing is hidden except to be made manifest; nor is anything secret except to come to light." (Mark 4:22 ESV)

Begin by spending time in prayer with pen and journal in hand. As you pray, invite the Holy Spirit into those intimate and secret places of your heart and mind. Ask Him to expose the lies you believe about yourself. (Start here and then move on to others such as your family, friends, church, community, society, etc.). Write these in your journal or on this page. Here are just a few examples of thoughts that may come to mind:

- *"I don't matter."*
- *"I am unlovable."*
- *"I am damaged."*
- *"I am alone."*
- *"I am unworthy of God's love."*

As you move onto the lies that others have spoken to you, consider these examples:

- *"You are worthless."*
- *"You have to be perfect."*
- *"You will never be good enough."*
- *"You are stupid."*
- *"You are a failure."*

Finally, move onto our society. It is full of false messages we all can fall for if we are not careful. Here are a few of its lies we should watch out for:

- *"God doesn't exist."*
- *"You must change to fit in."*
- *"You must cheat to get ahead."*
- *"Follow your heart. If it feels good, do it."*
- *"You are in charge of your own destiny."*

You may have recognized some familiar lies as you read these, but I would venture to say some of yours may still be tucked away for safekeeping. Mine were. Why is that? Because change is hard, even when it is for our own good. It took time for Jesus to peel back the layers of behaviors I had adopted as defense mechanisms that kept me in denial... and my life functioning. You will need to go way back and dig deeply to unearth these well-buried secrets. I understand it is tempting to leave well enough alone. But not where God is concerned. He knows keeping these lies hidden will do us no good and ignoring them is not an option. As He exposes them, you will most likely experience some intense emotions. Jesus is not bringing them to the forefront to cause you pain, although experiencing pain may be part of the process. He is bringing them to your attention to heal you and set you free.

Let's face it. No one wants to feel shame or disgrace. When it comes to our personal failures, past sins, or false beliefs, we would rather keep them secret than risk others using them against us. But the Lord does not reveal our shortcomings so that others can shout them from the rooftops. His intention is to provide us with lasting freedom. To do so, He must expose the lies we carry with us that are negatively affecting our beliefs, behaviors, and how we relate to others. Expose the lie, and it loses its power. We do so by learning to think like God thinks.

THINK LIKE GOD THINKS

I want you to take a walk with me down memory lane. Take a moment to reflect on your childhood. In celebration of Christmas, did your parents teach you to believe in Santa Claus? Mine did. My mother used the Naughty or Nice list to keep me in line months before St. Nick made his way to our house.

On Christmas Eve, we placed cookies and milk next to the fireplace for Santa to snack on. Next, we opened our first gift of the season, holiday pajamas, which we changed into before climbing into bed. Once Mom tucked us in, without our knowledge, Dad would crawl up onto the roof, shuffle around, and yell, "Ho-Ho-Ho!" Hearing the commotion and convinced it was Santa, we lay there, too excited to fall asleep.

While we learned the story of Jesus' birth in church, like most kids, I lived for Christmas morning and the excitement of unwrapping my presents. As I grew older, I began having doubts about the bearded man in a red suit who could magically deliver gifts all over the world in one night with only a sleigh and nine flying reindeer. Perhaps hearing that Santa wasn't real from an older kid in the neighborhood made me question his existence. Or maybe I overheard a conversation between my parents. Whatever it was, the day came when I didn't believe in Santa Claus anymore. Discovering this truth was like a bittersweet rite of passage. Along with no longer believing in the Tooth Fairy or the Easter Bunny, the road from childhood to adulthood was paved with disappointing truths.

The little white lies our parents told us to make our childhoods enchanting and magical were innocent enough. While I taught my children the true meaning of Christmas and Easter was to celebrate Jesus rather than to believe in Santa or the Easter Bunny, it doesn't mean I was always honest with them. There were plenty of other times I made promises I didn't keep, denied saying what they thought I said, or lied to protect their feelings. Sadly, I am ashamed to admit that once addiction entered our lives, there were times I also lied for them.

The reasons people justify lying vary among individuals. The line between right and wrong becomes less clear when considering minor indiscretions, misinformation, fabrications, and deceptions. Whatever the reason for lying, God never condones it. And while there may be occasional exceptions to the rule such as personal protection, public safety, or national security, this is rarely the case. The Bible warns us we will be held accountable for the words we speak.

"I tell you, on the day of judgment people will give account for every careless word they speak, for by your words you will be justified, and by your words you will be condemned." (Matthew 12:36-37 ESV)

So far, we have learned to identify and expose the lies we believe. But it's not always that easy, is it? Because the devil is a craftsman at cunningly disguising lies as truth, it can be difficult to tell the difference. Lies are powerful weapons in our adversary's hands. In his war against God, he yields his ultimate weapon, counterfeit truth. Determined to deceive us, he mixes just enough truth with a lie to make it enticing to us. The good news is Jesus defeated Satan and his lies with the most powerful weapon of all, the Word of God. With three simple words, "It is written," He put the devil in his place (see Luke 4).

Jesus sets the standard for truth because He is the Truth (John 14:6). As believers in Jesus, we are not to be bound by the lies of the enemy. What this means is we are to strive to think like God thinks about everything. Not just some things, but everything.

Because Satan wants us to doubt God's Word, he will do everything in his power to keep us from knowing the truth. However, changing how we think is not as hard as you might expect. These four practical steps will help you renew your mind so you can live in the truth:

4 Steps to Embracing the Truth and Overcoming Lies

1. **Know** the truth—**Recognize** the lie.
2. **Believe** the truth—**Reject** the lie.
3. **Speak** the truth—**Replace** the lie.
4. **Live** the truth—**Reverse** the lie.

Let's trim these steps down into bite-size pieces. As you review these steps, I have added a sample of a scripture that applies to each step of truth. I recommend memorizing these or choosing one of your own.

Step 1 - Know the Truth. In order to know the truth, we begin by examining what the Word of God says on the matter. Once we know the truth, it's easy to recognize a lie. How does what you believe line up with the Word of God?

"For the word of God is living and active, sharper than any two-edged sword, piercing to the division of soul and of spirit, of joints and of marrow, and discerning the thoughts and intentions of the heart." (Hebrews 4:12 ESV)

Step 2 - Believe the Truth. When we believe the truth, we think like God thinks and are empowered to reject the lie. We start by renewing our minds. What thoughts consume your mind? Do you believe them?

> "Do not be conformed to this world, but be transformed by the renewal of your mind, that by testing you may discern what is the will of God, what is good and acceptable and perfect." (Romans 12:2 ESV)

Step 3 - Speak the Truth. It's time to replace the lie. We do this by speaking the truth. Speaking the truth empowers us to change our thinking. Are the words you speak true?

> "Do not lie to one another, seeing that you have put off the old self with its practices and have put on the new self, which is being renewed in knowledge after the image of its creator." (Colossians 3:9-10 ESV)

Step 4 - Live the Truth. Genuine change happens when we reverse the lie. The last step in knowing the truth is living the truth by taking our thoughts captive. Do you live according to the truth?

> "We destroy arguments and every lofty opinion raised against the knowledge of God, and take every thought captive to obey Christ." (2 Corinthians 10:5 ESV)

Practical Application:

I will give you a practical example of how to apply this in your everyday life. We will start with a negative thought common to moms of wayward prodigals. This is one I remember sharing with my counselor as I faced the devastating reality of my son's addiction.

"I will never be happy again. How can I be happy when my child is suffering?" This thought may seem extreme, but ask any mom with a struggling child if she has thought it, and the majority will say, "Yes."

Next, here is an example of overcoming this lie:

Thought (Lie): *"I will never be happy again."*

1. Know the truth: *Compare your thought to what God's Word says, "For everything there is a season, and a time for every matter under heaven: a time to weep, and a time to laugh; a time to mourn, and a time to dance" (Ecclesiastes 3:1,4 ESV).*

Recognize the lie: *"I will **never** be happy again…"*

Apply the truth: Remember that there are seasons in our lives. Some are seasons of pleasure, and others are seasons of pain. This hard season you are going through won't last forever. If you're feeling sad and hopeless about your future, seek wisdom through your pastor, Christian counselors, and godly friends to encourage you to have hope.

2. Believe the truth: *"The Bible says there is a season for everything. This season of grieving will not last forever."*

Reject the lie: *"I reject the lie that I will never be happy again, and instead choose to believe I will experience seasons of happiness again."*

Apply the truth: Accept that grief is part of the process. Allow yourself to grieve what you have lost to addiction. Renew your mind with the promises of God. Next, find reasons to celebrate and have hope. Practice gratitude for what you have by keeping a gratitude jar. A prayer journal is a way to maintain hope while you wait.

3. Speak the truth: *"I will speak the truth of God's Word. 'Oh, taste and see that the LORD is good! Blessed (Happy) is the man who takes refuge in him!'" (Psalm 34:8 ESV).*

Replace the lie: *"I will not speak the lie, 'I will never be happy again.' Instead, I will replace it with the truth. 'I can be joyful because God's plans for me are good.'"*

Apply the truth: Write Bible verses and affirmations on cards and carry them with you. This is not a "name it and claim it" mindset. It's believing the promises of God for both you and your child. Carry your cards with you to read out loud throughout the day. Be accountable for your speech by asking a family member or close friend to help you recognize and address habitual complaining.

4. Live the truth: *"I believe I can be happy even while I grieve because I am blessed by God, and He is my refuge."*

Reject the lie: *"I will no longer accept these false beliefs. If my thoughts contradict God's Word, they are a lie."*

Apply the truth: Look for opportunities to cultivate truth in your life. Whatever the lie is, stepping outside your own painful circumstance to bless and encourage others is the perfect way to live God's truth. Serving at your church, volunteering at a local food bank, or helping your neighbor are a few ways you can overcome negative thought patterns and bless others.

Following these steps will help you overcome any lie you believe. If you are not sure what is the truth and what is a lie, listen for thoughts that contain words like "always" or "never." You should be on alert for self-blaming statements such as, "It's all my fault" or "I should have seen the warning signs." Also, be aware of toxic thoughts that blame others or make excuses for wrong behaviors. *"If he didn't_____, then I wouldn't have _____."*

Finally, to overcome the lies you believe, cling to this truth. *God loves you.* His love for you and your child is immeasurable. No lie or false belief the enemy shoots at you can withstand the power of God's love. Hold on to this truth. It will set you free.

"And you will know the truth, and the truth will set you free." (John 8:32 ESV)

Reflection Questions

1. Has your addicted child ever lied to you? How did you feel about it? How did you react?

2. Has the Lord exposed lies you believed since childhood? What has He shown you? How has learning of these lies affected your life and faith?

3. Do you find it difficult or easy to recognize lies when praying for discernment concerning your child?

4. What steps will you put into practice moving forward to help you believe and live according to the truth of God's Word?

CHAPTER 9

Let's Get Spiritual

"Behold, I have given you authority to tread on
serpents and scorpions, and over all the power of the
enemy, and nothing shall hurt you."
Luke 10:19 (ESV)

ENEMY TERRITORY

It was the middle of the night, and I was awake again. "Awakened" is more like it. Sensing a rustling of the sheets and the weight of something on the mattress, I rolled over to see what was going on. Still half-asleep, I rubbed my eyes and tried to focus. No one was there. Frustrated, I said out loud, "Not again," as I rolled over and tried to go back to sleep. This was the third night in a row the invisible intruder had paid me a visit. I couldn't tell if it was a bad dream, an overly active imagination, or something far more sinister. One thing was for sure. It wasn't my husband. He wasn't home, nor would he be for several weeks or months...if at all.

I shared earlier that Steve began using pain meds after sustaining back injuries from a car accident. Because of his disability, he was no longer working and became depressed and bored. He also turned to gambling to pass the time. Soon, he was in bondage to both. He hid them from me even when I interrogated him about the changes in his personality and missing funds from our bank account. Because he functioned well while taking the medications, confronting him did no good. He insisted he was doing fine, our finances were manageable, and I was the one with the problem. Because he was always a loving and supportive husband and father, I believed him. It must have been in my imagination. That's what addiction does. It makes you think you're the one with the problem.

In desperation, I cried out to Jesus to show me what was going on. I knew the man sitting in front of me was not the one I married, not the man I trusted. I didn't have to wait long before He revealed my husband's secret life. I heard the Lord say to my spirit, "Go to the pocket of his old jacket. Look inside." The closet contained an assortment of winter coats and casual jackets, but I knew exactly which one to look through—the old brown plaid jacket he had outgrown years ago. I examined its pockets and found a bundle of receipts from his gambling winnings. What? I had never seen Steve put so much as a nickel in a slot machine before. This was the last thing I expected. Dumbfounded, I stared at the pile of papers in my hands. *"So this is where our money has been going,"* I thought to myself.

After confronting Steve with the evidence, he finally confessed to a problem he had concealed for years. Hysterical, I demanded answers. "How could you let this happen? Why did you lie to me repeatedly?" The strongest man I knew remained speechless, unable to explain this thing that had power over him. I gave him an ultimatum: get help or get out. Humbled and grateful to be "ousted" by God, Steve agreed to do whatever it took to get his life and our marriage back on track.

Because I had plenty of experience with addiction and alcoholism, I knew there was no time to waste. We headed off to our local church recovery program for support. Together we created an accountability plan for our finances and how he would spend his free time. He joined a men's Bible study and met regularly with his friend, a local pastor, for discipleship. Steve also agreed to go off the pain meds that were doing more harm than good. Now that his "problem" was under control, we resumed our focus on our eldest son's addiction, which continued to wreak havoc on our family.

For several years, everything was going well, but eventually I noticed subtle changes in Steve's behavior. Facing another back surgery, his pain had reached intolerable levels. Along with being in pain, he seemed moody and on edge. It wasn't long before Jesus revealed to me that Steve was once again addicted to substances and gambling. Just as He did before, He showed me exactly where to go to find the evidence needed to confront him about his actions.

Finally reaching my breaking point, I lost it and screamed at him to get the "not-so-nice expletive" out, or I would take our daughter and go. If he wanted to save our marriage, he would need to get help. We did not allow our son to live in our home and abuse drugs. It wouldn't work for our marriage either. To be honest with you, I was "over" being more concerned about my family's addictions than they were. My broken man willingly packed his bags and departed, leaving me behind to deal with my own brokenness. In over forty years of marriage, except for occasional short solo trips, we were never apart. This was the first night in many years that Steve was not home. It turned out to be the same night the nocturnal intruder paid me a visit. Without realizing it, our entire household was under spiritual attack.

To help you better understand how the enemy uses drugs to attack our families, let's look at the definition of the Greek word *pharmakeía*, which is where we get the word "pharmacy."[19] In the Greek, *pharmakeía* primarily signified *"the use of medicine, drugs, spells; then poisoning; then sorcery (or witchcraft). In "sorcery" the use of drugs, whether simple or potent, was generally accompanied by incantations and appeals to occult powers."* In the Bible, sorcery or witchcraft refers to the use of drugs for hallucinogenic and mind-altering purposes. Sorcery is one of the "works of the flesh" warned against in Galatians 5:20 and in the book of Revelation.[20]

> "The rest of mankind, who were not killed by these plagues, did not repent of the works of their hands nor give up worshiping demons and idols of gold and silver and bronze and stone and wood, which cannot see

or hear or walk, nor did they repent of their murders or their *sorceries* or their sexual immorality or their thefts." (Revelation 9:20-21 ESV, emphasis mine)

The Bible warns us against abusing substances to avoid giving the enemy access to our lives. Satan did not force our loved ones to abuse drugs or alcohol, but he tempted them to follow after their desires. They came to believe that substances were the answer to their problems. Once hooked, these drugs became their idol. It's understandable how demonic forces have access to and can torment the life of someone bound by drugs.

In his book, *Biblical Counseling: A Topical Index for Christian Living,* Chuck Smith wrote:

> "So many people are dying a slow death because their addiction has a hold on them, almost as if it were demonic; and the only thing that can free a person from this hold is Jesus Christ. Jesus came to open the eyes of those that are blind, and 'to heal the brokenhearted, to proclaim liberty to the captives, and the opening of the prison to those who are bound' (Isaiah 61:1). 'Therefore if the Son makes you free, you shall be free indeed'" (John 8:36).[21]

The whole idea of drugs, demons, witchcraft, and sorcery may seem far-fetched. I get it. It's hard to imagine. But we believe in an invisible God, don't we? We believe in a Savior we have never met in person. And we believe the Holy Spirit lives inside us. When the Bible says that spiritual forces of evil are at work in this world, we'd better take heed. Pay attention to what is going on in your child's life. What are they into? What are they talking about? Listen and observe. If Jesus tells you something is wrong, believe Him. No, you're not losing your mind. The Lord is revealing the truth, the truth that can set your child free.

Looking back, I usually had a keen sensitivity to the spiritual battles raging in our home. While this strange bedfellow caught me off guard, this was not our first experience with spiritual warfare. There were other occasions when I was aware of a sinister presence that had entered our home on addiction's heels. Some of you may dismiss these experiences as my brain snapping under the weight of stress, but others will understand all too clearly the spiritual forces bent on destroying our families. When I questioned whether my mind was playing tricks on me or if I needed to resort to sleeping on the couch, I held onto this verse, believing God placed it in the Bible for a reason. What was happening was real. This was spiritual warfare.

"For we do not wrestle against flesh and blood, but against the rulers, against the authorities, against the cosmic powers over this present darkness, against the spiritual forces of evil in the heavenly places." (Ephesians 6:12 ESV)

Even though I was physically and emotionally exhausted, my faith grew stronger as the Holy Spirit renewed my mind and refreshed my spirit. He was strengthening my faith and preparing me for battle.

Now, back to our home invasion. These nighttime intrusions continued intermittently for several days. This was more than a dream or a vision. This was an actual evil spirit invading my bedroom. As if being separated from my soulmate wasn't hard enough. I felt abandoned and alone, trying to deal with this on my own.

In an attempt to catch it in the act, I started feigning sleep. Although it took on no form, I could sense its presence when it entered the room. Even in its silence, it was determined to convince me it had full access to our home. While I felt powerless against it, I knew Jesus had full authority over it. I commanded it to leave in Jesus' name, and it left, but not for long. Satan was after my faith. He wanted me to doubt God's power in the presence of evil. Was I going to choose to believe in the authority given to me by Jesus Christ, or would I continue to hide under the bedcovers?

No. There would be no more of that. It was time to take authority over the enemy and his menacing spirits.

"Behold, I have given you *authority* to tread on serpents and scorpions, and over all the power of the enemy, and nothing shall hurt you." (Luke 10:19 ESV, emphasis mine)

I could no longer sit back and let this thing run the show. It was time to do battle. My daughter and I began praying over the rooms of our house. She also believed something had invaded our home that didn't belong there. We played worship music as we prayed and praised Jesus. We anointed the thresholds of the rooms with oil, asking Jesus to remove any unwelcome spirits assigned to harass us and steal our peace. As we prayed in Jesus' name, we felt the Holy Spirit fill every room with His presence. From that point on, I slept peacefully through the night.

Let me assure you, I am not one to look for a demon under every rock. But, like it or not, we live in a world where the spiritual is just as real as the physical. These rulers, authorities, cosmic powers over this present darkness, and spiritual forces of evil in heavenly places aren't playing around. They are waging war against our families, homes, and communities. We need to take them every bit as seriously as they take us. We have no reason to fear, though, because Satan and his demons are under God's authority. The Lord has equipped us with spiritual weapons to fight back against them, including the mighty name of Jesus. As we enter into warfare, we should pray in Jesus' name. When saints of God get on their knees and start praying in His mighty name, the demons tremble.

"Therefore God has highly exalted him and bestowed on him the name that is above every name, so that at the *name of Jesus* every knee should bow, in heaven, and on earth and under the earth, and every tongue confess that Jesus Christ is Lord, to the glory of God the Father." (Philippians 2:9-11 ESV, emphasis mine)

In the meantime, Steve was having a spiritual encounter of his own. After he left, I could not imagine how we would ever have a life together again. I forgave him, but I didn't know if I could ever trust him. Given that trust in my spouse was at the top of my list of needs, I convinced myself that our marriage was beyond repair. I was numb from the shock of what we were going through and on the verge of giving up. To be honest, I was angry. Between him and our son, I was burned out from dealing with addiction.

Still, there remained in me a seed of hope. We had been married for over 40 years. Steve loved the Lord and cherished me. He would take a bullet for me. My husband and our marriage were worth fighting for. Therefore, I did what any godly wife does when she catches her husband lying to her. After plotting his murder, I decided it would be better if I prayed for him. The Holy Spirit prompted me to convey a message to him while he was staying out of state with our son, Kyle. He was to go to church, find a pastor or elder, and ask for prayer. I remember asking the Lord which church he should attend. I could almost hear Him chuckle as he replied, "Any church that worships Me will do." After relaying the message to Steve, the ball was in his court. This was between him and God.

The following Sunday, Steve and Kyle attended his local church. Not normally one to stay after and socialize, Steve was determined to wait around until he found someone to pray for him. Apparently, the Spirit had been speaking to him as well. After the service was over, he asked around and was directed to the corner of the church where the elders were praying for people. It turned out to be almost an hour's wait, but Steve wouldn't leave. He had the faith to believe God was going to meet him in the corner of the church that day, and he wasn't going anywhere.

Finally, it was his turn for prayer. As he poured out his heart to this young couple, he told them of the excruciating pain he lived with, his gambling and substance use problems, and how hopeless he felt. I am sure they were hungry and ready to get out of there, but faithfully they placed their hands on his shoulders and began to pray. What happened next was nothing short of a miracle. Feeling an overwhelming sense of God's presence, Steve heard the Holy Spirit speak these words audibly, *"I forgive you."* At that moment, he saw all his sins flash before his eyes. He hadn't gone up there to receive forgiveness, but in the blink of an eye, Jesus forgave him and set him free from desire for substances and gambling. He was a changed man, made new by the power of God's grace and His forgiveness.

In this war against addiction, never be hesitant to ask for prayer from your church leadership. There is power as we pray together and look to Jesus for the freedom and healing of our families.

> "Is anyone among you sick? Let him call for the elders of the church, and let them pray over him, anointing him with oil in the name of the Lord. And the prayer of faith will save the one who is sick, and the Lord will raise him up. And if he has committed sins, he will be forgiven." (James 5:14-15 ESV)

As Steve shared his testimony with me, I was cautiously optimistic. I was happy about his encounter with Jesus, but would these changes last? For the first time in our marriage, he had an insatiable desire to spend time in God's Word. Even though miles apart, we started reading the Bible together over video chat.

After six weeks, he moved back home and our journey to healing as a couple began. But while he had experienced a life-changing divine encounter, I had not. I was still reeling from the events of the weeks prior, not only because of his relapse, but also because of the enemy's invasion of our home. I was exhausted from the emotional stress and spiritual warfare I had been through. It would take time for me to let go of fear of the unknown and trust Jesus to fight my battles for me.

FAITH IN THE BATTLE

This experience made me realize how determined Satan was to convince me he had control over my family. Despite everything we had been through, I never doubted God's power to overcome evil. But the enemy succeeded in persuading me that even if my loved ones overcame their addictions, inevitably they would relapse and be back under his control.

While my faith was resolute in most areas of my life, when it came to addiction, I waffled. I believed God's Word was the final authority on everything, but the disease narrative of "once an addict, always an addict" got stuck in my mind, hijacking my seemingly rock-solid faith and replacing it with fear and dread. After saturating my mind with scriptures like this one from 1 Corinthians, I believed God would not inflict a disease on someone that would force them to sin against Him. So why did I have my doubts concerning addiction?

"No temptation has overtaken you that is not common to man. God is faithful, and he will not let you be tempted beyond your ability, but with the temptation he will

also provide the way of escape, that you may be able
to endure it. Therefore, my beloved, flee from idolatry."
(1 Corinthians 10:13-14 ESV)

Once I figured out the harassing spirit in my house was
there on assignment, I still failed to connect the dots and recognize that my faith was also under attack. The enemy continued to do everything in his power to entice me to take my eyes
off the Lord. I was trapped in a mindset of unbelief because
I believed a lie—well, probably a lot of lies. It was time to go
to battle. I would no longer passively stand by, convinced that
my family could never triumph over their addictions. No longer would I allow our home (or my mind) to be the enemy's
territory. It was time to accept God's mission: to help other
moms be victorious in the face of one of the most terrifying
attacks the enemy could ever wage against their families.

Jesus had already placed the idea for this book in my heart.
Now, He was preparing me to declare His truth against a system of lies that has convinced millions of people they will
never be free from their addictions. To proclaim the good
news that freedom is possible, I would need to understand
and believe what the Bible says about addiction and spiritual
warfare. I would no longer be fighting this battle with earthly
weapons. It was time for me to stop being wishy-washy about
my faith and learn to stand on the Lord's promises in the face
of enemy attacks.

"For though we walk in the flesh, we are not waging war
according to the flesh. For the weapons of our warfare
are not of the flesh but have divine power to destroy
strongholds." (2 Corinthians 10:3-4 ESV)

For starters, I needed to put down my earthly weapons once and for all. Nagging, pleading, manipulation, yelling—you name it, I tried it. Nothing worked. Why? Because I was reacting out of fear instead of faith. I was terrified my son would die, so I nagged and pleaded. I panicked because he might end up in prison, so I tried to save him and control his every move. I feared he would bleed us dry financially, so I yelled and threatened. None of my weapons worked. In fact, they only made matters worse.

Then came the moment when Jesus showed me that by fighting in my own strength and with earthly weapons, I lacked the faith to trust Him to fight for me. I always believed I had faith in God to fight my battles, but He revealed to me that none of my actions were grounded in faith. My prayers, although zealous, were powerless. I consumed the scriptures fervently, but still lived in fear and unbelief. I often reminded my son of God's love when, truthfully, I was the one who needed reminding. Nothing about my behavior resembled anything close to offensive faith-filled warfare. I might as well have been hiding out in a cave.

Does what I am sharing sound painfully familiar? If it does, don't beat yourself up. This is one of the toughest battles you'll ever face. When we are battle weary, our faith either grows stronger or gets weaker. It all depends on who we place our faith in, Jesus or ourselves.

When we look at the scriptures, we find we are not the only ones who struggle with our faith. Christ's disciples followed Him around for a few years, observing His teachings and miracles. As they spent time with Him, their faith grew.

You would think they would have extreme faith, the kind that comes from being in the presence of God Himself. This didn't prove to be the case.

Once ready for their mission, Jesus sent His disciples out to proclaim the kingdom of Heaven, heal the sick, raise the dead, cleanse the lepers, and cast out demons (Matthew 10:7-8). It must have been thrilling for them to be used by God in such miraculous ways. However, their faith was tested when they encountered a demon who refused to do as it was told. The bewildered disciples asked Jesus why they couldn't cast the demon out of the boy (Matthew 17:14-19).

> "He said to them, 'Because of your *little faith*. For truly, I say to you, if you have faith like a grain of mustard seed, you will say to this mountain, "Move from here to there," and it will move, and nothing will be impossible for you.'" (Matthew 17:20 ESV, emphasis mine)

Faith was, and still is, a big deal to God. The disciples were eyewitnesses to the miracles of Jesus, but they grew weak at the knees in the presence of this demon-possessed boy. I can almost picture the scene as Philip shoved Thomas towards the lad and said, "You do it," only for Thomas to throw his hands up and shout, "No way, man! You do it!"

It's easy to have faith when we feel in control, isn't it? But it sure gets tested when we face challenges beyond our ability to handle alone. And that's exactly how God wants it. I suspect this is how the disciples felt when Jesus sent them out at the start of their ministry. Their mission would be impossible for them to accomplish on their own. They would need to exercise faith, not in themselves, but in Jesus and His power to work through them.

In the verses above, other Bible versions translate the words "little faith" as "unbelief." The Greek word for both English translations is *apistía,* which means "faithlessness, disbelief, unbelief."[22] When Jesus rebuked His disciples, it was not because their faith was small or weak, but because they lacked faith entirely. Weren't these the same disciples who just performed incredible miracles? What caused this shift in their faith?

As we read this story in the other gospel accounts, we learn the disciples were arguing with the scribes over why they could not heal the demon-possessed boy. Jesus walked into the chaotic scene where the desperate father confronted Him and begged Him to heal his son. While the disciples had given up on the boy, his father had not. How did Jesus respond?

"And Jesus answered, 'O *faithless and twisted* generation, how long am I to be with you? How long am I to bear with you? Bring him here to me.'" (Matthew 17:17 ESV, emphasis mine)

Jesus had just called the crowd out for being faithless. Now, He was chastising His disciples for their lack of faith. What? Was He comparing them to the same people he just called "twisted" (*lit. perverse, turned aside, and corrupted*)? He made it clear to the disciples that their unbelief did not differ from that of the scribes they were arguing with. Somehow, they lost whatever genuine faith they had when they first set out on their mission.

The book of Hebrews reminds us that without **faith,** it is impossible to please God *(Hebrews 11:6 ESV, paraphrased).* Here, the word for "faith" is *pístis,* meaning "full assurance, firm persuasion, and conviction."[23] This is an uncompromising faith that doesn't waver but believes Jesus is who He says He is and can do what He says He can do.

This was a resolute faith shown by a persistent father who never gave up even when all hope seemed lost. Instead, by faith, he ignored the ones who couldn't save his son and directed his attention to the only one who could. I love the interaction between this desperate man and Jesus, as recorded in the book of Mark. After detailing the torment his son had endured from the demon since childhood, the father looked to Jesus with what little faith he had left and said, *"But if you can do anything, have compassion on us and help us.' And Jesus said to him, "'If you can"! All things are possible for one who believes.' Immediately, the father of the child cried out and said, 'I believe; help my unbelief!'" (Mark 9:22b-24 ESV).*

This is the cry of a father's heart! "I believe, help my unbelief!" And this is also the cry of a mother's heart, isn't it? How many times have we cried out to Jesus, "Please save my child!" How many doors have we knocked on? How many calls have we made? Doctors, insurance companies, rehabs. "Help my son!" "Save my daughter!" Cries from a relentless father who would go to the ends of the earth to rescue his son from intense suffering and a persistent mom who would do the same. This father knew the demon was determined to kill his son. And you know the enemy is set on destroying yours.

So where does this leave us as we fight for our addicted children, for our families, and for ourselves? What can we learn by observing the disciples as they wavered in unbelief and from this precious father who held on to what little faith he had left? Perhaps the disciples lacked faith because they listened to the hopeless reports about the demoniac, the ones that said he was beyond help, too far gone. Or they may have approached him confidently, only to be taken aback by his dire condition. Whatever the reason for their unbelief, we can relate, can't we?

The challenge here is for each of us to examine our own faith. Is it strong and unwavering? Is it more of a mixture of doubt and wishful thinking? Or is it weak and almost non-existent? For some, have you given up altogether? If it's the latter, hold on to this truth: God hasn't given up on you. When you are at your weakest and feel you can't go on, He is there with you, holding you. Jesus is working in your life to give you hope and strengthen your faith.

Another question we should ask ourselves is, "What am I focusing on?" Are you focusing on Jesus, or are you focusing on the bad reports? If your eyes are on your child's erratic behavior, their physical deterioration, their constant relapses, or their declining mental stability, your faith will weaken. But the Bible reminds us to walk by faith and not by sight (see 2 Corinthians 5:7). This is key to winning the battle of our minds as we enter into warfare for our families.

Finally, remember that even if we engage in spiritual warfare for our children, it does not guarantee they will be free from their bondage to substances or self-destructive behaviors.

Our kids still have free will. But it does mean the Lord will give them every opportunity possible to have victory over this bondage in their life. So don't give up. As the song says, "Don't stop believing." Because with God all things are possible for those who believe.

IF GOD IS FOR US...

The idea of spiritual warfare may seem overwhelming. In fact, it might sound like something straight out of a Sci-Fi movie. But the Bible is clear that the battle in the heavenly places is real. There is a war raging in the spiritual realm between God and His angels and Satan and his demons, a battle between good and evil. Satan, however, is already a defeated foe. Not only did Jesus pay the debt for our sin at the cross, He also *"disarmed the rulers and authorities and put them to open shame, by triumphing over them in him" (Colossians 2:15 ESV).*

As believers, the Lord has given us authority over the enemy in our lives. Because Satan comes to steal, kill, and destroy our families, we must be aware of his tactics. Our children are trapped in his snare. The drugs have taken them hostage, and their minds are the devil's playground. Don't think for one moment he isn't sneering in their ears, "Look what you've done. You've made a mess out of your life. How can anyone love you? God doesn't love you. He doesn't care about you. You will never be free. You are mine." With his sinister attacks against our children's minds, he intends to destroy their lives and, ultimately, claim their souls. If your child is a Christian, the devil cannot steal their salvation. He can, through the power of persuasion, torment them, devastate their lives, and pull them into his dark world. When we engage in this battle against addiction, we must guard against the enemy as he attempts to do the same to us. I am thankful that God has a better plan, as written in the book of John. *"The thief comes only to steal and kill and destroy. I came that they may have life and have it abundantly"* (10:10 ESV).

But what should we do when we don't have this abundant life God promised us? When I launched into writing this book, I pledged to be honest with you at all costs, so I have to confess that for most of our addiction journey, I lived anything but abundantly. I was miserable. I felt alone in the battle against my son's addiction, like God had dropped me in the middle of the war zone and abandoned me there to fend for myself. While I was still going through the motions of engaging in spiritual warfare, as time went on with no end in sight, I soon grew weary of fighting. It seemed we'd already lost the battle, and our family had raised the white flag of surrender, but no one told me.

There had to be a better way to remain in the spiritual battle and still experience the abundant life Jesus offered me. When I finally reached the point of complete exhaustion, I couldn't take one more step or pray one more prayer. Raising my hands in the air, I cried out, "Jesus, I surrender! I can't do this on my own. Please fight this battle for me."

Have you ever been in a situation where you were in over your head? Your only options were to fail miserably or ask for help. That's how I felt as I fought for my son's life. I was in way over my head. No wonder I wasn't experiencing abundant life. I was worn out from fighting this war on my own. Remember the saying, "Mommy knows best?" I learned the hard way that when it comes to spiritual warfare, that statement doesn't hold water. What I thought was spiritual warfare was actually me just fighting in my own strength, praying and confessing scriptures, and asking God to bless my efforts. That was a big mistake on my part, a painful lesson that Mommy doesn't know best after all.

If we stand a chance of winning the war between light and darkness, we must recognize that God is in control, relinquish our right to do things our way, and release our own expectations for the outcome. In other words, we aren't in control. God is. He gives the commands, and we follow them. In order to fight and win our spiritual battles, we must surrender to our Commander and obey His orders.

As I slowly accepted the idea that I was not Chief Mom in Charge of My Child's Destiny, I started letting go of the burden I had carried for a long time. The battle I was engaged in was not meant to be fought alone. While I may have believed I was the lone man standing, I was wrong. Jesus was there fighting for me, and He was no stranger to battle. He also felt the painful blows and heard the taunting jeers of His enemies. Not only was He with me in the battle I was facing, He understood what I was going through. While Christ was alone during His final hours of agonizing suffering, He would never allow me to face my suffering without His presence. This is His promise to all His children. *"It is the LORD who goes before you. He will be with you; he will not leave you or forsake you. Do not fear or be dismayed"* (Deuteronomy 31:8 ESV).

It's hard to believe we can experience an abundant life while we are experiencing intense suffering. But we can because Jesus is with us even as the battle rages on. He is with us when we've exhausted all our efforts and our children are still entrenched in their addiction. He is with us through one relapse after another. He is with us when our son or daughter hasn't spoken to us in years. And He is with our children, not just when they are serving Him and free from addiction, but also when they are at their worst. That is God's love, grace, and mercy in action.

Our children are never so far gone that the outstretched hand of the Lord cannot save them. His Spirit penetrates places in their hearts and minds our words cannot reach. He alone knows if and when they will be ready to accept His invitation to turn to Him and receive the help they desperately need.

Jesus never gives up on His children and neither should we. But when we are in the middle of a spiritual battle for the lives of our kids, waiting is the hardest part, isn't it? We're moms. We must do something. We can, and we will. In the upcoming chapters, we will learn more about how to fight our battles God's way. But what do we do in the meantime? We have prayed and asked God to intervene. We have immersed ourselves in the scriptures and stood on their promises. We've resisted Satan and rejected his lies. Now what? What do we do while we anguish in the silence of unanswered prayers?

It's here in this place of praying and waiting that God tests our faith. It's in this place that doubt creeps in and our patience wears thin. This is the place where we surrender and cry out, "I give up!" But this is also the place where we meet Jesus. This is the place where we come to Him with our wounded and wayward children and cry out for mercy. It's in this place of absolute surrender we pray, "Lord, I believe. Please help my unbelief!"

Reflection Questions

1. What is your understanding of spiritual warfare? What is your understanding of it based on Ephesians 6:12 and 2 Corinthians 10:3-5?

2. Have you ever experienced spiritual warfare because of your child's addiction? In what way? How did you handle your spiritual battle?

3. How has your faith held up in this battle for your child's life? Has it been weak, strong, or non-existent?

4. In what ways has Jesus ministered to you when you felt like giving up? Does it help to know you are not alone, and the Lord is fighting your battle for you?

PART FOUR

Let Go and

Let God

CHAPTER 10

Battle Ready

"Then he said to me, "This is the word of the LORD to
Zerubbabel: Not by might, nor by power, but by my
Spirit, says the LORD of hosts."
Zechariah 4:6 (ESV)

NOT BY MIGHT

D o you remember the day you were born again? What
was it like? Did you feel differently after you asked Jesus
to forgive your sins and be Lord of your life? I certainly did.
Even though I met Jesus when I was a very young child, it
wasn't until I was about 12 years old that I heard and accepted
His invitation to be born again.

When I responded to the altar call at a youth event, I didn't
expect anything to change. After all, I had always believed in

Jesus. But this time, something was different. While the pastor at the Lutheran church I attended as a child taught me about Jesus' immaculate conception, miraculous birth, sacrificial life, incomprehensible suffering, and glorious resurrection, he never shared the one thing that changed everything for me—Jesus wanted to have a personal relationship with me. Me, Dawn.

As far back as I can remember, no one ever tried to get to know the real me, the girl I was inside. Not my parents. Not the kids on the street. No one. Sure, I had friends and family, but honestly, no one made an effort to understand who I truly was or how I felt deep down. Because I exuded self-confidence, they didn't see the fragile girl who blamed herself for the family turmoil. But Jesus saw me, and He wanted a relationship with me.

When I rushed forward to ask Jesus into my heart, everything changed. I was clean. I was no longer to blame. I was brand new. Only a short time later, I learned what it meant to be baptized in the Holy Spirit. I wanted everything Jesus had for me. I wanted the same gift He promised His followers prior to His ascension when He said, *"Do not leave Jerusalem, but wait for the gift my Father promised, which you have heard me speak about. For John baptized with water, but in a few days you will be baptized with the Holy Spirit" (Acts 1:4-5 NIV).*

Can you imagine their anticipation as they waited? But how would they know when the Holy Spirit came upon them? Jesus continued by telling them they would receive power to be His witnesses throughout Jerusalem and even to the ends of the earth (see Acts 1:8). The Greek word used here for "power" is *dunamis,* which means "miraculous power, might, and force."[24] Jesus promised to baptize them with His power, the same power by which He rose from the dead!

> "If the Spirit of him who raised Jesus from the dead dwells in you, he who raised Christ Jesus from the dead will also give life to your mortal bodies through his Spirit who dwells in you." (Romans 8:11 ESV)

You may find this hard to believe with where your life is right now, but God has empowered you to be His witness to those who are lost, weary, and broken, including your children. He knew there would be days when, as mothers, we would question our ability to share His love with anyone. I mean, if other people had a bird's-eye view of our home life, they might run in the other direction! But Jesus didn't ask us to be perfect witnesses. He asked us to be obedient witnesses. That's why He sent the Holy Spirit as a gift to help us do His will.

> "And Peter said to them, 'Repent and be baptized every one of you in the name of Jesus Christ for the forgiveness of your sins, and you will receive the gift of the Holy Spirit. For the promise is for you and for your children and for all who are far off, everyone whom the Lord our God calls to himself.'" (Acts 2:38-39 ESV)

When we became born again, Satan was not thrilled with our decision. The last thing he wants is a Holy Spirit empowered church sharing the message of freedom with the rest of the souls he is holding captive. Through his relentless scheming and attacks, he determines to distract us and keep us so focused on our problems, we neglect to connect to our Power Source to fight our battles. There is no better way for the enemy to disable believers than to keep us so distracted, discouraged, or disgruntled that we fail to connect daily with the Spirit of God. In doing so, we cease to be effective witnesses of Christ's power to save, heal, and set free those who are lost.

We cannot stand against the spiritual forces of wickedness raging against our families without the Holy Spirit. If you haven't yet encountered His life-changing power, ask Him to fill you today. If you have already experienced His life-changing power, are you fully living in it? Are you continually seeking a fresh infilling of God's Spirit to empower you for the battle ahead? Or are you still trying to do it in your own strength, only to find yourself discouraged by your own limitations? For me, the struggle is real. One day, I am filled with the Spirit and my faith is strong. The next day, chaos breaks loose, and I am once again consumed with fear, resorting to my old measures to save my son. How I long to have resilient faith in the hard times, especially in the hard times.

Speaking of faith, let me tell you a story about my friend Tracy. I met Tracy many years ago when our sons were young and attended the same Christian school together. In high school, her son Jason started dabbling with drugs. Shortly after, he became addicted to opiates. As you might expect, Tracy kept her son's addiction secret.

Because our boys were close friends, it didn't take long for us to notice changes in Jason's appearance and behavior. By the time the boys graduated, his problems had escalated. Because we didn't see him regularly, we figured at the very worst he was smoking marijuana. Our sons' lives took different directions as mine started college and hers continued to decline.

It took several years before Tracy talked to me about Jason's addiction. In her attempt to help him, she sent him to live with his father in another state. He found a job and seemed to be doing better until he relapsed, and the problems started again. Next, she moved him in with his brother. That worked for a while until it didn't. Jason started getting in trouble with the law, so there was a stint in jail, then drug court and outpatient treatment. Nothing helped for long.

I understand Tracy's dilemma. When we first suspected our son's drug use, I did not know there was such a thing as an over-the-counter drug test to verify my suspicions. Instead, I interrogated him, assessed his physical condition, and searched the internet hoping to figure it out. Both Tracy and I were driving in the dark with no headlights, no navigation system, and no clue where we were headed.

This is where the faith part of the story comes in. Because we were naïve about addiction, we both had to rely on the Holy Spirit and our gut instincts as moms. As we talked about those early days, Tracy recalled to me a time when she suspected something was off, but was clueless to what it might be. Assuming her son was on drugs, she searched his room and car but found nothing. That's when Tracy got desperate and started praying.

"Jesus. Please show me what Jason is involved with. I have looked everywhere. I need your help!"

In her heart, she felt the Holy Spirit prompting her to go into his room and remove the backplate from his computer. There, she found a bag of pills. On another occasion, Jason went for a visit to her sister's house. By then, the family knew of his drug use, but thought it was a thing of the past. After he left, her sister noticed a bottle of pain pills was missing. She had just recently undergone surgery, so she needed them for pain management. Having searched everywhere and suspicious over Jason's recent visit, she called Tracy to ask her to question him.

"Mom! I can't believe she would think I took her pills. I would never do that," Jason insisted, storming out of the house and slamming the door behind him.

Tracy had enough experience at this point to recognize a lie when she heard it, so she leaped into action and searched his room, but found nothing. Frustrated, she headed out of the room, but paused when she once again heard the Spirit speaking.

"Go search his dresser again."

"Jesus, I emptied every drawer. Nothing is in there," she responded.

"Go search it again," He insisted.

Reluctantly, she placed her fingertips on the top-drawer knobs and opened it. Just then, she heard His voice again.

"Not there. Go to the bottom drawer and remove it. Look behind it."

"Now we're getting somewhere," Tracy thought as she sprang into action. She knew the voice of the Spirit of God when He

spoke to her. Why had she doubted him? She pulled the drawer out hastily as its contents spilled to the floor. As she peered inside, she discovered the bottle of missing pills.

"Clever guy," she thought to herself. *"But not clever enough to outsmart Jesus and one determined mom."*

Because Jason's addiction was confusing to Tracy, she knew she needed the Holy Spirit's guidance to help her make wise decisions. During the process, Jesus gave her multiple opportunities to tune into His voice as He spoke to her heart. While she learned that being obedient to the Lord didn't always result in the outcome she hoped for, she discovered a newfound sense of peace as she tuned into his voice. Like my friend Tracy, the Holy Spirit will also be our guide if we are open to listening to and obeying Him.

BY HIS SPIRIT

I am often questioned about how to recognize when God is speaking to us. In the busyness of everyday life, it's hard enough to hear the Lord's voice, but it becomes increasingly difficult amidst the chaos and confusion of addiction. Gratefully, despite all the chaos, God is not a God of confusion but of peace (see 1 Corinthians 14:33). It all comes down to our relationship with Jesus. When we are in a relationship with someone, we get to know them by spending time together. We learn what they like and don't like. We become acquainted with their personality traits and communication style. The same is true of our relationship with Jesus. We get to know

His character and the manner in which He speaks to us by spending time with Him.

At this point in the conversation, a few discouraged moms usually respond with, "How am I supposed to know when the Lord is speaking to me? I have never heard His voice. I wish He was here in person."

Oh, my friend, actually, He is here in person. You just can't see Him. When Jesus prepared to leave the earth, He didn't leave His children alone. He promised His disciples help was on the way.

> "And I will ask the Father, and he will give you another *Helper*, to be with you forever, even the Spirit of truth, whom the world cannot receive, because it neither sees him nor knows him. You know him, for he dwells with you and will be in you." (John 14:16-17 ESV, emphasis mine)

Isn't that incredible? Jesus was about to go through the most intense persecution and suffering imaginable, yet He was concerned for His kids. He wanted them to know He would not leave them alone.

In Greek, the word translated "Helper" is *paráklētos,* meaning "Comforter, Consoler, or Advocate."[25] Jesus provided encouragement to these men by explaining that God would speak directly to them through His Spirit.

> "When the Spirit of truth comes, he will guide you into all the truth, for he will not speak on his own authority,

but whatever he hears he will speak, and he will declare to you the things that are to come." (John 16:13 ESV)

When you accepted Jesus as your Savior, the Holy Spirit came and made His home in your heart (see 1 Corin. 3:16, Acts 2:38, Eph. 1:13). Do you know what this means? It means God Himself lives in you. The Holy Spirit is not just a sidekick to God the Father and Jesus Christ the Son. He is God the Spirit and is equally part of the Trinity. He was with the Father and the Son at creation as God spoke, *"Let us make man in our image, after our likeness" (Genesis 1:26 ESV, emphasis mine).* It was the Holy Spirit's breath that gave man life *(Genesis 2:7 ESV).*

When you first asked Jesus into your heart, you didn't come up with the idea on your own. Because Jesus wants a relationship with you, He invited you to follow Him. You accepted His invitation, experienced forgiveness, received eternal life, and His Spirit now lives in you forever. This is a guarantee.

Because we are moms of struggling prodigals, it is critical for us to know this truth. The enemy will come into our thoughts, hurl accusations, and heap tons of guilt, shame, and blame on us because he wants us tone-deaf to the voice of the Holy Spirit. He doesn't want us praying because he doesn't want us hearing from God. He would rather beat us down to the point where we are hiding out in our closet having a pity party.

This is why it's important you understand who you are in Christ. You see, before you were the mom of a wayward son or daughter, you were God's child. He is your Abba, your Father.

He wants you to come to Him for everything. If your child were to come to you and ask for advice, would you give it to them, or would you tell them to go figure it out for themselves? We long to pour our wisdom and knowledge into our children when they come to us open to our advice, don't we? It's no different with God who offers us wisdom when we ask for it.

> "I keep asking that the God of our Lord Jesus Christ, the glorious Father, may give you the Spirit of wisdom and revelation, so that you may know him better." (Ephesians 1:17 NIV)

Jesus wants us to know Him. He doesn't impart His wisdom only to those whose children are walking the straight and narrow. He doesn't hold back on the imperfect mom with a past. When you accepted Jesus, He blessed you with the gift of His Spirit. There are a few ways we can learn to tune into the Spirit's voice as He speaks to us. We do so by spending time in His presence by reading, studying, and meditating on the Word. We are also taught to pray at all times. We do so by bringing our requests to Jesus and waiting silently for Him to speak to us. Prayer is not a one-way street. Make room for the Lord to speak as you sit at His feet and listen intently. You will become more aware of how the Holy Spirit speaks to you as you grow intimately closer to Him.

As you learn to discern the Lord's voice, don't forget how Satan caught Adam and Eve in his snare. He cleverly twisted God's word, causing them to doubt His instructions. Always check what you believe you are hearing with the Bible. If you are still not sure, ask a wise Christian friend, pastor, or trusted advisor for their input. Because God is not a God of confusion, you can trust He will give you peace as you seek wisdom and understanding.

All this sounds well and fine. If only it were that easy, right? I can count on one hand the number of times addiction reared its ugly head, and I could still think straight, much less hear from God. But we must remember we are in a war. We don't get a pass on prayer just because it's hard. Instead, because this is a spiritual battle, we need to learn how to go into our war rooms and pray fervently for our children and for our families. Within that room, we will learn how to tune into the voice of God when He speaks, so we are prepared to obediently follow His orders when He gives them to us.

You may be asking yourself, "All this talk about stepping out in faith is great. But how does it help me handle the spiritual warfare I am dealing with at home?" Good question. Now is the time to change how we fight our battles. Curious? God has equipped us to fight for our children in a more powerful and effective way than we are used to. We will not fight our battles by focusing on our children. Instead, we will focus on Jesus. We are now fighting a spiritual battle with spiritual weapons. Since this battle is not for the faint-hearted, God has prepared us through the Holy Spirit. This time, we are armed and dangerous.

ARMED AND DANGEROUS

At 5:45 a.m. EST on September 11, 2001, two men passed through security at the Portland International Jetport in Maine, where they boarded a commuter flight to Boston Logan International Airport. While the majority of the country was still asleep, American Airlines Flight 11 departed for Los Angeles, California, at 7:59 a.m. with them onboard. The North Tower of the World Trade Center was struck by Flight 11 at 8:46 a.m. There were no survivors.

Our nation's citizens watched in shock as news broke that three other planes were also hijacked. By 10:02 a.m., all three planes had crashed, two into targeted buildings and one, because of the heroism of its passengers, into an open field, missing its target of the White House or the U.S. Capitol. After months of careful planning, nineteen al-Qaeda terrorists slipped through airport security unnoticed and took control of four planes, filled with hundreds of passengers, using only small knives, box cutters, and cans of pepper spray. The attack on U.S. soil took years to plan and prepare for. It lasted slightly over four hours and left 2,977 people dead.[26]

As a nation, our lives were radically changed due to the tragic events of 9/11. Where once we felt safe to move freely about in our country, our false sense of security bubble had burst. Our enemy hated us. He would stop at nothing to destroy our country, our economy, and our people. On May 2, 2011, our military captured and executed the operation's ringleader, Osama bin Laden. No longer would we allow ourselves to be caught off guard. To keep our country safe, our government would need to remain on the offensive.

While the events of that tragic day rocked our world, the truth is we, as Christ's followers, face the enemy's attacks every day. Our enemy, while invisible to us, is every bit as real as the terrorists who hijacked the planes over twenty years ago. And while we are fast asleep, he creeps into our lives and invades our homes when we least suspect it.

Have you ever observed how a lion hunts his prey? Without making a sound, he prowls around, waiting for just the right time to attack. The Bible compares Satan to a lion in 1 Peter. *"Be sober-minded; be watchful. Your adversary the devil prowls around like a roaring lion, seeking someone to devour"* *(1 Peter 5:8 ESV).* What this tells us is that Satan, like a lion, doesn't announce to his unaware victim, "Hey, I'm going to attack you. You better take off running. I'll even give you a head start." Instead, he patiently and intentionally waits for the perfect opportunity to strike the poor unsuspecting creature. But unlike the deer or gazelle, whose only hope is to outrun the lion, the Lord has given us His spiritual armor as protection when the enemy attacks.

"Therefore take up the whole armor of God, that you may be able to withstand the evil day, and having done all, to stand firm. Stand therefore, having fastened on the belt of truth, and having put on the breastplate of righteousness, and, as shoes for your feet, having put on the readiness given by the gospel of peace. In all circumstances, take up the shield of faith, with which you can extinguish all the flaming darts of the evil one; and take up the helmet of salvation, and the sword of the Spirit, which is the word of God, praying at all times in the Spirit, with all prayer and supplication." (Ephesians 6:13-18a ESV)

This is a very impressive list, isn't it? Notice we are told to take up the whole armor of God so we can stand firm. No soldier goes into battle, leaving any of his armor behind. He is fully prepared for battle. Because this is spiritual armor, we need to dress ourselves in it every day. As you pray and put on your armor, remember each piece requires an act of obedience on our part. We aren't just saying we are putting on armor. We are actually applying the armor and joining Christ in His warfare against the enemy. I always struggled to understand what it meant to put on the armor of God. Maybe you have as well. This list describes each piece of armor and the protection it offers:

The Armor of God

- **Belt of Truth** – The devil caused the fall of man with a lie. It's one of his favorite weapons. Don't lie, distort the truth, or speak falsehoods. Speak the truth in love to each other (Ephesians 4:15, 25).
- **Breastplate of Righteousness** – Satan is determined to cause you to doubt who you are in Christ by accusing you. Put off your old self with its sinful habits. Put on the new self in the true righteousness of Christ (Ephesians 4:22-24).
- **Shoes of the Gospel of Peace** – Satan wants God's people silenced, not proclaiming the gospel of peace with boldness and authority. Share the message of peace with the world and live in peace with each other (Ephesians 2:1-22; 4:1-3).

- **Shield of Faith** – Our enemy seeks to steal our faith. Stand firm in your faith as you face pain, suffering, and possibly death (Hebrews 2:14).
- **Helmet of Salvation** - Satan goes after our thought life. He attacks our minds with doubts, fears, worries, anxieties, and lies. We counteract his attacks by renewing our minds (Romans 12:2).
- **Sword of the Spirit** – This is the Word of God and is our offensive weapon against every lie, scheme, and temptation of the enemy. When he tries to condemn, confuse, and intimidate us, we go on the offense by declaring scriptures and claiming God's promises for our lives (2 Corinthians 10:5).
- **Pray in the Spirit** – This is our direct communication with our Commander, who instructs us to pray without ceasing. When we don't know what to pray, the Spirit intercedes for us according to God's will (Romans 8:26-27).

Mom, Jesus has fully equipped you for this battle you are facing. He has blessed you with faith for this journey and the keen ability to tune into His Spirit and understand His will. The enemy wants you to believe this battle is too big for you, but it's not. Why? Because you are not fighting it alone. Begin today by activating your faith and putting on your spiritual armor. Next, we will learn from Jesus how to make a radical difference in the lives of our addicted children by asking the question, "What would Jesus do?"

Reflection Questions

1. Have you ever received the baptism of the Holy Spirit? If so, in what way is it different from the baptism of salvation?

2. How does the Holy Spirit help you as you deal with your child's addiction? Are you able to recognize His voice when He speaks to you?

3. Have you had a similar experience to Tracy, where the Holy Spirit gave you a specific word of knowledge about your child? Explain how you recognized His voice and how you responded.

4. How can you put on the full armor of God each day to arm yourself against the enemy as you go to battle for your child?

CHAPTER 11

What Would Jesus Do?

"This is my commandment, that you love one another
as I have loved you."
John 15:12 (ESV)

LEAD BY EXAMPLE

When we first learned of our children's substance use,
one of the biggest challenges we faced was who to
tell and who not to tell. Assuming we knew their response,
we avoided sharing our family's dilemma with anyone we felt
wouldn't understand or might judge us.

When our younger son started using drugs, my parents
and family were the last people I wanted to tell. While I grew

up in a home where alcohol was abused, my father never saw himself as having a problem with it. Even though he drank at every family gathering, it was as though no one noticed but me. We never mentioned his drinking outside our home, as our family business was to stay private.

Matthew was also a very private person and didn't want me sharing his business with others in the family. He fought hard to overcome his problem and achieve success in life. He didn't want his past defining him or hindering his future. Because it was his story to tell, I respected his wishes.

My father often called to check in and always asked about the kids. Wanting details about his grandson's plans following graduation, he asked all the normal questions one would expect. "What are his plans for the future? Where is he going to college? Has he received an acceptance letter yet?" It was all I could do not to respond sarcastically with quips like, "How about where is he going to rehab? Does he have a sober living house lined up once he gets out? Does he have a sponsor?" It was getting harder to bite my tongue when he called.

Both my list of excuses and my nose grew longer as I tried strategically to avoid my father's questions and divert his attention elsewhere. One thing I've never been good at is lying. While we focused on his plans to attend college upon graduation, we avoided the subject of drugs altogether. When he moved to California, we let his grandfather know he was going to school to become a certified addiction and mental health counselor, but we never revealed his past problems. Upon returning to Las Vegas, he put that part of his life behind him as he entered college to further his education. Besides confiding in my mom, who was always supportive and a good listener, the rest of the family didn't know about his experience.

A few years later, we found ourselves in the same dilemma with his brother. Because Kyle had just graduated from a Christian drug program and was already living in California, we made the excuse that he had moved there to pursue his film career. Once again, I told a partial truth. I was becoming skilled at the art of evading the subject. While he moved to launch his career, in my effort to shield his privacy and spare me more shame, I omitted crucial details.

When his grandpa managed to reach him, Kyle would excitedly tell him about all the work he was doing in Hollywood, while still pretending everything else in his life was going great. He told us the same story when we called. Little did we know, his sobriety would be short-lived, and soon he would be spiraling into another relapse. We suspected there was a problem when we couldn't reach him for several days at a time. It became clear after he totaled another car, and his dad drove to California to help him.

Right about this time, we got word that my dad's wife of 36 years, Barb, had late-stage lung cancer. Her doctors estimated she only had a few months to live. It was then I knew I had to come clean. I knew both she and Dad suspected something wasn't right. After all, we never came to visit them even though they lived only three hours away. I dreaded the day we made the drive to their small town to speak to them, convinced they would judge my son and add to my already huge mound of maternal guilt.

Because Barb wasn't up to cooking, we met together at the town's one and only cafe. When Dad asked about his grandson, I knew it was time to confess. As I poured out my heart and apologized for avoiding them, tears welled up in their eyes. With genuine concern, they both asked what they could do to help. I didn't go there wanting anything from them, but as we continued to talk, Kyle's grandmother offered to pay for him to attend the same program that had helped his brother. At my protest, she insisted, "We are family, and family sticks together."

My father and Barb, both unbelievers, poured grace and kindness into our lives when their own lives were falling apart. How had I misjudged them? Both had their own struggles with drinking, but instead of judgment, we received mercy. I have no words to express the love they showed us. I had let my own preconceived ideas of how they would respond keep me from sharing our family's painful trial with them years earlier. Instead, both were the hands and feet of Jesus to us.

A few days later, I received a check in the mail along with a note I have held close ever since. The card written in Barb's perfect penmanship read:

Dear Dawn,
Reassure Kyle that he should never feel embarrassment or humiliation from his family. Strong family bonds are not created overnight, nor do they abandon you in a time of need. I have so much empathy for the poor souls on this earth who struggle daily with no family to turn to. We'll be with you every step of the way.
Love you, Dad and Barb.

WHAT WOULD JESUS DO?

Barb lost her battle with cancer only three short months later. My father's and Barb's kindness taught me a valuable lesson about keeping family secrets a secret. Although avoidance may appear to be the best approach, we must not assume we know how our family will react to the news of our child's addiction. It's important that we remain open to what the Lord wants to do in their lives and who He may use to help them. I am humbled and grateful for the love and support shown to us by our family throughout the years.

As I look back, I see the handwriting of God's grace all over our lives during those painful and rocky years. More than once, my pride almost kept my children from receiving blessings from some of the most unlikely people in their lives. God can use ordinary people to do extraordinary things if we are open to give and receive as He leads us.

While there were several occasions on our journey when God provided for our needs, one stands out to me. This time the Lord blessed our son, Matthew, through someone he met while attending a recovery program in our city. You know, the one that only the rich and famous can afford? Hey, only the best for our boy! Who cares if we had to empty our savings account and max out our charge cards to get him there? (Never do that, by the way). While there, he became acquainted with a man who was using an alias because he was prominent in our city. They hit it off and stayed in contact after completion of the program.

The story continues. Earlier, I wrote about being employed as a Licensed Aesthetician in a medical practice. While working there, I became friends with a skincare patient who was also a Christian. During one of our discussions, she revealed to me that her husband had received treatment for a pain pill addiction and was now doing well. She asked me to keep his situation confidential because he was well known in our city. Of course, I respected their privacy. During our conversation, I shared with her that we were experiencing a similar situation with our son. While swapping stories, we soon realized our family members had attended the same facility and may have crossed paths. Because people in the recovery community are good at respecting each other's anonymity and her husband was there under an alias, we had no way of knowing for sure if they ever met.

One day she came to my office for a facial. After settling in, she immediately asked, "How's Matthew? What's he up to?"

It wasn't unusual for us to update each other on how our families were doing. However, it was interesting to learn she wasn't asking for herself, but for her husband. It turns out they did know each other from the program and had stayed in contact. He had been thinking about Matthew and how he was progressing. I filled her in on how well he was doing and shared his desire to enroll in a program that would equip him to grow in his spiritual walk and prepare him to become a mental health and addiction counselor.

"Why isn't he there, then?" Her voice carried a tone of curiosity.

Reluctantly, I confessed, "We're tapped out financially."

Without hesitation, she responded, "Well, why didn't you call me?"

"*What, and ask you for money? No way,*" I thought to myself.

"Well, why would I call you about that?" I asked her cautiously.

"Never mind," she quipped. "How much does he need?" She wasn't backing down. Stumbling over my words, I told her the amount.

"We are not taking your money. Thank you, but no way," I insisted.

"That's not really up to you, now, is it? My husband asked me to find out how he's doing, and I'm just delivering the message."

After finishing her facial, she ran out the door, calling behind her, "I will get back to you in a few hours."

What happened next was a miracle. At lunch, I checked my phone and found a message from our son's counselor, requesting that I return his call. Turns out he also counseled my patient's husband, who had contacted him about sponsoring the program Matthew wished to attend. They both believed it was to his advantage, so they contacted Matthew to share the news. He gladly accepted his generous offer and was excited to start right away. While I was still resistant to the idea, our counselor emphatically reminded me that this was not my decision. Matthew was an adult, and I needed to support what God was doing in his life. Talk about a God-smack!

No sooner did I hang up, my patient and her husband arrived with a check made out to the program he would be attending. They had already called ahead to check availability and make all the arrangements. They announced to the Director that we would soon be on our way. My only job was to get him there. My son had prayed in faith and believed God would provide for his program costs, and that is exactly what happened. Through the generosity of these earth-angels, Jesus changed the course of Matthew's life forever.

"And my God will meet all your needs according to the riches of his glory in Christ Jesus." (Philippians 4:19 NIV)

I am forever grateful for the people God used to help our sons on their journeys. Both boys received blessings from people who genuinely cared about them. However, I first had to humble myself and get out of God's way. In both cases, my pride almost prevented them from receiving their blessings. It wasn't about me. It was about Jesus showing my children that He loved them and would provide for their needs.

The Lord can do the same for your children if you will make room for Him to work. As their moms, it's normal to think we have to have all the answers. We feel responsible for solving their problems. And it's our job to figure out a way to pay for it. In this way, we prevent others from being the hands and feet of Jesus to our children. As I said earlier, this doesn't mean we abandon our children or reject them. Instead, we ask the Holy Spirit to reveal whatever is hindering us from releasing them to Him. In this way, we make room for God to work in their lives. This is only possible when we open our faith-filled eyes to believe He is working in places and ways we cannot see. I never imagined Jesus would use unexpected people to minister His love and faithfulness to my sons, but He did.

When we become mothers, along with loving our children, we are called to train them in the way they should go (see Proverbs 22:6). We do this by teaching them the Word of God and by leading them by example. It's not what we say that matters most. It's what we do. I remember how painful it was to hear my son call me a hypocrite for not practicing what I preached. He said to me, "Mom, you tell me to trust Jesus, but you don't trust Him. You worry all the time about everything." Sadly, he was right. I was leading my children with fear instead of faith. I was worried about everything. He saw it and called me on it. It was easier for me to preach to my son about trusting the Lord than it was to turn the narrative around and receive these hard truths for myself. While I had built my faith on the firm foundation of Jesus Christ, I had allowed my feelings to go unchecked and take control of my words and actions.

The Bible instructs us to build our houses on a firm foundation with a faith that withstands the storms of life. You know, the ones that make us quake in our boots? But even when we are afraid, there is no better way to be a witness to our children than for them to see us stand in faith in the face of adversity and obey God no matter how intense the storm.

Not too long ago, we had a severe storm in our town. These don't occur often in the desert, but when they do, they usually involve high winds. On this day, the weather forecast was for a sunny day with medium winds, which is not out of the ordinary. What we did not expect was rain and sustained winds of about 50 mph with 75 mph gusts. As the storm intensified, we started feeling uneasy. Living here most of our lives, neither Steve nor I remembered our city having winds of this intensity. As we heard the patio furniture being tossed around outside, the windows rattling, and the neighbors' car alarms sounding, we knew this was a big storm, at least for us desert-rats.

I was experiencing some pain because of a recent back injury, so I went upstairs to my bedroom to lie down for a few minutes. One of my frightened dogs followed me to hang out and seek comfort. Things didn't go as planned. Because of the howling winds and rain pounding against the windows, resting was out of the question for either of us. Suddenly, out of nowhere, our large bedroom window, located only three feet from where we lay, was sucked out of its frame and fell outwards, shattering on the ground two stories below. It reminded me of a scene from the Wizard of Oz as the curtains and shades blew out the window but remained attached to the rods mounted on the wall inside. As my sweet pooch bolted towards the door, I rushed to anchor down anything that could blow out the hole left by the missing window.

Once we boarded up the window and assessed the situation, we found the culprit was a pressure change in the attic access in my closet that caused enough force against the window to push it out. This all happened in a split second without enough forewarning for us to run for cover. What sounded like a vacuum was actually the pressure releasing once the window flew out. Thankfully, no one got hurt, and the incident was nothing more than an expensive inconvenience.

I share this story because it took place the very night Kyle went back into a detox facility following another relapse. A storm was not only raging outside our home, but on the inside as well. Like the winds that forced the bedroom window out of its frame, I felt like the wind had been knocked out of me. However, like our house that is built on a firm foundation, I am still standing. I am thankful for the firm foundation I've built my faith on, the rock of Jesus Christ. This is the same faith we all can stand on, and the one we are called to demonstrate to our children.

> "Everyone then who hears these words of mine and does them will be like a wise man who built his house on the rock. And the rain fell, and the floods came, and the winds blew and beat on that house, but it did not fall, because it had been founded on the rock." (Matthew 7:24-25 ESV)

How do we exemplify the kind of faith Jesus is talking about here? By trusting in Him and following Him obediently as He leads us. When Christ walked on this earth, He called His disciples to follow Him. While doing so, they carefully observed every move He made and heard every word He spoke.

No matter what problem we face in life, following Jesus' lead is always the answer. When we are facing any trial, before we take action, it's wise to ask the popular question, "What would Jesus do?" One of the first observations we can make from Christ's example is that He was a leader, not a follower. He didn't run with the crowd or succumb to peer pressure. He listened to His Father and submitted to Him (see John 5:30).

God has also placed us in a position of leadership in our child's life, a position of significant influence. He has called us to be leaders instead of followers in our families. What this means is we are to follow Christ's example, not the world's, and then lead our wayward children by our example. For starters, let's begin by letting God handle it.

LET GOD HANDLE IT

When you hear the phrase "Let go and let God," what comes to mind? Do you picture yourself releasing all your cares to the Lord as you dance through a meadow of fresh spring flowers? Or do you imagine that you're slumped over in your chair, bawling your eyes out as you throw your hands up in surrender? Does letting go mean ignoring the person hurting themselves and causing you pain and frustration? Does it mean giving up or pretending you don't care? It's challenging to find the sweet spot between caring too much and not caring at all or doing too much for someone and wanting nothing to do with them.

For the mother whose son or daughter is in the throes of addiction, hearing those five words "let go and let God" can sound like nails on a chalkboard. I mean, just because our child is running wild doesn't mean we abandon our motherly duties, does it? Not necessarily, but it doesn't mean we chase after them, either. But how do we know when to get involved or when to let God handle it?

Because we have chosen to follow Jesus' lead, it's wise to observe how He handled difficult people and challenging circumstances. First things first. We need to check our motives. Jesus did everything in complete obedience to His Father. He never had selfish intentions or a desire to help others for personal gain or to alleviate His own suffering. Even though we love our children with every fiber of our being, when it comes down to it, we also want out of pain ourselves, don't we? Therefore, if relieving them of their pain helps relieve us of ours, we are more than willing to do whatever is necessary.

One thing is for certain: Jesus didn't run from pain. He pressed into it. His plan all along was to lose His life to save ours. He is the one who made our momma's hearts. He understood how deeply we would hurt. He knew the lengths we would go to save our children. He created us with bonds that could not be easily broken. That's why "let go and let God handle it" is not code for "giving up." It is what we do when we realize His way of getting things done is much better than ours, even when it hurts.

Back to the story about the window crashing to the ground the same night my son went into a detox facility. As I rested later and tried to take in all the events of the day, the Holy Spirit brought this part of Isaiah to mind. *"When the enemy comes in like a flood, The Spirit of the LORD will lift up a standard against him"* (Isaiah 59:19 NKJV).

Contemplating these words, I pictured the Lord preventing Satan from pressing in on me and causing me harm. More than just a coincidence, he reminded me that Satan comes to steal, kill, and destroy. The enemy wanted that window to crash in on me. Instead, God sent His angels to push back the powers of darkness. While I was feeling alone and forgotten, God was working on my behalf to protect me. I was completely powerless against the raging storm outside and could not stop the window from crashing to the ground below. But I could control my thoughts, so instead of being afraid, I reminded myself that my life is in God's hands.

When we face the storms of life, it's important to keep in mind that we see only in part. More often than not, things are not as they seem, especially where our children are concerned. It's times like these we need to remember Jesus is moving in their lives in ways we cannot see or understand. We can do the hard work of letting go because we can trust that Jesus is in control.

The Lord gave mothers the strength to do hard things. He sent the Holy Spirit to empower us, the Bible to teach us, and the armor of God to protect us. We're fully prepared for this mission. I know it doesn't always feel like it because we are completely exhausted, but it's true. You might remember the car manufacturer's slogan, "Built Ford Tough®." Well, Christian moms of addicted children should have the slogan, "Built Lord Tough."

You also may be familiar with the term "tough love." It's often associated with the idea of kicking our kids out until they are ready to get help for their addiction. I find most parents are divided on whether they should practice tough love with their child. While it's painful for the child to learn their parents will no longer rescue or enable them, it's excruciating for the parents to administer it. I've since learned there is a love that hurts us more and cuts us deeper than tough love. It is called "rugged love."

In their book, *Letting Go, Rugged Love for Wayward Souls*, the authors describe rugged love as "love with teeth." They write:

> *"Rugged love is the way God engages and reaches sinful people. We are all wayward, dead, and trapped in our sin. So the way we love prodigals must be patterned after the rugged love of God.*
>
> *What is this rugged love? Love is rugged when it's strong enough to face evil;*
> *tenacious enough to do good;*
> *courageous enough to enforce consequences;*
> *sturdy enough to be patient;*
> *resilient enough to forgive;*
> *trusting enough to pray boldly."*[27]

This is the kind of love that empowers us to live sacrificially. It was this self-sacrificing, rugged love Christ demonstrated as He lived, suffered, and died to reconcile us to Himself. As we learn to follow Christ's example, let's start by looking at His relationship with God His Father. What a beautiful relationship they have, one built on unconditional love, the same love Jesus has for us. *"So now faith, hope, and love abide, these three; but the greatest of these is love" (1 Corinthians 13:13 ESV).*

Jesus's time on earth exemplified faith, hope, and love. Observing how He related to His Father and to His followers,

I discovered four biblical ways to lead my children that also helped me in my efforts to let go and let God. Along with faith, hope, and love, we also need grace as we seek to follow Christ's example and love others as He loves us. I will address the first three ways to love our children biblically in this chapter.

4 Ways to Biblically Lead Our Children
1. *Prayerfully (in Faith)*
2. *Patiently (in Hope)*
3. *Purposefully (in Love)*
4. *Practically (in Grace)*

Because love is the greatest gift, it's the foundation on which we are to build our relationships with God and each other. It's easily assumed that love comes naturally for us as moms, but not in this case. This is not an emotional love, but an unconditional, sacrificial love that purposefully chooses to love regardless of our feelings. The Greek word used in this verse is *agápē*,[28] the same word for "love" as in 1 John 4:8 that reads, *"God is love."* This type of love, while impossible to create on our own, is given to us as a fruit of the Spirit (see Galatians 5:22).

When we lead our children with *agápē* love, it is God Himself loving them through us. Whoa! Go back and read that again. When we ask God to love our children through us, we begin by asking Him to empty us of ourselves and our wants, needs, and desires. We ask Jesus to show us how to see our children through His eyes and how to love them like He does. This love surrenders them to the Father no matter how much it hurts or costs us. There is no better way for us to lovingly lead our children than for us to demonstrate lives of complete trust and surrender to God.

Next, we lead our children with faith. If anyone knew how to live by faith, it was Jesus. He did so by staying in constant communication with His Father. He lived a life of surrender and obedience to His Father's will. When his disciples asked Him to teach them to pray, He led them in what we know as The Lord's Prayer, which is found in the books of Matthew and Luke. Depending on the version we read it in, some verses are excluded. I still prefer to pray it the same way I learned it as a kid during confirmation class in my Lutheran Church.

The Lord's Prayer
Our Father which art in heaven,
Hallowed be thy name.
Thy kingdom come.
Thy will be done
in earth, as it is in heaven.
Give us this day our daily bread.
And forgive us our debts,
as we forgive our debtors.
And lead us not into temptation,
but deliver us from evil:
For thine is the kingdom,
the power, and the glory,
forever.
Amen.

When you read this prayer, did you see how Jesus demonstrated His faith and trust in God? He did so by surrendering His own will in obedience to His Father. Then, just prior to His death, He spoke these words and prayed this prayer of ultimate surrender.

> "And they went to a place called Gethsemane. And he said to his disciples, 'Sit here while I pray.' And he took with him Peter and James and John, and began to be greatly distressed and troubled. And he said to them, 'My soul is very sorrowful, even to death. Remain here and watch.' And going a little farther, he fell on the ground and prayed that, if it were possible, the hour might pass from him. And he said, 'Abba, Father, all things are possible for you. Remove this cup from me. Yet not what I will, but what you will.'" (Mark 14:32-36 ESV)

It takes faith to pray a prayer of surrender, doesn't it? This is not a simple "bless our food" prayer at the dinner table. This is a gut-wrenching plea that cries out from the depths of our soul, "Father. If there is any other way, please take this cup, this pain, this burden from me. But it's not my will that matters. May Your will be done in my life and in the life of my child." This is a prayer of faith, not a prayer that demands God to do things our way and in our timing. This is a prayer of release that whispers, "I know You can restore my child and remove this burden from me, but not my will, but Thine, be done."

Once we've decided we will live prayerfully by faith, we are ready to lead our children by example. Our actions, words, and feelings will change as we walk by faith. Fear can't control us anymore when we live by faith. Because Jesus is the author and perfecter of our faith (see Hebrews 12:2), we look to Him to lead the way. We then lead our children by following His example.

One way Jesus prepared to hear from His Father and equipped Himself to withstand temptation was by fasting. The Bible mentions fasting over seventy times. But is it necessary for Christians to fast today? Although fasting is not specifically commanded in the New Testament, Jesus and His disciples practiced it as a discipline, as stated in the book of Matthew.

"And when you fast, do not look gloomy like the hypocrites, for they disfigure their faces that their fasting may be seen by others. Truly, I say to you, they have received their reward. But when you fast, anoint your head and wash your face, that our fasting may not be seen by others but by your Father who is in secret. And your Father who sees in secret will reward you." (Matthew 6:16-18 ESV)

By reading these verses, we can conclude that Christ's followers should be fasting. Jesus was clear that we should not fast publicly to impress people but in secret, so our focus is on God, the Father. Fasting is about subduing our flesh from good things like food, so we are humbled and strengthened in our spirit. Other reasons we fast are: to worship God, to express repentance over our sins, to resist demonic temptation, to seek the Holy Spirit's guidance and strengthening, for deliverance of the oppressed, for a revival in the church, and for the repentance and protection of our nation.

We prepare ourselves through fasting for the temptations we will face personally and while praying for deliverance for our children. When we fast, it is not intending to get God to do what we want. It is to align our thoughts and intentions with God's will. There are many types of fasts you can take part in depending on your personal health requirements and lifestyle. I recommend doing some research on fasting and seeking the Lord's direction prior to starting your fast.

Because we are waging war for our addicted children, you can bet Satan will come against us in full force when we fast. The last thing he wants is for us to fast because he knows it will strengthen our faith to stand against him. There is power when we fast to break the chains of evil, keeping our children bound to their addiction and us imprisoned in depression, fear, and despair. Nothing threatens him more than when we fast and pray in faith for God to set the prisoners free.

"Is not this the fast that I choose: to loose the bonds of wickedness, to undo the straps of the yoke, to let the oppressed go free, and to break every yoke?" (Isaiah 58:6 ESV)

When we pray for the deliverance of our children, we do so with the hope that they will cry out to Jesus and repent of their sins and self-destructive behaviors. But what do we do when we have exercised faith, prayed, and fasted for our children, yet they remain trapped in their addiction? How do we remain in faith when we have persisted in prayer, and it seems God has turned a deaf ear to our pleas? This is where hope comes in. Hope is the energy that keeps our faith alive. The word "hope" in the New Testament Greek means "favorable and confident expectation, the happy anticipation of good."[29]

When everything around us seems hopeless, it's difficult to remain optimistic. We've cried, prayed, and pleaded with God, but our circumstances have gotten worse instead of better. It's tempting to take matters into our own hands, especially when God is silent or says, "No" or "Not yet." But our hope is not cultivated in the garden of impulsivity. Instead, we nurture it by patiently waiting for God to answer. *"But if we hope for what we do not see, we wait for it with patience"* *(Romans 8:25 ESV).*

Still, the question remains, "What do we do when we don't know what to do?" Let's delve into the answer as we explore how to have hope while we patiently wait for our prayers to be answered.

WHAT TO DO WHEN YOU DON'T KNOW WHAT TO DO

The book of 2 Chronicles 20 includes one of my favorite stories of hope in the Bible, one that strengthened my faith in the early days of our family's journey. I call it my "Victory Chapter." I encourage you to read the story of King Jehoshaphat and the nation of Judah as they faced enemy invasion from three countries who joined forces against them. As you might expect, the King feared for the safety of His people.

Instead of panicking, he did what any wise king should do and determined to seek the Lord as he proclaimed a fast throughout all Judah (verse 3). Rather than hiding out at home, all the cities of Judah responded by coming together to seek help from God. This leads us to our first tip on what to do when you don't know what to do.

What to Do When You Don't Know What to Do

- **Tip #1–Don't do it alone.** Ask for support from people who will seek the Lord, pray, and fast with you.

    "And Judah assembled to seek help from the LORD; from all the cities of Judah they came to seek the LORD" (2 Chronicles 20:4 ESV).

Next, Jehoshaphat called the people together to worship the Lord. There, he proclaimed that He alone was God of Heaven and ruler over the kingdoms. He remembered how God drove their enemies out of the land promised to His people, the same nations He had previously shown mercy towards. What the King understood is when his enemies threatened to attack God's people, they were really going after God Himself.

- **Tip #2–Pray as you remember God's faithfulness, deliverance, and protection in your life.**

    "O LORD, God of our fathers, are you not God in heaven? You rule over all the kingdoms of the nations. In your hand are power and might, so that none is able to withstand you" (2 Chronicles 20:6 ESV).

The entire time the King prayed, the people stood with him, determined to put their trust in the Lord, regardless of the outcome. As he petitioned God on behalf of Judah, he

WHAT WOULD JESUS DO?

was not in denial about the direness of their situation, but remained resolute in his faith.

> "'If disaster comes upon us, the sword, judgment, or pestilence, or famine, we will stand before this house and before you—for your name is in this house—and cry out to you in our affliction, and you will hear and save.'" (2 Chronicles 20:9 ESV)

I love the King's faith when he cries out to God, "You will hear and save." When we pray these surrendered prayers, we release our battle and its outcome to the Lord. This is a resolute faith that says, "Lord, I trust you even if Your answer is not the one I hoped for, because I know You hear me and will save me." Take Jehoshaphat's prayer and personalize it to your circumstances. I encourage you to write your prayer down and pray it daily.

- **Tip #3–Humbly admit you are powerless to fight this battle on your own, but your hope is in the Lord.**

    "O our God, will you not execute judgment on them? For we are powerless against this great horde that is coming against us" (2 Chronicles 20:12a).

As the King continued to pray, he humbly acknowledged his own powerlessness against his enemies as he asked God to execute judgment against them. And now for my favorite part of his prayer, *"We do not know what to do, but our eyes are on you" (2 Chronicles 20:12b).*

Mom, this is a hope-filled cry of desperation that says, "We can do nothing on our own. We will not look to anyone else for salvation. Our eyes are on You only, Lord."

As the people stood and waited, the Spirit spoke through one of His prophets these reassuring words, *"Do not be afraid and do not be dismayed at this great horde, for the battle is not yours but God's"* (2 Chronicles 20:15).

- **Tip #4—Stand firm and do not fear, for the battle belongs to the Lord.**

"You will not need to fight in this battle. Stand firm, hold your position, and see the salvation of the LORD...Do not be afraid and do not be dismayed" (2 Chronicles 20:17a ESV).

The prophet gave them these instructions. They would not need to fight in this battle. Instead, they were to stand firm, hold their positions, and see the salvation of the Lord. Hallelujah!

The next morning, the King gave his people one last pep talk to help them avoid discouragement as they faced their enemies head-on. As he rallied all of Judah together, he encouraged them with these words, *"Listen to me! Believe in the LORD God, and you will stand firm. Have faith, and you will succeed"* (2 Chronicles 20:20 ESV, paraphrased).

This is when it can get hard for us. Standing firm requires patiently waiting on the Lord. But when nothing seems to happen and the battle rages on, it's easy to lose hope. What battle have you been fighting in your own power? Or should I say, "What battle have you been losing because you tried to fight it on your own?" It could be the Lord wants you to sit this one out. If He has not given you marching orders, be still and wait for further instructions.

Finally, Jehoshaphat called the singers to praise God for His holiness and faithful love. As soon as they began to sing and praise, the Lord set up an ambush against their enemies. The result? Their enemies destroyed each other. God delivered Judah from their hands and gave them victory as they praised and worshiped Him.

- **Tip#5–Praise Jesus with songs of praise and thanksgiving.**

    "Give thanks to the LORD, for his steadfast love endures forever" (2 Chronicles 20:21 ESV).

One of our most powerful weapons we can pick up as we fight our battles is praise, but sometimes we underestimate its power. When we're overwhelmed and afraid, prayer comes naturally. But in our brokenness, praise is often surrendered through gritted teeth. It is during the dark moments, our praise is a sweet incense to our Lord. With our praises, we surrender our hearts and lives to God, acknowledging that He alone sits on the throne. Not the enemy. Not an addiction. Not even our children. Only Jesus is worthy of our praise.

As we learned from King Jehoshaphat, even when we don't know what to do, the Lord has a battle plan prepared for us. Sometimes, it requires us to take action. Other times, we are called to wait patiently for Him as He fights our battles for us. Either way, we can trust Him to show us how to lead our children by example with faith, hope, and love. Next, let's learn how to fight our battles God's way.

Reflection Questions

1. Do you feel you have done a good job leading your child by example in life and faith? Describe why or why not.

2. In what ways has Jesus led you by His example? How can you follow His example as you lead your child?

3. Do you agree with the saying "Let go and let God?" Explain how doing so has hurt or helped your relationship with your child.

4. As you review the story in 2 Chronicles 20, what lessons did you learn that will help you fight spiritually for your child and family? What will you do when you don't know what to do?

CHAPTER 12

This is How We Fight Our Battles

"What causes fights and quarrels among you? Don't
they come from your desires that battle within you?"
James 4:1 (NIV)

FIGHTING THE GOOD FIGHT

In our last chapter, we looked at leading our children by
Christ's example. We do so by leading them prayerfully,
patiently, and purposefully with faith and hope on the foundation of love. Next, we are going to look at leading them
practically with grace. The word for "grace" in Greek is *charis*.
It means "grace, as a gift or blessing brought to man by Je-

sus Christ, favor, gratitude, thanks, a favor, kindness."[30] Grace is the key that unlocks the door to open, honest, and loving communication. This is where we will need to talk the talk and walk the walk. Jesus led His disciples by showing, not just telling them, how to be His witnesses. We can do the same for our children.

It's incredibly challenging to maintain our composure when dealing with the stress brought on by our addicted children. Sometimes, feeling angry is justified, and we have to address the problem immediately. We can't wait until things cool down because of the urgency of the situation. It's especially difficult to have a productive conversation when both parties are emotionally charged. Ephesians 4:26 instructs us to *"be angry and do not sin,"* but how is this possible when the situation is escalating?

I often hear family addiction recovery specialists warn against causing our children shame or embarrassment. But the fear of confronting them for their actions only delays the inevitable and fosters resentment between both the parents and their addicted children. Our children use drugs to numb their emotions, shame being one of them. Bringing up their dire condition does not make them ashamed. They are already burdened under a cloak of shame because of their lifestyle and spiritual condition. Keeping this in mind, when we as their parents expose their sin, we should do so in an attitude of love because *"love covers a multitude of sins" (1 Peter 4:8).*

We can learn how to speak into the lives of our children by observing how the Lord handled the fall of humanity. When Adam and Eve partook of the forbidden fruit, they immediately realized they were naked and experienced shame for the first time. God did not neglect to *confront* their disobedience because He wanted to spare their feelings. Instead, He *convicted* them of their sin and explained the *consequences* they would suffer. He then relieved their shame by *covering* their nakedness (see Genesis 3:7-20). What we can learn from this story is that God *cherishes* His children and handles their disobedience carefully, always with their redemption in mind.

As we prepare to speak to our children, we should have the same heart and intent as the Lord has towards us as His children. To do so, we must...

- Be willing to *confront* them honestly about their sin and destructive choices.

- Allow the Holy Spirit to *convict* them about their sinful conduct without judging them or trying to control them.

- Permit them to experience natural *consequences* or those that result from breaking God's or our boundaries.

- Do not expose or add to their shame by embarrassing or humiliating them. Remember, love *covers* a multitude of sins.

- Always *cherish* them and uphold their worth as a child of God.

It is possible to have challenging conversations with our hard-to-reach adult children about their actions while still being supportive and respectful of their thoughts and feelings. If our only goal is to persuade them to get help for their addiction, we are most likely desperate enough to say and do just about anything. But if their salvation and restoration to God is our highest priority, our words and actions should mirror Christ's love, grace, and mercy towards them. The one thing we should never do is fail to speak the truth to them for fear of hurting their feelings. Speak the truth in love, but by all means, speak it.

"Rather, speaking the truth in love, we are to grow up in every way into him who is the head, into Christ." (Ephesians 4:15 ESV)

Satan is a master at causing family strife and division by playing on the emotions of everyone involved. The burden placed on parents with addicted children is heavy enough. It is especially painful when the enemy coming at you is your own child. I have heard it said in some addiction recovery circles that it is not your child lashing out at you. It's their addiction. No, it's your child, under the influence of their addiction, saying those hateful things to you. And right now, they mean every word they're saying because their agenda is to get you to give them what they believe they need for their survival.

"But what comes out of the mouth proceeds from the heart, and this defiles a person. For out of the heart come evil thoughts, murder, adultery, sexual immorality, theft, false witness, slander." (Matthew 15:18-19 ESV)

If we excuse their behavior because they were high when they said those hurtful things to us, we are allowing them to continue in their sin unchecked. This is a form of enabling that doesn't hold them accountable for their words and actions. As parents, turning the other cheek only goes so far when it's our God-given responsibility to train them in the way they should go. See, we are never off the hook as parents. Whether we are actively involved in their lives or loving them from a distance, we are still their moms. We may not have control over their lives, but we still have influence. This doesn't mean we retaliate with harsh words or are unforgiving. Instead, we treat them with respect, speak truth into their lives, and trust that the Holy Spirit will convict them of their wrong actions.

The Holman Bible Dictionary defines "conviction" as "a sense of guilt and shame leading to repentance."[31] The Greek word for "convict" is *elégxō*. It means "to expose, convict, reprove, generally with the suggestion of shame of the person convicted."[32] We are not to try to protect them from feelings of shame by avoiding the subject of sin. But we should not cast stones of condemnation, either. That's where grace comes in. It is God's loving kindness that is intended to lead them to repentance.

"Don't you see how wonderfully kind, tolerant, and patient God is with you? Does this mean nothing to you? Can't you see that his kindness is intended to turn you from your sin?" (Romans 2:4 NLT)

Nothing exposes our weaknesses as humans like loving someone struggling with addiction. It challenges everything good in us as it picks at every unhealed area, exposing old wounds. We want to be godly examples to our children, but we leak humanity from every pore. Our powerlessness to do anything to save them wreaks of the stench of past failures. We know we should trust God, but what if doing so means our child's story won't end well? Surely, giving them just one more good talking to would be enough to set them straight and get them back on track. If only it were that easy. But it also doesn't have to be that hard either. We can begin by asking Jesus to help us see our child as He sees them, to show us the face behind the mask of addiction.

Our children are more than their addictions. Ask any mom, and she will sing her child's praises. I should know. I ask the moms in our support group regularly to tell us about their son or daughter's greatest character attributes, gifts, and talents. They gush as they share story after story of their child apart from their addiction. Most tell of how kind, respectful, and generous they are towards other people. But addiction has clouded their view of their child. They now struggle to see these qualities when they look at their loved one. Instead, they see them through the lens of disappointment, pain, doubt, and fear. While we may struggle to remember who our son or daughter was before addiction took them hostage, the Lord remembers the person He created them to be.

"I praise you, for I am fearfully and wonderfully made. Wonderful are your works; my soul knows it very well." (Psalm 139:14 ESV)

Our first step in preparing to have these challenging conversations with our children is to see their identity through His eyes. By doing so, we will move from hopeless to hopefilled and will carry this newfound hope into our relationship with them. Next, we will learn to choose our battles wisely.

CHOOSE YOUR BATTLES WISELY

We attended a church for many years where Steve and I served in leadership roles. Initially, it was great. Steve served on the Board of Directors where he could use his construction and business experience to serve the church body. I served in the Women's Ministry and on the worship team. I loved using my gifts and talents to minister to the congregation. But over the years, a shift took place. The pastor and leadership of the church were involved in misconduct, and nothing was being done about it. Knowing we were facing a church split, we did our best to confront the issues and tried to expedite a resolution. Not only were our efforts in vain, we then became the target of gossip and rejection from not only the leadership, but the people who caught wind of the scandal. No longer were we invited to the leadership meetings or get-togethers. While they didn't kick us out of the church, they made us feel very unwelcomed. For many of you who have been in church leadership before, I am sure all this sounds too familiar.

Months went by and, as expected, the church split happened with a few assistant pastors leaving, taking half the members to start their own churches. Still, the church drama continued as if no one could see it but us. Steve wasn't one to put up with such nonsense and kept insisting we pull our kids from the church's school and get the heck out of dodge. Not wanting to uproot our children, I was more resistant, believing if we kept trying, we could bring this nightmare to a peaceful resolution. But as the months went on, I grew weary of explaining myself or trying to mediate one conflict after another. One day, as I was crying my eyes out before the Lord, I heard

Him speak to me, "Dawn, if you are not part of the solution, you are part of the problem." Convicted, I knew immediately I was the latter. While I was only trying to help the situation, by not controlling my tongue, I was making matters worse.

"Whoever keeps his mouth and his tongue keeps himself out of trouble." (Proverbs 21:23 ESV)

The Holy Spirit then gave me a vision of a wheel on a bicycle. He told me to focus on the rim and the spokes of the wheel. He instructed me to pull each spoke out one at a time. The wheel stayed intact initially, but as I continued to remove the spokes, it eventually crumpled and could no longer hold the tire. It was then I realized I was one of many spokes keeping the wheel spinning and the bike operable. My staying meant I was part of the problem, not the solution. How convicting and humbling! It was not my responsibility to fix the other people keeping the drama wheel in motion. It was time to obey the Lord, listen to Steve, and leave the church.

Through that experience, I learned a valuable lesson about choosing my battles wisely. The Spirit revealed to me I would soon face spiritual warfare against my family. He told me staying in that church would "shipwreck my children's faith," as they were also subject to scrutiny there. He was preparing me for a battle much more intense than the nonsensical drama of the church. It was time I learned how to detach from battles that were not mine to fight.

This lesson holds true for our addicted loved ones as well. There will be occasions where we must run onto the battlefield fully armed to engage in warfare. There will be other times when God's battle plan will be for us to sit back, watch, and pray. In this way, we remain engaged in the battle, but will be fighting with different weapons. But how do we disengage from the drama addiction brings into our families? I admit, it's easier said than done.

Back to Jesus and His example of how to deal with broken people. Everyone He encountered had a story of what brought them to their place of brokenness. Some had demonic spirits, others had ailments considered by society to be brought on by sin, and others who engaged in sinful lifestyles faced the rejection of being social outcasts. Because Jesus' mission was to glorify His Father, He never got caught up in their drama or that of His critics. Instead, He either helped the people who wanted out of their mess, or He walked away from those who were only there to make trouble.

This was the defining line Jesus drew in every situation. Perhaps the conversation went something like this. *"Either you want my help, or you don't. I am offering you abundant life. Take it or leave it. I love you, but I won't force you to change."* This doesn't mean Jesus never engaged in conflict or addressed those who opposed Him. Jesus always spoke the truth to those who wanted to hear it and even those who didn't. But He also knew when to stay silent or walk away, a skill that will serve us well as we seek to speak to our children who would prefer to tune us out.

When we disengage from drama, we learn to respond thoughtfully rather than reacting in the heat of the moment. Most altercations with our addicted children don't require a screaming match to get our point across. While sometimes, it is necessary to make quick decisions and take action, it is wise to approach most situations with careful thought and prayer. These words spoken by James give us instructions on how to keep ourselves from anger.

> "Know this, my beloved brothers: let every person be quick to hear, slow to speak, slow to anger; for the anger of man does not produce the righteousness of God." (James 1:19-20 ESV)

What does this look like in our everyday lives as we try to maintain our composure so we can communicate with our loved ones? For us to speak effectively into the lives of our children, we will need to be emotionally and spiritually prepared. Emotionally, because they know how to get under our skin and push all our buttons. Spiritually, because this is a spiritual battle. Remember, our end goal is for our children to accept the love of Jesus, who desires to set them free, save them, and bring them healing. Our communication should address both their spiritual state and their emotional, mental, and physical well-being.

In order to be prepared for tough conversations, first we need to ask the Lord to reveal the places of brokenness we are struggling with or in denial about. Remember, God has work to do in your heart as well as your child's. We can get so caught up in our own agenda of trying to help them, we can't see the areas where we need healing. This doesn't mean we have to have it all figured out before we talk to them, but we will need to be open and humble ourselves before speaking into their lives.

I encourage you to spend time in prayer and journaling as you prepare for your conversation with your son or daughter. Ask the Holy Spirit to reveal to you any old wounds that are festering because of your child's addiction. Are you holding onto past trauma, unforgiveness, or bitterness towards someone who hurt you long ago? Are you bringing these hurts and hangups into your relationship with your child? When you sit down to share your heart with them, you want to be fully present and focused on God's best for them. As you enter into a time of reflection and self-examination, ask His Spirit to search your heart and make you aware of any negative beliefs causing you anxiety. Ask Him to reveal to you any areas where your heart and mind need to be renewed. One way to do so is to pray these words from the book of Psalms.

"Search me, God, and know my heart; test me and know my anxious thoughts. See if there is any offensive way in me, and lead me in the way everlasting." (Psalms 139:23-24 NIV)

In Chapter 10 of this book, we examined how to put on the armor of God. Along with suiting up, we become spiritually prepared by being filled with the Spirit of God. This is evident by the fruit of the Spirit in our lives. Galatians reads, *"But the fruit of the Spirit is love, joy, peace, patience, kindness, goodness, faithfulness, gentleness, self-control; against such things there is no law"(verses 5:22-23 ESV).*

When we are burned out from the worry and stress addiction causes us, it's like our fruit has spoiled on the vine. Instead of a sweet taste and fragrant aroma, it is bitter and rotten. At my worst, this verse should have read, *"But the fruit of Dawn's flesh is hatred, sorrow, turmoil, impatience, cruelty, meanness, unfaithfulness, and out of control."* Ugly, right? Sometimes, the only fruit displayed in my life was the fruit of my flesh. Definitely not one of my finest moments. When you are preparing to speak with your child about their addiction and reckless behavior, come prepared with the fruit of the Spirit.

Finally, before sitting down to have that tough talk with your rebel, remember things aren't always as they seem. When circumstances have escalated and are out of control, we often paint the worst-case scenario. Much like the story-book character Chicken Little, a drop of rain means "the sky is falling!" But what we must remember is that in all the chaos, God is still in control. Jesus never panicked, and neither should we. Most non-life-threatening situations allow us time to step back and think before we speak. I like to call these temporary breaks or pauses **God's Divine Interruptions to Satan's Disruptions.** The scenarios look something like this.

- **Scenario 1** – Fran's son, Zack, calls asking for a ride to a recovery meeting. She gets a gut-check that "meeting" is code for "drug dealer." Instead of interrogating Zack, she tells him she will get back with him after she gives it some thought. That check in her spirit is a divine interruption.

- **Scenario 2** – Sue's daughter, Mandy, asks for money to buy black pants and shoes for her first day on the job. Sue offers to take her to the mall to buy them, but Mandy insists she wants to go alone and is hurt that her mom doesn't trust her. Sue's reservation about handing Mandy money is a divine interruption.

- **Scenario 3** – Laura's son, David, just lost his job, claiming his boss has it out for him. From previous experience, Laura knows David's story doesn't line up and suspects a relapse. Laura's suspicion is a divine interruption.

God's divine interruptions to Satan's disruptions come in many forms. But they are easily recognizable as a "check" in our spirit. These checks should not go unchecked. Rather, they are indicators we need to take a pause, step back, pray, and do a bit of investigating if necessary. During these pauses, observe how you are handling the situation. Will you be able to treat your child with grace and kindness? Or will you get upset, fly off the handle, and say things you will later regret?

If you are prone to panic and react without thinking, have an action plan in place. This is when I can't stress enough not to do it alone. Text your husband, phone a friend, or reach out to your counselor. Old habits and reactions die hard, so recognize when you need help. God is sending you a warning signal. Listen to it. Satan would rather you ignore that warning and do or say something you later regret. But Jesus is calling you to listen to His "still, small voice" as He speaks to you in the chaos. As you learn to take these pauses, you will find yourself better equipped to disengage from addiction's drama, choose your battles wisely, and extend grace to your struggling child.

FIGHTING FAIR

The home I grew up in was anything but peaceful. Both my parents were prone to angry outbursts, especially when my father was drinking. As I grew up, I learned that while anger was acceptable, crying was not, so I started hiding my fear and pain behind anger. Anger was a normal reaction to just about anything around our home. Whether it was us kids tracking dirt on the newly cleaned floor, an overly inflated electric bill, or the slow driver on the road ahead of us, my parents always seemed to be angry about something. Even when my parents' anger reached epic proportions, I accepted it as normal, assuming everyone else lived the same way.

Raising my kids, I pushed back the tears to avoid feeling broken. Instead, I would nag Steve or scold my kids about something insignificant. Sadly, I was becoming like my mom who came home from work every night angry about something. While we kids were the brunt of her disapproval, I now realize she was hurting because of my father's drinking and infidelity. She had never learned to express her feelings with anything but anger. Then she passed her poor coping skills onto her kids.

When my kids started using drugs, my anger intensified. I couldn't bear staying up all night crying, but I sure knew how to give them a piece of my mind. While I wasn't one to blow up and lose my temper often, I was controlling and demanding. Every word that came out of my mouth was some sort of threat. The governing emotion behind my constant aggravation was fear. I carried that fear into every conversation I had with them. It took several years, countless prayers, and a ton of practice for me to learn how to speak to them without screaming or threatening to get my point across. I will spend the rest of this chapter sharing what worked for me and offering practical advice on how to have a reasonable and (hopefully) effective conversation with your prodigal child.

When we set off on a mission to speak into the lives of our children, let's not forget we are the parents here. We need to be prepared to say what we need to say and stick to our word. Therefore, we will need to rehearse our lines, so to speak. We are not to go into any conversation unprepared. If we do, they will twist every word we say, and it will turn into an argument with disastrous results. It's up to us to make sure we settle matters in our own minds before trying to change theirs. We do this by determining ahead of time the primary objective and desired outcome of the conversation. Is your son self-destructing because he is abusing drugs or alcohol? Are you concerned for his life? Keep the conversation focused on your desire to see him get help before it's too late. Don't go off on a tangent about why he can't keep a job or stole your debit card. Stay direct and focus on the issue at hand. Is your daughter staying in an abusive relationship so she can feed her habit? Don't nag her about how thin she is or how terrible she looks. Focus on getting her out of that relationship by discussing her needs and having a plan available if and when she is ready.

When fighting fair, we should strive to keep our children's spiritual and emotional well-being at the forefront of every battle plan we make and conversation we have with them. Satan is the real enemy here. Addiction is his weapon of mass destruction. Remember, our children are in there somewhere. Addiction has stolen their identity and sense of self-worth. However, their true identity is found in being a child of the Creator of the Universe.

Taming my tongue was one of the hardest skills I learned, but also one of the most effective. These are some of the invaluable skills I have learned through experience and put into practice when communicating with my children.

- **Fight Fair:** Don't have a conversation when you are angry or upset. Wait until you can stay calm and think clearly. The Bible teaches us to be angry, but not sin. It is also wise to not try to speak to your child when they are under the influence or detoxing, as they won't be in any condition to talk. It is better to wait and reschedule than to blow up. But don't wait too long. The conversation still needs to take place.

- **Self-Control or Out of Control:** The fruit of the Spirit is self-control. If you are in an emotionally charged state of mind, you most likely are not in control of your emotions, thoughts, or words. Threats, intimidation, and manipulation are warning signs you're out of control. Take a break, pray, calm down, and return to the conversation later.

- **Safety Net:** Have a safety net in place to stop the spiraling if the conversation is heading south. Examples of safety nets are: bringing someone with you when you speak to your child, preparing a written script to keep you on subject, setting a timer to limit the length of the conversation, or having a code word either of you can say to stop or shift the conversation before it spirals out of control.

- **Fire Starters and Fire Quenchers:** Be aware of triggers from past hurts, present trauma, or negative life experiences. When our children feel cornered and are in a defensive posture, they may say things that trigger your pain points. Ask the Lord to prepare your heart so you don't lash out or retaliate. We also want to avoid saying hurtful things that could be a trigger for them. The tongue is a flame. Our careless words are like throwing kerosene on a forest fire. Statements like "you always" and "you never" are examples of fire starters. An example of a fire quencher would be a defusing comment like, "I am sorry for saying that to you. It won't happen again."

- **Green, Yellow, and Red-Light Conversations:** This is one of my favorite conversation tools.

  —**Green-light conversations** flow naturally and are un-restricted. These conversations center around pleasant circumstances, happy memories, and neutral events. Green-light conversations are safe to have anytime and anywhere. They include sincere compliments and accolades for well-earned accomplishments.

  —**Yellow-light conversations** are to be approached with caution because they can go either way. These conversations need to occur, but how we perceive them is based on our tone, temperament, and timing. These conversations usually involve subjects like getting a job, doing chores, maintaining their sobriety, and seeking treatment for their addiction. While the conversation is necessary, if we are off on our timing or tone or are in a bad mood, it is probably not a good time to talk to our loved one. With yellow-light conversations, always have an exit strategy. Yellow-lights can turn red with one word or glance. But as healing occurs, they can also become green-light conversations.

—**Red-light conversations** should be considered a "no-go-zone" and should never occur. These include name-calling, derogatory remarks, threats, and coercion. For either party to feel safe to have green or yellow-light conversations, they need to be assured they will never become red-lights. If almost every conversation you try to have with your child becomes a red-light one, I recommend you find a counselor or pastor to mediate these conversations with you.

- **Peace Treaties:** Learning to disagree agreeably is an important and effective communication skill. Peace treaties should be made without a winner and loser in mind and be in the best interest of both parties involved. You should initiate a peace treaty when you have reached an impasse in a disagreement with your child. For example, while you know your child is lying about staying out past curfew, they are upset because they feel you don't trust them. It soon becomes a shouting match as both of you try to make your point. This is when it becomes necessary for you both to agree to disagree. Instead of calling your child a liar and widening the gap between your already strained relationship, you can say something like, "Please forgive me for not handling this well. From now on, I ask you to respect your curfew, and I will do my best to trust that you are where you say you are." Forgiveness is fundamental when forming a peace treaty. When your loved one says or does something that hurts you, extending forgiveness is the first step in coming to a peaceful resolution.

"Put on then, as God's chosen ones, holy and beloved, compassionate hearts, kindness, humility, meekness, and patience, bearing with one another and, if one has a complaint against another, forgiving each other; as the Lord has forgiven you, so you also must forgive." (Colossians 3:12-13 ESV)

Finally, I said earlier, before you speak with your child, remember to pray, asking the Lord to guide your conversation. Ask the Holy Spirit to give you clarity as you listen and speak with your child. Pray for spiritual eyes to see and ears to hear what is really being said in their words and tone, and for the discernment to know if the conversation is veering off course.

One way I recognize when something is out of order is when I experience confusion. The Bible tells us, *"For God is not a God of confusion, but of peace" (1 Corinthians 14:33 ESV).* The Greek word for "confusion" *is akatastasía,* which means "instability, disturbance, upheaval, revolution, almost anarchy."[33] This type of confusion is brought on by the enemy and needs to be guarded against in our conversations.

"For where envy and self-seeking *exist,* confusion and every evil thing *are* there." (James 3:16 NKJV)

When all your attempts to fight fair have failed, leaving you feeling baffled and at a loss for what just happened, most likely confusion is at the root of the problem. And not just any confusion, but the kind that brings with it every evil work. What this means is the enemy knows how to make black look white and upside-down appear right side-up. Praying against the evil one's lies and confusion before, during, and after you speak with your child will help refute his mind games and bring clarity to these otherwise confusing conversations.

But how do you know when you are experiencing confusion? This is what I call a "gut-check moment." I am sure you have experienced an uneasy feeling in your stomach during a conversation with someone before. While you can't put your finger on it, you sense something is just not right. As the conversation continues, your head starts pounding and feels fuzzy. Next, you become tongue-tied or at a loss for words. Experiencing this level of confusion can even occur when you are alone. As you ruminate over a distressing situation, your mind plays out every possible worst-case scenario. More than likely, you have a sense of uneasiness in the pit of your stomach, making it impossible to think straight or make wise decisions.

Because God is not a God of confusion, but of peace, He is not in that confusion you are experiencing. What this means is Satan is present and is waging war against your mind. This is not just a red-light moment. This is when you must stop what you are doing, sound the alarm, and get into the presence of God. You will not be able to handle it any other way. There is no staying in the conversation and trying to figure it out. Take a break and go into your prayer closet. Ask others to pray and intercede for you and for your child. Wait for the Lord to restore your peace and bring clarity to your mind before making another attempt at the conversation.

Because Jesus is our peace, as we abide in His presence, we can trust He will bring peace to our hearts and minds and order to the chaos in our families.

These practical communication skills have been tried and tested by yours truly. By keeping them in mind as I face challenging conversations with my children, I was able to keep the lines of communication open in the most trying of circumstances. Putting them into practice will help ensure you fight fairly for, not against, your children.

Reflection Questions

1. When communicating with your addicted child, in what ways have you shown God's grace practically in their life? In what ways have you struggled with grace?

2. As you consider what practical grace looks like on a scale of 1-5, with one being the worst and five being the best, score yourself in the following areas: Confronting, Conviction, Consequences, Covering, and Cherishing.

3. Are you good at choosing your battles wisely, or do you feel this is an area that needs improvement? Explain your answer.

4. Which of the communication skills listed in the section Fighting Fair will be most helpful in future conversations with your child? In what way(s) will it be helpful?

PART FIVE

All Things New

CHAPTER 13

Past Pains and Present Promises

"When I am afraid, I put my trust in you. In God, whose
word I praise, in God I trust; I shall not be afraid."
Psalm 56:3-4a (ESV)

DADDY'S GOT YOU

"*D*awn, let go and jump! I'll catch you!"

I could barely hear my coach's encouraging words
above the ringing in my ears. The muffled sound of "Wah,
Wah, Wah" was all I could make out as he pleaded with me
to take the plunge from the high dive into the pool of water
below.

My teammates also tried cheering me on, although they were not quite as patient or understanding. It was hot, and they were eager to take a dip into the cool refreshment, waiting fifteen feet beneath my toes. Even with calling me a few choice names, they couldn't get me to budge off my perch.

For the first time in my life, at twelve years old, I was paralyzed with fear. Minutes before, I had courageously made my way to the top. Now, my only thought was, *"I'm going to die."* What was happening to me? I had taken this dive many times before. It was easy. It was fun. So why was I stuck here now?

As my coach made his way towards me, I heard him say firmly, "Just let go." It took some serious persuasion on his part to coax me to release my grip, grab his hand, and allow him to guide me to safety. It seemed like hours as he carefully inched us off the board, down the ladder, and back to the reality that I had failed in a big way. The pain of the searing concrete burning the bottoms of my feet paled compared to the agony of my bruised ego.

I wish I could put my finger on the source of that paralyzing fear, but I never figured it out. Perhaps witnessing my sixteen-year-old cousin drown in the lake at summer camp that same year triggered my panic. Maybe I was traumatized when I watched a neighborhood friend fall from that same diving board the summer before, resulting in several lost teeth and two broken wrists. I don't know, but I suspect that before there was an official diagnosis for it, I had a case of PTSD, post-traumatic stress disorder, bringing with it episodes of debilitating fear. Back in those days, no one really understood the effects of trauma on people, much less on children. It was easier to believe we could just get over a traumatic situation by forgetting about it and moving on. In our house, once it was over, it was best to leave it in the past and not bring it up again.

After the high-dive incident, I made up my mind that fear would never control me again. Lofty vow, I know. I still had plenty of traumatic experiences, from my chaotic home life to neighborhood bullies to the loss of loved ones, but I put on a mask and tried to be the brave one who looked out for everyone else. I also became skilled at avoiding anything that caused me fear, like the high dive at that pool or swimming in the deep waters of a lake. Whenever possible, I tried to avoid feelings of intense fear by controlling my circumstances around me. Although I lived in a constant state of anxiety, at least it was better than being afraid all the time.

My determination to control my fear meant that everything needed to be in perfect order. Because I feared rejection, I not only wanted my life to be perfect, I wanted to be perfect. The perfect daughter, perfect friend, perfect student, and perfect Christian. I carried that same attitude straight into adulthood. I loved the Lord and had surrendered my life to Him, but I still struggled with the need to control my actions, my emotions, my surroundings, even my family.

Most of us have experienced trauma in our lives. The chaos and uncertainty around addiction is very traumatic. How can it not be when our children are engaging in risky behavior every day? To help us better understand how addiction can cause us trauma, let's start with its definition. "Trauma" is defined as "any disturbing experience that results in significant fear, helplessness, dissociation, confusion, or other disruptive feelings intense enough to have a long-lasting negative effect on a person's attitudes, behavior, and other aspects of functioning."[34] Trauma always occurs from an actual event, one outside the normal realm of human experience. It overwhelms our normal coping mechanisms and our ability to function.

Today, there is extensive research being done in the field of trauma and how it affects people. Many people have unexpected flashbacks of the situation, causing them to relive their traumatizing event as if it was happening all over again. Others experience symptoms including insomnia, nightmares, severe anxiety, depression, hyper-vigilance, irritability, or social isolation. They may also suffer from stress-related physical symptoms like headaches or digestive issues. While many people experience traumatic events, to be diagnosed with PTSD, the symptoms must last longer than a month and be severe enough to interfere with aspects of daily life, such as work and relationships. It's understandable how the ongoing trauma caused by our children's addictions can lead to PTSD symptoms in many moms.

When I first learned about the diagnosis of PTSD, I thought it was reserved for veterans who had faced life and death in combat situations. I eventually came to realize post-traumatic stress affects millions of people who have experienced traumatizing events of varying types and degrees. Each of us responds to trauma in different ways. While how we respond to a traumatic incident varies, the brain automatically reacts to what it perceives as imminent danger with a fight-or-flight response. In some situations, the brain will freeze and the person will become paralyzed or stuck. My go-to response was usually to fight. Flight wasn't an option because that meant admitting to myself I was afraid. It never occurred to me that freezing like I did on top of that high dive was also a possibility.

The diving board incident would not be the only time childhood trauma affected how I handled stressful situations. Sadly, I carried these trauma responses into adulthood and into how I coped with addiction in my family.

The day Steve spoke the words to me, "Our son is using drugs," all those fears came flooding in again. Suddenly, I was back on top of that diving board, unable to move or hear my coach's voice as he tried to talk me down. Like before, I was frozen in fear. I couldn't speak. I could barely breathe. My need to control was desperately trying to take the reins. I needed to fix him. I needed to fix us. Instead, I breathed a desperate prayer.

"Jesus, Jesus," I whispered.

I was powerless to get off the floor, much less put two words together. In despair, I cried out to the only One truly able to rescue a panicked girl from the high dive or lift up a broken mom and give her the courage she would need to face her worst fears. In that moment of sheer terror, Jesus was there.

"Just let go, Dawn. I'll catch you," He spoke with calm assurance.

Then I remembered the words of the psalmist. *"Even though I walk through the darkest valley, I will fear no evil, for you are with me"* (Psalm 23:4 NIV).

In my darkest valley, with fear overwhelming me, Jesus was with me. Paralyzed by fear, there was no controlling this. There was no fixing it. I couldn't rely on my old standby coping skills for this one. My only choice was to let go and cling to Him. But how? While I desired to let go, I wrestled with doing so. It was late in the evening. There was no one we could call at that hour. That's when I realized my only option was to let go of my need to fix my son, pray for strength to get through the night, and trust the Lord to show me what to do the following day. I would soon learn that letting go would not be a "one and done, once and for all" event. Like climbing up on the diving board to give it another try, it would be a process I would have to go through many times in the future.

As moms of children who are on a life-destructive path, trauma is part of our new normal. For someone who hasn't walked in our shoes, it's easy to say, "Don't worry. Just trust God." Seriously, they just don't get it. And let's pray they never do. I have heard stories that would bring the strongest, most faith-filled people to their knees. Living in the unexpected means never knowing what news we will receive when we answer a knock on the door, receive a late-night phone call, or open a text message. With repeated episodes and the resulting adrenaline rush, we become easily triggered by noises, sirens, or other external stimuli.

I recently asked the moms in our group how addiction has most negatively affected them. With over fifty responses, the majority said they had developed PTSD from the constant barrage of traumatic events they've gone through. Although not every mother of an addicted child develops PTSD, the trauma they undergo has a profound impact on them. Those who have endured adverse childhood experiences as children are especially vulnerable to developing PTSD. Although these women are believers, they can't help but bear the consequences of the burden they have been carrying for so long. They love the Lord and trust Him, but their minds and bodies are suffering intensely because of the stress they are under.

While the Bible doesn't specifically mention PTSD or trauma, it often discusses fear. With "Do not fear" being the most frequent command in the Bible, as people of faith, it's hard to imagine how it's possible that fear can have this much control over us. Yet, because of our circumstances, we accept living in a perpetual state of fear as normal. While occasionally feeling afraid is justified, being controlled by it is not God's plan for us. Instead, Jesus wants us to come to Him when we are afraid, so He can comfort us and strengthen our faith. In contrast, Satan's agenda is to keep us overwhelmed by fear. He does so by continually reminding us of these painful experiences. He will even distort our memories so that when we replay them, we become increasingly fearful.

"for God gave us a spirit not of fear but of power and love and self-control." (2 Timothy 1:7 ESV)

Over time, our brains and bodies develop coping mechanisms to adapt to past, present, or future trauma. Remember the diving board story I shared with you earlier? Recently, I remembered a situation where I responded similarly. A few years ago, my oldest was struggling deeply with his mental health and substance use. His girlfriend had just broken up with him, and he was in a deep depression. Because of his despair, he sent a text message to his brother threatening to commit suicide, but he did not read it until a few hours later. He immediately phoned his dad for help. Steve called 911, who dispatched the police and emergency responders to our son's apartment. At that point, Steve contacted me at work to tell me what was going on. Do you know what I did? Absolutely nothing! Faced with a life and death crisis, I kept working on my patient as though everything was well and fine at home.

After a while, my phone rang, displaying an unknown number on the caller I.D. I asked my patient to excuse me and stepped out of the room to retrieve the call. On the other end was a man identifying himself as the police officer who had responded to the call. To my relief, my son was alive, but because the officer felt he was a danger to himself, he was being transported for medical observation and psychiatric hold. Thanking the officer, I hung up, returned to my room, and went back to work, apologizing to my patient for the interruption. I never breathed a word of what happened to anyone until much later.

A few months ago, I recalled the agonizing events of that day. I began thanking the Lord for the outcome and for granting me the strength to endure that traumatic incident. Do you know what He said? Well, instead of patting me on the back and exclaiming, "Well done, daughter! You really know how to keep your cool under pressure," He chastised me.

"What part of any of that was okay, Dawn?" He asked firmly. "If there was ever a time when you should have left work to be with your family, that was the time." *Ouch!*

My cheeks turned bright red as I embarrassingly realized the error of my ways. While I thought I was being strong and stoic, the Holy Spirit reminded me of that young girl frozen in fear, clutching the diving board decades earlier. If there was a right time to fall apart, that was it. Even excusing myself to have a meltdown in the bathroom would have been okay. But to pretend it wasn't happening? That was more than me keeping it together. That was me denying the dire reality of our current crisis by trying to work through it. While growing up, I witnessed these same coping mechanisms modeled by my mother. Like her, the more I disassociated from the traumatic situation, the less pain it could cause me. But Jesus didn't want me to deny my fear. He wanted me to listen to His voice and obey Him as He called out, *"Just let go."* Do you hear His voice calling out to you as well?

GETTING PAST YOUR PAST

While I have studied trauma and its effects on our brains, I am not an expert on it, nor will I suggest that getting over it is easy. The more I learn about trauma, the more I understand how complex it is. I understand its negative effects on our brains and bodies personally. When we live in a constant state of fight, flight, freeze, or waiting for the next crisis to hit, it's almost impossible to give our adrenals a rest. The brain gets stuck in hyper-drive, always on high alert. Once triggered, it responds with feelings of panic, a normal reaction for a brain that perceives it's in danger. But this should not be a common occurrence. So, how do we resolve these uncontrolled feelings and flashbacks when the Bible repeatedly warns us to not be afraid? We begin by seeking the Lord and inviting the Holy Spirit to reveal those places where lingering fear, pain, and trauma are hiding out.

"I sought the LORD, and he answered me and delivered me from all my fears." (Psalm 34:4 ESV)

Do you remember a time when you were busy doing life as normal and something startled you unexpectedly? How did you react to these sudden surprises? Think back to your childhood. The game "Hide and Seek"[35] was all about hiding to keep from getting caught and then jumping out to scare our friend. As a child, I was notorious for hiding in closets, under tables, and behind bushes for what seemed like hours, so I could jump out and surprise one of my siblings or friends. I even caught my mom and grandparents off-guard a few times. The walloping I received was well worth it just so I could see their reactions!

One thing that stands out to me is how easy it was to get an extreme reaction out of my mom or grandma. I now have a better understanding of how their brains were programmed to have a more intense fight-or-flight response than us kids. Now that I am an adult, I would not appreciate someone jumping out at me just to get a laugh. Our past experiences play a big part in how we react to playful frights or genuine emergencies. You have probably heard someone say, "I hate surprises!" Many people feel that way. They don't like being caught off guard, even if it is for something fun, like a surprise birthday party. For moms of self-destructing children, our bodies have been programmed to react to pleasant surprises in the same way they respond to an unexpected call from the police or emergency room. How then can we move beyond our past, so that the shocking events of today are less traumatizing? While there is no way to avoid taking these hits when they come our way, we can learn how to better handle them and lessen their negative impact on us.

Like my mischievous childhood shenanigans aimed at taunting my family, the devil looks for every opportunity to terrorize us. He patiently lurks in the darkness for the moment we are distracted to catch us off guard. Hopefully, as we become more aware of his tactics, he won't be as successful as I was at startling my poor mom. You'd think she would have figured out my hiding places or realized that if I was being quiet, I was probably up to no good. But the secret to my success was not that I had discovered clever new hideouts. It was my timing. I knew when Mom was preoccupied and her mind was elsewhere, so I learned to wait patiently to make the most of these opportunities. This is how the enemy works in our lives. He knows exactly how we are hardwired. He understands our brains are programmed to react to fearful situations with an automated fight-or-flight response. He also knows our brains store these past traumas in their memory banks, so he uses the element of surprise to keep us in a perpetual state of high alert. The only way we can render his attacks powerless is by preparing ourselves in advance.

While it hurts to dig up previous painful experiences, I encourage you to ask the Holy Spirit to reveal any past trauma or hidden fears you might not be aware of. My paralyzing reaction to jumping off the high dive was not rooted in a fear of heights or a fear of falling. I had been on and off that diving board many times. Instead, something totally unrelated caused what happened on that hot summer day. Somewhere along the way, I stopped feeling safe. By then, I had experienced or witnessed multiple traumatic events, and something clicked in my brain, making me believe I was in danger and needed to protect myself. While I can't put my finger on the exact moment it occurred, it was most likely caused by a series of adverse events rather than just one. This is the key to understanding our trauma responses as adults. When we don't address our fears, they will eventually be beyond our ability to manage.

Today's mental health professionals are experienced in helping people process trauma. Whenever there is an emergency or crisis, trained first responders dispatched to help victims of a crime or natural disaster process these traumatic experiences. That wasn't the case for most of us growing up. Instead, we dealt with it by doing our best to forget what happened and move on. But long before there were therapists and counselors to help those suffering from trauma, the Lord knew His children would experience deep pain and overwhelming fear. Jesus, while on His earthly mission, took on human form, suffered intensely and grieved deeply. This means that He felt the same heartbreak and emotional pain we experience. A few days before His crucifixion, Jesus prayed, *"My Father, if it be possible, let this cup pass from me; nevertheless, not as I will, but as you will"* (Matthew 26:39 ESV).

I am filled with awe and gratitude as I consider the Lord's compassion towards His wounded children. The Bible tells us He is near to the brokenhearted and saves those who are crushed in spirit. Jesus devoted His life to ministering to people who were hurting and in need of His help. Rich or poor, Jew or Gentile, if they asked for help, Jesus showed them mercy. And as His servants, I am thankful that our churches are becoming better equipped to meet the needs of the hurting people who walk through their doors. In my case, I became a certified mental health first responder and trauma coach through a board-certified Christian counseling program. Many churches now have mental health teams set up to help those in crisis access the resources they need in their church and community.

What if you have limited or no access to professional help in your area? I understand from experience that it can be a challenge to find good counselors and therapists due to lack of accessibility or affordability. If this is the case, contact the churches in your area and ask about their counseling programs, as well as a list of available community resources. They often network with professionals who will work with you at low-cost or on a sliding scale.

Thankfully, our inability to access professional counseling does not hinder God's power to heal us. Because of all the information out there, we can fall into the mindset of believing that without professional therapy, we will never be free from the grip trauma has on us. This is where I want to assure that the Lord will not leave you high and dry. Personally, after investing in my children's treatment and therapy, it wasn't feasible for me to meet regularly with a therapist. Support groups and family counseling were helpful, but I received true inner healing through the comfort and counsel of the Holy Spirit.

Jesus has consistently been a very present help in my time of need. He knows my heart better than anyone, and His Word has sustained me in my darkest days. As I abided in the Lord's presence and in His Word, He revealed to me those deeply wounded areas of my heart only He can heal.

"For the word of God is alive and powerful. It is sharper than the sharpest two-edged sword, cutting between soul and spirit, between joint and marrow. It exposes our innermost thoughts and desires. Nothing in all creation is hidden from God. Everything is naked and exposed before his eyes, and he is the one to whom we are accountable." (Hebrews 4:12-13 NLT)

What are some signs you may need to seek professional help? If you can no longer work or perform your daily functions because of the debilitating impact of trauma on your life, I strongly encourage you to seek medical care and professional therapy, as well as spiritual support. If you have experienced trauma but can function normally, don't ignore it, hoping it will go away. Ask Jesus to help you process and heal from your past trauma, but don't hesitate to seek professional help if necessary. By doing so, you can heal from these experiences and be better prepared to face future adverse and traumatic events when they occur.

It's also important to get spiritual guidance as you process the impact your trauma has had on your faith. Whomever you speak with, whether it is a pastor, a counselor, or a biblical mentor, be honest with them. Do not be ashamed of your feelings, your emotional struggles, or any of the events of your past. You will need someone to help you as you walk through this journey and keep you accountable as you seek to make progress.

As I processed the trauma I was going through as the result of my child's addiction, I soon discovered that past traumas were getting in the way of my healing. Most of us, as children, did our best to cope with what happened, forget about it, and move on. We were unaware that the ghosts of these painful experiences remained hidden in the closets of our minds. As adults, when they resurface, we brush them off like menacing gnats instead of using a flyswatter on them and getting rid of them once and for all. While we will never forget the painful ordeals of our past, we can have victory over their lasting negative impact on our lives.

To begin with, trauma not only leaves an imprint on our minds, we also feel it in our physical bodies. Therefore, it is crucial that we address past trauma rather than ignoring it. As we heal from these adverse experiences, we will grow in our ability to deal with the unforeseen challenges that lie ahead. Regardless of whether we choose to seek professional help, it is comforting to know our help comes from the Lord, who can relate to our suffering and is always with us in the most painful moments of our lives.

> "But to our wounds only God's wounds can speak,
> And not a god has wounds, but Thou alone."
> ~ Edward Shillito, a Free Church Minister in England
> during World War I.[36]

Throughout my healing journey, I discovered that embracing these spiritual practices and lifestyle changes is beneficial in dealing with and overcoming past traumas. You may find them helpful as you process yours.

- **Grief Prayers** - a lament is a prayer that comes out of grief, trauma, tragedy, and sorrow. When we lament, we face our feelings and pour out our pain before Jesus by asking Him the hard questions like, "Why?" "How long?" "Where are You?" As you pray, read the books of Lamentations and Psalms for examples of how to lament. One helpful way to lament is to use the Psalms as a writing prompt, rewriting it in your own words. After pouring out your heart, always close in praise as you thank the Lord for hearing your prayer (see 2 Corinthians 7:10. For examples of laments, see Psalms 3 and 4).

- **Pen Your Pain** - journaling is a way you can engage with God by writing your thoughts and expressing your feelings. Some journals leave space for free-form journaling, while others include specific prompts and prayers. One helpful type of journaling is called "protest or grievance" journaling. Here, you write about the traumatic event you are going through, your thoughts and feelings surrounding it, and the impact the pain is having on your emotions. Dig deep, be truthful, and don't censor yourself. Once you finish writing and processing in your journal, destroy it so no one will see it. Finally, spend time in God's presence as you reflect on His love and mercy (see Habakkuk 2:2; Exodus 17:14).

- **Forgive and Release** - forgiving and forgetting is hard, but forgiving and releasing are necessary practices as we process our trauma. Confessing our sins to Jesus and receiving His forgiveness will release us from feelings of shame and guilt. Forgiving those who hurt us will release us from the bonds of bitterness and resentment. When we forgive others, the Lord will also forgive us (see Matthew 6:14-15).

- **Grateful Reflection** - reflecting on God's faithful presence and goodness in our lives moves us away from the pain and toward our healing. Spend time each day thanking Jesus for your many blessings (see 1 Thessalonians 5:18; Colossians 3:15).

- **Meditation Moments** - the Bible is rich in verses encouraging believers to meditate on the Lord's character, His Word, His promises, and His presence in our lives. When meditating on the Lord, I encourage you to practice deep breathing and remain in an attitude of silence to allow space for Jesus to speak into your heart and heal your soul (see Psalm 19:14; Joshua 1:8; Philippians 4:8).

- **Practice Self-care** - your body is a temple of the Holy Spirit and taking care of it is essential as you process trauma. Get proper rest, exercise, and nutrition. Be aware of circumstances that add undue stress to your life. Seek to simplify your schedule and the demands you place on yourself (see 1 Corinthians 6:19-20).

- **Get Moving** - exercise is a necessary part of the healing process. Getting outside in the fresh air and taking a walk is one way to reconnect with God and spend time in prayer. Going to the gym and working up a sweat helps to release tension and take your mind off your worries for a while. Also, dancing to praise music can heal and restore your body and mind (see Romans 12:1; Proverbs 31:17).

- **Rest and Relax** - this includes physical, mental, and spiritual rest. When we rest, we give ourselves a break to restore our minds and bodies and revive our spirits. If you are not getting enough sleep, make some necessary lifestyle changes such as reducing time on your devices, limiting your caffeine intake, going to bed earlier, taking a warm bath, and taking short naps to rest and refresh during the day (see Psalm 22:2-3; Mark 6:31).

- **Lean on Others** - Jesus places people in our lives who can be there to encourage us and help us through traumatic events. Whether it is family, friends, church groups, neighbors, a counselor, or pastor, find your people, and lean on them for support (see Galatians 6:2; Ecclesiastes 4:12).

- **Slow Down** - practice patience as you heal from your trauma. While you want all the hurtful memories to go away and stay gone for good, most healings take time. Remember, you are a work in progress, so be patient with the process (see Romans 12:12; Ephesians 4:2).

FACING THE UNKNOWN

For moms with self-destructive children, dealing with past trauma is hard enough. The thought of the trauma that possibly awaits is unbearable. As we go through one crisis after another, we may start experiencing an anticipatory anxiety caused by playing out all the "what ifs" in our minds. Because of past traumatic experiences due to our child's addiction, we ruminate over the endless possibilities of tragedies that might occur. If we let these anxious thoughts go unchecked long enough, they can become obsessive, stealing our hope and robbing us of our peace. Because of these past traumatic events and the negative emotions tied to them, anything that reminds us of what has gone wrong or what might go wrong in the future easily triggers us.

Facing an unknown future can cause us to fear, especially when we've read the latest reports on addiction. Unfortunately, the statistics and reports on substance use are not written with our mental well-being in mind. Living with addiction is scary. The more we learn about it, the more terrifying it becomes. The news reports project the crisis will only get worse. The statistics prove they're correct. It's no surprise that we fear for our kids. However, as Christian mothers, we must not allow these negative reports to dictate what we believe about the futures of our kids or ourselves.

To keep from becoming stuck in the past or fearful for our futures, it's helpful to remind ourselves that our lives are more than just a dash between two dots on a piece of paper. Many people believe that our life is defined by the time between our birth and our death. However, the Bible teaches us we are sojourners passing through on our way to our eternal home.

> "For we are strangers before you and sojourners, as all our fathers were. Our days on the earth are like a shadow, and there is no abiding." (1 Chronicles 29:15 ESV)

When we keep an eternal perspective, we are no longer slaves to fear of the "what-ifs" in our lives. Instead, we can choose beforehand to stand and say, "Even if the worst-case scenario happens, I will trust You, Lord."

Mom, this means even if the worst possible thing happens to our children. That thing we have no control over. That thing that will break us, crush us, and cause us such deep grief that we believe we won't survive. The death of a child is every mother's worst nightmare. Sadly, too many have lost their children as death snatched them away before their time. This is the "even-if" I am talking about, the one we might someday face, and the one God our Father has already faced.

While we were still sinners, God demonstrated His love for us by giving His Son Jesus to die for us (see Romans 5:8). He made the ultimate sacrifice so we can live forever with Him. Death no longer has power over us because Jesus has granted us eternal life. Because of this hope, the "what ifs" in life no longer have a hold on us. And they no longer need to have a hold on our children, either. When we set our eyes on eternity, we can let go of our fear for our children's future and embrace the One who holds their future. We read in Revelation the words of Jesus: *"Behold, I stand at the door and knock. If anyone hears my voice and opens the door, I will come in to him and eat with him, and he with me" (Revelation 3:20 ESV).*

What a promise we can hold on to. Our Lord will never give up on knocking on the door of our children's hearts. Even on their path of self-destruction, He is there, relentlessly pursuing them. Jesus is offering them eternal life. He is the only one who can promise them victory over death and over their addictions.

"'O death, where is your victory? O death, where is your sting?' The sting of death is sin, and the power of sin is the law. But thanks be to God, who gives us victory through our Lord Jesus Christ." (1 Corinthians 15:55-57 ESV)

Once we commit to moving past the "what ifs" that hold our minds hostage and decide to trust Jesus, "even if" things don't turn out the way we hope, we can shift the dialogue to "what now?" True transformation takes place when we confront our fears, focus on Jesus, and follow the Holy Spirit's guidance. Now, instead of living in paralyzing fear, we can face an uncertain future with a secure faith that asks, "What would You have me do now, Lord?" When we change our mindset, there is nothing the enemy of fear can do to stop us.

Reflection Questions

1. Have you previously experienced trauma in your life prior to your child's addiction? Write as much or as little as you can to describe the event.

2. How has it affected how you handle the ongoing trauma caused by your child's addiction?

3. What spiritual practices and lifestyle changes will you implement in order to heal from previous trauma and prepare for future traumatic experiences?

4. As you look over the verses in this lesson, is there one that resonates with you as you face uncertainty in your future? Explain why it encourages you.

CHAPTER 14

A Work in Progress

"Many women do noble things, but you surpass them all."
Proverbs 31:29 (NIV)

YOU'RE SUCH A CHARACTER

*I*n the book of Exodus, we read about the nation of Israel's enslavement to Egypt. While in captivity, the Lord blessed and multiplied His people. Because of their booming population, the king of Egypt was concerned an uprising would break out. To prevent this from happening, he ordered the Hebrew midwives to kill all the male babies they delivered. But the midwives feared God and refused to follow the king's command. When questioned, the midwives cleverly stated that the Hebrew women labored quickly and delivered their babies before they could arrive.

This displeased the king, so his next move was to order that all the Hebrew baby boys were to be thrown into the Nile River. Can you imagine how despondent these new mothers must have felt? They were helpless to save their babies. But this wasn't the case for one Levite woman who had just given birth to a son. Instead of following the king's edict, she kept her newborn hidden for three months to protect him. When she could no longer keep him hidden, she came up with another plan to save her son's life. Rather than watch the Egyptians murder her child, she crafted a papyrus basket, gently packed her precious cargo in it, and placed it in the reeds of the river. She then gave his sister the task of keeping watch from a distance to see what happened next.

As the story continues, the Pharaoh's daughter went to bathe in the river. Noticing the basket, she sent her servant to fetch it from the water. Inside, she found the crying baby and took pity on him. No longer did she only hear of Hebrew male babies drowning in the river. She now had to face the reality of what was going on right before her eyes. Because the baby's big sister "just so happened" to be there at the right moment, she offered to go and bring a Hebrew woman to nurse the infant. That woman "coincidentally" turned out to be the baby's mother. The Pharaoh's daughter named the baby boy Moses because she said, "I drew him out of the water." God preserved the life of the baby Moses who would one day be the man who would lead the nation of Israel out of slavery to Egypt (see Exodus 1-2).

As we look back at this story, we observe courage in the face of crisis, as these women dared to obey God when doing so meant risking their own lives. The two midwives, Moses' mother, and his sister all resisted being accomplices to this evil attack against God's children. I have to consider the bravery of the midwives. How genius of them to say, "No" and devise such a clever excuse that no man on the planet could argue with them! And Moses' mother? She was not afraid of the king's edict and determined to do whatever was necessary to keep her child safe. The apple didn't fall far from the tree when the baby's sister bravely made sure he was well cared for by his own mother. Even the Pharaoh's daughter unwittingly was part of God's plan to save baby Moses.

Each of these amazing women had one thing in common. They exemplified strength of character during perilous times. As for Moses' mother, because of her courage, she was listed among the heroes of faith in the book of Hebrews.

"By faith Moses, when he was born, was hidden for three months by his parents, because they saw that the child was beautiful, and they were not afraid of the king's edict." (Hebrews 11:23 ESV)

As a mother, I can relate to the fear Moses' mother must have felt. I am sure she feared for his life and for her own safety. But she didn't let fear stop her. She was a woman of faith. She looked at her son and knew he was special. She believed God had a plan for his life, so she acted according to her faith, not her feelings. Still, can you imagine the anguish she must have felt as she placed her newborn into the water with only a basket to protect him? What unimaginable pain she must have endured as she let him go and prayed to the Lord for his safekeeping. What does this story have to do with us as moms of addicted and wayward children? After all, our children are adults making their own choices, not helpless babies. We can't make their decisions for them. While this passage shares the faith of Moses' mother in a crisis, it also encourages us to conquer fear by taking action. Our trials can make or break us. When faced with a crisis, we can either give up and give in, or we can walk by faith through the fire of adversity as the Lord builds His character in us.

"Not only that, but we rejoice in our sufferings, knowing that suffering produces endurance, and endurance produces character, and character produces hope." (Romans 5:3-4 ESV)

As we read words like suffering and endurance, there is no doubt we will face times of intense adversity in our lives, times when we feel like giving up because of sheer exhaustion. But before raising the white flag to surrender, consider the call to action in these verses. We are told to rejoice in our sufferings because doing so results in a chain reaction that produces endurance, which then produces character, which ultimately produces hope in us. But how does having hope in our hardships help make them any easier? This verse answers this question well.

"and hope does not put us to shame, because God's love has been poured into our hearts through the Holy Spirit who has been given to us." (Romans 5:5 ESV)

When God's love is poured into our hearts, we are no longer ashamed. His love sets us free from shame. But what if we can't feel God's love because of the pain we are experiencing? It's easy to feel loved by God when everything is going great, isn't it? Who hasn't heard someone say before, "Of course she's happy. Everything is perfect in her life." But without first experiencing hardship, we will never experience the hope promised us in this verse. The Greek word for "hope" is *elpís,* which is translated "expectation (of what is sure–certain), trust, confidence. "[37] Tribulation builds in us a kind of hope that will not leave us disappointed. Re-read the first part of the verse, *"hope does not put us to shame."* The biblical word for "hope" here is "a hope that does not cause us to *"blush with shame."*[38]

We have all hoped for something, only to be disappointed before, haven't we? We question why we keep hoping, just to be let down over and over again. I have felt myself losing hope a few times. I actually told Steve that I had lost all hope that my son would ever be free from his addiction. But, in those moments when I felt like giving up, Jesus reminded me of this verse.

> "May the God of hope fill you with all joy and peace in believing, so that by the power of the Holy Spirit you may abound in hope." (Romans 15:13 ESV)

Because of His love for us, the Lord made sure we wouldn't have to conjure up some wishful thinking to get through this battle. Instead, we have an imperishable hope that is given to us by the Holy Spirit. Our hope is not in other people. It is not in our circumstances. It is not even in our child's ability to stay drug free. Our hope is in Jesus. And He is the reason we never lose hope!

Still, it's hard to feel hopeful when things look hopeless. I hear the weariness in the voices of moms as they speak of enduring their trials for 10, 20, and for some, even 30 years. These moms have spent countless hours on their knees crying out to God for their child, only to have their prayers go unanswered and their hopes dashed. In their brokenness, they cannot fathom how persevering through their trials will strengthen their faith and mature their character.

As I write this book, I do so with these moms in mind. I write it with you in mind. I never want the words I pen to come across as me having it all figured out already. I am right here with you. Like you, I want to grow in character. And like these brave women of the Bible, I want to live courageously and come through my trial victoriously. But like you, I also get weary.

PERFECTLY IMPERFECT

My heart's desire has always been to please the Lord. Instead, I accepted the lie that if I failed in any area of my life, motherhood being one of them, I would be a disappointment to Him. Although I knew in my head that I was not a complete failure as a mother, deep in my heart, I felt I needed to tell Jesus how sorry I was for all the times I failed miserably at it. The times I yelled at my kids when I should have been patient with them. The days when my imperfection demanded their perfection. The moments when I held them back out of fear they might fail. It was on those occasions the Lord tenderly reminded me that other than Himself, no one is perfect. We are all a work in progress. Still, for women like me who struggle with perfectionism, it's hard to wrap our minds around scriptures like Matthew that tell us, *"You therefore must be perfect, as your heavenly Father is perfect" (Matthew 5:48 ESV).*

In this verse, the word "perfect" means "having reached its end, fully grown, mature, and complete." It is used in this verse to demonstrate *completeness of Christian character.*[39] Being "perfect" for us as believers does not mean we will never sin, make a mistake, or fail in our lives.

How does understanding this help us if we are still blaming ourselves or feeling guilty for the suffering of our children? First, we should remember that the Lord is empathetic to what we are going through. He is a perfect Father in every way, and yet, His children go astray. He understands what we are up against trying to raise children in a fallen world. Next, we have to guard against comparing ourselves to other mothers who seem to have it more together than we do.

While friends, family, and even social media influencers offer their advice on how to raise good kids who become great adults, it can leave us reeling in self-doubt if we aren't careful to consider the source. Remember, most of what's displayed on social media is all smoke and mirrors. I would guess that what goes on in their homes is every bit as real and hard, although uniquely different, as what goes on in ours. Still, it doesn't make it any easier to be on the receiving end of thoughtless advice or criticism. Whether intentional or unintentional, an insensitive comment becomes a weapon in the enemy's hands as he targets our already fragile egos.

Because I did skincare in a Plastic Surgery office, many of the patients I treated lived affluently. They could provide their children with the finest schools, the best nannies, personal tutors, studying abroad, and every other advantage money has to offer. Almost all of them ended up attending the best universities in the country as a result of the excellent college preparatory education they received. I want to emphasize that I am not speaking from a place of envy. I knew them well enough to know their lives were far from perfect. I am simply stating the fact that we came from two very different worlds. I remember the stress each mother faced as she helped her son or daughter apply for the schools of their choice and the relief she felt when they received their acceptance letters. As she beamed with pride, I was genuinely happy for her and for her child. After my congratulatory response, it almost never failed that some of these moms would boastfully respond, "Thank you. He turned out to be such a great kid! I must have raised him right." Gulp! That's when I felt like I had just been sucker punched. Although she didn't mean to hit a raw nerve, the list of all my mommy shortcomings started falling from my memory bank like ticker tape in a parade.

"Maybe if I had raised my sons right, things would have turned out differently for them," a voice sneered in my head in its all-too-familiar accusatory tone. *"Hmm. Maybe if I had a crystal ball, I wouldn't have made all the mistakes I made."* But that wasn't the case. While I loved my children and did the best I could raising them, there came a point when they made

their own choices. It was time for this imperfect mom to admit she raised imperfect kids in a world that says anything less than perfect is subpar.

How I longed for a do-over, a second chance to make it right, to do it better. In my dreams, I would be able to provide my children with everything they needed to have an "easy" life, one free from all the pain they have experienced. I would make sure they were happy, successful, and didn't struggle with perfectionism and self-doubt like I do. Or would I? What if doing it over my way meant doing it without Jesus? What if striving to please people meant failing to please Him? Paul wrote in Galatians, *"For am I now seeking the approval of man, or of God? Or am I trying to please man?"* His answer reveals that we can't do both. *"If I were still trying to please man, I would not be a servant of Christ"* (Galatians 1:10 ESV).

Who do you live to please, my friend? Like me, has your frail humanity screamed at you, *"You have to do better!"* Do you beat yourself up because you believe somehow this whole mess is your fault? If so, stop. You don't have that much power. None of us can control another person. I was a slow learner where that was concerned. I always strived to please God by doing more instead of becoming less. I could barely tolerate my own weaknesses, much less expose them to others. But the Lord doesn't want us to live our lives striving for the world's version of perfection. He allows us to be weak, so that His power will rest upon us. Because of His grace, we can embrace our imperfections and release our desire to please anyone but Him.

"But he said to me, 'My grace is sufficient for you, for my power is made perfect in weakness.' Therefore I will boast all the more gladly of my weaknesses, so that the power of Christ may rest upon me." (2 Corinthians 12:9 ESV)

THE LABELS WE WEAR

Do you remember the first time someone called you a name? "Stupid!" "Ugly!" "Fatty!" You may have been too young to know what the words meant, but by the looks on the faces of the name-callers, you guessed they weren't being nice. It might have been the neighborhood kids or school bully who labeled you "Four-Eyes," making you feel self-conscious about your first pair of glasses. Maybe your own siblings called you "Miss Goody-Two-Shoes" as they dared you to throw a rock at the neighbor's window. Some of you may have felt the bitter sting of disappointment when your parents insensitively called you names like "Worthless," "Failure," or "'Mistake."

Not all the words (or labels) others put on us are bad. Some make us feel better about ourselves: "Beautiful." "Smart." "Kind." How about the first time you heard someone say you were their "Best Friend!" From the moment we come into the world, the labeling starts. Boy or girl, healthy or sick, rich or poor, advantaged or disadvantaged, normal or different... all labels, while meant to describe us, should never define us. The labels put on us by other people, if we let them, have the power to propel us forward in our God-ordained purpose, or they can hinder us, keep us stuck, or set us back from being the person the Lord created us to be. The only labels we are to embrace are the ones God has placed on us: "Loved," "Redeemed," "Forgiven," "Worthy." He is our Creator, the One who made us. Only He has the authority to label and define us. I like to call these "God's Designer Labels." While God's labels are always founded on the truth, man-made labels are often based on lies or half-lies because they come from a place of personal bias. The question is, "Whose labels are you wearing?"

To understand the difference between man-made labels and God's designer labels, it's important to understand their intent. Proverbs 18:21 says that *"death and life are in the power of the tongue,"* so we can see how powerful labels can be. Man-made labels describe and place value on people based on their appearance, performance, ability, behaviors, or roles. God's labels define who we are and declare our worth based on our identity as His children.

"See what kind of love the Father has given to us, that we should be called children of God, and so we are." (1 John 3:1a ESV)

The problem with man-made labels, especially the negative ones, is they tend to be sticky. God's labels, on the other hand, slip off us like butter on a hot pancake. Who hasn't received several compliments and then one harsh criticism, only to forget all the accolades and let the insult bother them for days? Why is that? I believe I know the answer, but to figure it out, let's take one final trip back to the Garden of Eden.

"Then God said, 'Let us make man in our image, after our likeness. And let them have dominion over the
fish of the sea and over the birds of the heavens and
over the livestock and over all the earth and over every creeping thing that creeps on the earth.' So God
created man in his own image, in the image of God
he created him; male and female he created them."
(Genesis 1:26-27 ESV)

The truth we find in these verses is often overlooked. The
Lord God made us to be His image bearers. When He created
Adam and Eve, they were free from sin, and thus, free from
shame. They saw themselves only through their Creator's eyes.

"And the man and his wife were both naked and were
not ashamed." (Genesis 2:25 ESV)

But things did not stay that way for long. After partaking
of the forbidden fruit, their eyes were opened, and they knew
they were naked. For the first time, they felt uncomfortable
in their own skin. To hide their nakedness, they wove together fig leaves for clothing. But their physical coverings weren't
enough to conceal their shame, so they did what any sinful,
shame-filled man or woman would do. When they heard the
Lord walking in the garden, they were afraid and hid themselves from Him (see Genesis 3:7-11).

The first two negative emotions experienced by Adam and
Eve after they sinned were shame and fear. Let me add a few
more to the list. They felt exposed, vulnerable, and unpro-
tected. This is what sin does to us. It makes us self-centered,

self-conscious, and self-absorbed. It separates us from God, so we act independently of Him. When God created humans in His image, He created us to be righteous like Him. We were not meant to carry sin around in our earthly bodies.

One of the most insightful questions God asked in His encounter with His fallen children was, "Who told you that you were naked?" Sadly, no one had to point out their nakedness. Not only did they see it for themselves, but they also felt naked. The Lord knew the answer to His question before He asked them. His creation had sinned against Him. But because of His love for them and grace towards them, instead of exposing their shame, He made garments to cover them (see Genesis 3:21).

Since man's rebellion against God, people have done everything in their power to escape their shame. When we can't escape it, we try to cover it. Instead of fig leaves, we sew together labels of good works, achievements, and success to cover our negative feelings of guilt, failure, and self-loathing. But these man-made labels come with consequences. If someone places a positive label on us because of our accomplishments or attributes, we risk becoming prideful and acting independently of God. We may even feel like we are better than other people if we compare ourselves to them. If a negative label is spoken to us because of our failures or weaknesses, we may feel ashamed and hide from God. We can start to believe that we are worth less than others who seem better than us. Because our feelings pack a powerful punch, we must be careful not to allow man-made labels to hold more power over us than God's designer labels.

This is common with mothers of self-destructing or way-ward children. While we may not admit to feeling ashamed of our child or their behavior, we have no problem admitting our own feelings of shame for not being a better mom. We subconsciously start wearing a label bearing the scarlet letter "A" for "Addict's Mom," as though placing guilt on ourselves will somehow keep our children from feeling shame. How do I know this? Not only have I placed that label on myself, I have also had multiple conversations with other moms who've done the same thing. It never fails that most will start the conversation discussing their child's experience with drugs or alcohol, only to stop short and start making excuses for them. Next, the mom will shift the conversation from her child to herself and what she should have done differently. Before it's over, she is bearing full responsibility for her child's actions and donning the labels of shame and blame right along with it. Mom, can you relate? What labels are you now wearing because of your child's addiction?

As I write about the labels we wear as mothers of prodi-gals, let me emphasize that not all are negative. It's all about whose labels you're wearing. When Jesus sees you, He doesn't see you as a failure or disappointment. Instead, when He looks at you, He announces to His angels, "See that one? She is a mighty prayer warrior! A woman of faith. A daughter of the Most-High God! In My name, she has stood against the pow-ers of darkness, determined to destroy her child. She will never give up until her child is saved, delivered, and set free."

No longer should we allow these man-made labels to hold us back from seeing ourselves as God sees us. We find our identity in Him alone. But it can be difficult to recognize which labels are man-made and which are God-designed, especially when we've worn them for so long. If you are not sure, always compare them to the Word of God. Here are a few of the labels the Lord places on His children.

"But you are a *chosen race*, a *royal priesthood*, a *holy nation*, a *people for his own possession*, that you may proclaim the excellencies of him who called you out of darkness into his marvelous light." (1 Peter 2:9 ESV, emphasis mine)

This is how Jesus sees you, beloved one. You are chosen, royal, holy, and His own possession. You might find it hard to see yourself this way, but when Jesus looks at you, He sees Himself. Just as we look at our children and see the family resemblance, the Lord looks at us as His image bearers. As you recall, Moses' mother was an ordinary woman on an extraordinary mission. While enslaved in Egypt, she believed God had a plan for her newborn son. When the Pharaoh's daughter took the baby Moses to raise him as an Egyptian, his mother knew his true identity. He would always be her child. In his veins flowed Hebrew blood. Being raised by Egyptian royalty would never change his identity as a child of the Most High God. The same is true for you. You have the Spirit of God living inside you. It no longer matters how other people define you. You are a woman on a mission from God, and you are wearing His labels to prove it.

Speaking of labels, here's a bit of a backstory of why I call them "God's Designer Labels." Several years ago, Steve, Jadyn, and I went on our dream trip to Italy. One of our favorite visits was to the city of Florence. While there, we stopped by a leather factory where they made custom handbags, jackets, shoes, and wallets. What stood out to me most was the craftsmanship of these beautifully handmade items. First, the leather was carefully dyed with the finest natural pigments. Next, the pieces were cut out by hand and stitched together by a seamstress who painstakingly ensured that each stitch was precisely placed according to the designer's standards. Finally, when the piece was almost finished, she would stitch into the inside seam a label bearing the designer's name that included the inscription, *"Handmade with Genuine Italian Leather."*

Each design was unique and stunning. There was nothing cookie-cutter about it. These works of art were not made from man-made materials or sewn on an assembly line. They were authentic and genuine, as individual as a fingerprint. That little label carefully sewn into the inside of the garment bore the designer's certificate of authenticity. Without it, no matter how good the suit or purse looked on the outside, it was a fake. This is what Jesus does for us. Because of His grace, we are new creations. We bear the Master Designer's personal certificate of authenticity, a label that is permanently woven into our identity as His children. No longer are we identified by man-made labels. What others think about us or what we think about ourselves doesn't define us. Because we are His workmanship and we bear the name of our Maker, we can throw out those old labels permanently.

In the following verse, the Greek word for "workmanship" is *poiéma*, which means "a work, a product, i.e. **fabric** (literally or figuratively) - a thing that is made, workmanship."[40]

"For we are his workmanship, created in Christ Jesus for good works, which God prepared beforehand, that we should walk in them." (Ephesians 2:10 ESV)

Take a few moments to reflect on this verse and what it means to be God's workmanship. I love the example of fabric in the definition. The words came alive to me as I pictured the Lord carefully selecting the perfect fabric to weave into a masterpiece useful for his purpose. When God created each of us, He did not play favorites. He cut us all out of the same cloth. He did not pick and choose who would be made from the finest silks and linens, or who He would cut from a piece of cheap muslin. He created each of us with love and for His glory.

But why is it necessary to get rid of our man-made labels if we desire to make a difference in the lives of our children? For starters, our kids watch what we do more than they listen to what we say. They want to see if we practice what we preach. There is no better way for us to help our children break free from their bondages than for them to see us break free from ours. Once we were born again, we became new creations. Since the old person is now gone, why would we still wear those old labels? They defined us as who we *were*, not as who we *are*. It's time to bury them once and for all.

"Therefore, if anyone is in Christ, he is a new creation.
The old has passed away; behold, the new has come."
(2 Corinthians 5:17 ESV)

Dying to our old way of seeing ourselves can be harder than it seems. While our minds tell us that the negative labels we are wearing are lies, our feelings tell us otherwise. When we were kids, if someone negatively labeled us, it hurt our feelings, didn't it? We tried to ignore the name-callers or pretend their words didn't hurt, but they did. As the saying goes, "Sticks and stones may break my bones, but words will never hurt me." But that's not exactly true, is it? As I have gotten older, most of these labels don't hurt like they used to, but some still cut deep.

God created us to have feelings. If He only wanted us to think, He would not have created us with the capacity to feel. He loves us, and He made us to love Him in return. He also made us to love other people. Along with our ability to feel love, we also feel pain, sorrow, and grief. People can hurt us, and we can hurt them by the words we speak.

Right now, you may be wearing negative labels that are keeping you from moving forward in fulfilling your dreams and God's plans for your life. Maybe they are holding you back from intimacy in your relationships with other people or even with the Lord. While your child's addiction is not to blame for many of the labels you've worn since childhood, it has exposed them. If you grew up feeling like a failure as a child, it is possible you see yourself as a failure as a mother. If you felt like you were a bad kid, you might see yourself as a bad mom. Because our feelings deeply influence our beliefs, we must not let them go unchecked. When we compare these beliefs to the Word of truth and who God says we are, how do they stack up?

As I contemplated my own feelings of inadequacy, failure, and unworthiness as a mother, I began to realize that if I wanted to *heal,* I had to *feel.* I could only pretend I was okay for so long. Then, when the pain became bad enough, there was no more ignoring it. I cried out to Jesus, asking Him to show me why I felt so negative about myself. Instead of answering me directly, He nudged my spirit and asked me some hard questions. "Who told you that you were naked?" "Who told you to feel ashamed and cover yourself?" "Who made you feel afraid, so you hid from Me?" Each question seared my conscience as I answered "Me" to all three. I was the one who listened to the voice of the accuser, accepted his lying labels, and allowed them to define me. As the Holy Spirit revealed and removed each of these false labels, He presented me with a whole new wardrobe, arrayed with His designer labels.

"I am overwhelmed with joy in the LORD my God! For he has dressed me with the clothing of salvation and draped me in a robe of righteousness. I am like a bridegroom dressed for his wedding or a bride with her jewels." (Isaiah 61:10 NLT)

Because of the grace of Jesus, I no longer feel ashamed or to blame for my son's addiction. I am ready to trash the manmade lying labels once and for all. Are you with me? Let's start by changing our wardrobe and throwing out a few things. Think of it as doing some spiritual spring cleaning.

Out with the Old Labels

- **Reveal** – Ask the Lord to show you any false labels you are wearing and their source. Regardless of who labeled you, if their words are wrong or hurtful, those labels do not belong in your closet.
- **Reject** the negative label by speaking against it and not receiving it. This can be as simple as saying, "This label is a lie from the enemy, and I will not receive it."
- **Remove** – Ask the Lord to remove any lying labels and the false beliefs attached to them. This can be painful as lying labels are sticky. Ask Jesus to heal you and set you free from their negative effects.
- **Refuse** to let negative labels have control over you by forgiving those who labeled or hurt you. This also includes asking Jesus to forgive you for words you've spoken wrongfully about yourself.

Next, the fun part. Since those old labels are gone, let's get dressed for success!

In with the New Labels

- **Receive** your identity as God's daughter. Who does God say you are? Receive it and believe it. Claim and wear the gift of God's Designer Labels.
- **Renew** your mind by meditating on the Word of God. When you renew your mind, your feelings, beliefs, and words will follow.
- **Replace** stinking thinking with life-giving words of hope and faith. Speak kindly about yourself and others.
- **Remind** yourself daily to wear your new God's designer labels with grace, gratitude, and a new attitude!

When first putting these practices into action, you may feel like rushing right through them. Instead, take your time and ponder the suggestions within each one. The royal attire Jesus desires to clothe you in is far more beautiful than that holey sweatshirt you might be reluctant to throw out. But, I can guarantee once you do, you will never go back to those old man-made labels again. With God's designer labels, you will be a couture girl for sure!

Reflection Questions

1. When you read the account of Moses' mother and the other women God used to save Moses' life, can you see how the Lord used these ordinary women for an extraordinary purpose? Share your thoughts.

2. In what ways does rejoicing in our suffering produce hope in our lives? What would it look like for you to have a kind of hope that does not disappoint?

3. Have you struggled with perfectionism? In what ways? How can understanding the biblical definition of the word "perfect" help you overcome the world's standards of perfectionism?

4. Have you worn negative labels since your childhood that affected how you see yourself as the mother of an addicted child? How will you be able to recognize and replace these old labels moving forward? How does putting on God's designer labels help improve how you see yourself?

CHAPTER 15

Grace Becomes You

"In him we have redemption through his blood, the
forgiveness of our trespasses, according to the riches
of his grace."
Ephesians 1:7 (ESV)

THE GIFT OF GRACE

"*I* have tried to forgive him, but I just can't forget what he did to me!" How difficult it is to move past the pain and trauma caused us by another person. Even though we try to forgive and forget, the painful memories play on repeat in our wounded souls. When that someone we are struggling to forgive is ourselves, it's even harder.

We read in the book of Matthew, *"For if you forgive others their trespasses your heavenly Father will also forgive you, but if you do not forgive others their trespasses, neither will your Father forgive your trespasses" (Matthew 6:14-15 ESV).*

Notice the Bible does not teach the practice of self-forgiveness, which is a concept in secular psychology. Only Jesus can forgive us. If we desire to be free of the guilt and self-blame we are holding onto, we will need to accept the forgiveness He offers us.

Consider this. Jesus commanded us to forgive others. This includes forgiving our children for the pain they've caused us, right? Therefore, since Jesus requires us to forgive others as a condition for receiving His forgiveness, why would He allow us to hold on to unforgiveness towards ourselves? When the Lord forgives us, He no longer remembers the sins we committed. His blood washes us clean. We have only to receive His forgiveness and bask in his grace. Far too often, as mothers of addicted children, we drag our guilt around like a ball and chain, refusing to let it go. We claim we want to be forgiven and free from guilt, but when it comes down to it, if we no longer feel guilty, we then feel guilty for not feeling guilty. (If we were together right now, I would ask for a show of hands.)

Do you remember the Bible story about the invalid man at the Pool of Bethesda? Multitudes of sick people waited around the pool for the waters to stir, hoping that they would be the first one in so they could receive their healing. This man had spent the last 38 years of his life waiting to be healed, but never made it into the pool first. Then one day, he had an encounter with Jesus, who was about to change his life. As Jesus approached the man, He spoke these words to him, *"Do you want to be healed?" (John 5:6 ESV).*

Rather than answering Jesus with a simple "Heck ya," he gave an excuse. *"Sir, I have no one to put me into the pool when the water is stirred up, and while I am going another steps down before me."* Instead of catering to the man's excuses, Jesus did what He came to do and said to him, *"Get up, take up your bed, and walk"* (John 5:7-8 ESV).

Dear sister, my question for you today is the same as the one presented to this hurting man by Jesus Himself. "Do you want to be healed?" Do you want to be free from the emotional pain that, like this man's physical ailment, has kept you bound for years? Or, with Jesus standing before you, would your answer be, "I have an addicted child. I can't be healed while she is still bound by drugs." It's time for us to be honest with ourselves about whether we earnestly desire to be free from our emotional torment, especially if our child's situation is getting worse instead of better.

On the path from guilt to grace, it is crucial we consider our readiness to abandon excuses and accept the healing, forgiveness, and freedom offered to us by Jesus. Our relationship with Him is ours alone. It is not a relationship between Jesus, us, and our kids. Whether we accept or refuse His offer is solely ours to decide. He won't allow us to glance over our shoulder and ask, "But what about them?" With this in mind, I will ask you again, "Do you want to be healed, my friend?" I suspect your answer is a resounding, "Yes!" If so, you may also be asking, "But how does forgiving others for the pain they caused me help me heal?" or "How can I heal when, even after Christ forgave me, I am still carrying this burden of guilt and shame?"

By embracing forgiveness, our hearts and minds will experience healing. Let's first address forgiving others. Are you unable to forgive your child for the pain he or she has caused you? Perhaps you blame your child's father or someone else for their addiction. Maybe someone hurt you years ago, but you can't find it in your heart to forgive them. The Bible teaches us how to forgive in these verses from Ephesians. *"Let all bitterness and wrath and anger and clamor and slander be put away from you, along with all malice. Be kind to one another, tenderhearted, forgiving one another, as God in Christ forgave you" (Ephesians 4:31-32 ESV).*

The key to how to forgive is in the verse above, *"forgiving one another, **as God in Christ forgave you**" (emphasis mine).* Jesus never asked us to forgive those who hurt us in our own strength. He taught us to forgive others as He forgave us. Remember when Jesus taught His disciples how to pray, He also included forgiveness in His prayer, *"and forgive us our debts, as we also have forgiven our debtors" (Matthew 6:12).*

It's clear that to be forgiven, we will also need to forgive others. But what if we don't want to or aren't ready to forgive our offender? What if the offender is our child who continues to break our trust after promising us it will never happen again? We can forgive those who hurt us because Jesus wants us to. We do so in obedience to Him. We keep forgiving because He keeps forgiving us. But even when we want to, it's hard to forgive the people who have caused us immeasurable harm and pain.

With this in mind, here are five steps we can take to forgive others, even if they are not sorry or repentant for the hurt they've caused us.

1. **Decide to Forgive.** Forgiving someone who has hurt us is hard, even painful. In order to proceed, we must first have the willingness to forgive. Forgiveness starts with a decision, one that says, "Because Jesus forgives me, I choose to forgive this person who hurt me" (see Mark 11:25).

2. **Ask God to Help You.** Ask Jesus to teach you to forgive. Trust that Jesus will help you forgive those who have hurt you. Look up Bible verses and stories of people who forgave the person who hurt them (see Luke 23:34).

3. **Give Jesus Your Hurts.** Understand your emotions are normal. Share your pain with the Lord, and ask Him to heal you of the pain caused by the person who hurt you (see 1 Peter 5:7).

4. **Pray for Your Offender.** This can be hard because we don't want to think about, much less pray for the person who hurt us. But the Bible tells us to bless those who curse us and pray for those who abuse us. We can trust that if the Lord tells us to pray for our offender, He will bless us for our obedience (see Luke 6:27-29).

5. **Consider Jesus.** Forgiving those who hurt us may seem impossible unless we first consider Jesus and the suffering He endured to forgive us for our sins. As we gratefully contemplate the sacrifice He paid for us, we will find it easier to forgive those who hurt us (see Hebrews 12:3).

Now that we have looked at how to forgive others, we will address our own feelings of guilt and how receiving Jesus' forgiveness is the key to getting over them. Start by doing some soul-searching. What decisions or actions are you feeling guilty about? Are the reasons for your guilt justified? Why or why not? Review the following definition for the word "guilt." Do any of these describe you?

1: the fact of having committed a breach of conduct especially violating law and involving a penalty

2: a. the state of one who has committed an offense especially consciously

   b: feelings of deserving blame especially for imagined offenses or from a sense of inadequacy: self-reproach: harsh criticism or disapproval of oneself especially for wrong-doing, shame, self-loathing[41]

Did you notice the second part of the definition describes guilt as "feelings of deserving blame especially for imagined offenses?" Experiencing genuine feelings of guilt when we do wrong is normal. Believing and receiving false guilt is not. What's become known to us as "Mom-guilt" can be a false, exaggerated, or misplaced guilt. In other words, the guilt you're feeling is not based on facts or truth. Although these feelings may be rooted in some semblance of truth, they carry with them an over-exaggerated sense of personal blame for your child's actions and their consequences. While your feelings are valid, the way you remember the situation that caused these intense feelings may be skewed. Therefore, it is important for us to revisit our past and see if things are really as they seem.

I will share a personal example. As you are aware, both of my sons abused substances at various points in their lives. As their mom, while I understood I didn't cause this, meaning I didn't force them to use drugs, I couldn't help but wonder if or how I played a part in why they started using drugs. In my normal, direct fashion, I spoke with them on separate occasions and asked them what I could have done differently. Both assured me I was a good mother. It wasn't my fault. Somehow, while I appreciated their desire to ease my pain, guilt, and self-blame, I couldn't shake the idea that they were just trying to protect me. Isn't that so mom-like? Even when our kids insist it's not all about us, we make it all about us.

As we look back on our parenting skills or lack thereof, we will recall times we did something that hurt our child. I mean, it happens, doesn't it? We lose our cool and say something that we later regret. We point out their weaknesses instead of their strengths while trying to motivate them to improve. Sometimes our list of wrongs includes more serious offenses. Raising latch-key kids, marrying abusive stepfathers, or having an addiction problem of our own are some reasons we moms feel the added burden of responsibility for our child's addictions. I would be stopping short if I said we have little or no influence on our children and the decisions they make. But at some point, they become adults who are responsible for their own lives. Instead, we view them as children and treat them as if they cannot make their decisions without our input. This dysfunctional mother-child relationship is a breeding ground for guilt and shame. But instead of justifying or making excuses for our behavior, we can break free from our guilt by confessing to the Lord that we do not always trust Him with the lives of our children and asking for His forgiveness.

Once we ask Jesus for forgiveness, we must receive His forgiveness once and for all. No returning to ruminate over our sin again and again. Just because we don't feel forgiven doesn't mean we aren't forgiven. The Bible teaches us in 1 John 1:9 that *"if we confess our sins, Jesus is faithful and just to forgive us and to cleanse us from all unrighteousness."* There is no need to forgive ourselves or keep asking Jesus for forgiveness, because once He forgives us, it is done. We have only to accept His priceless gift of grace.

THE JOURNEY FROM GUILT TO GRACE

Guilt isn't the only emotion we experience on our journey from guilt to grace, is it? How about powering through with grit when we feel like giving up? Or the grief we feel as we mourn the death of all the dreams we had for our struggling children? The emotional ups and downs feel like an out-of-control roller coaster we can never get off. Our momentary joy breaks are fleeting, sustaining us only until we come to the next drop, and our world falls out from under us once again. We fight with every ounce of our strength, only to have it fail us. We grow weary of drying our tears and donning a fake smile before stepping out the door each day. Everyone says we are so strong, but except for the grace of God, we would collapse out of sheer exhaustion. The Lord knows the toll all this has taken on us. He didn't create us to carry such a heavy load. Instead, He calls us to come to Him to find rest. *"Come*

to me, all who labor and are heavy laden, and I will give you rest"
(Matthew 11:28 ESV).

For most of us, addiction affects our lives for many years, if not indefinitely. Anyone with an addicted child knows it is a marathon, not a sprint. Evil is relentless in pursuing its goal of complete annihilation of our children and everyone else in the family. When we find out our child's life is at stake, we rush onto the battlefield to save them. The problem is, we stay there. We never take a break. We ignore our Commander as He shouts above the chaos, "Retreat! Retreat!" Instead, with sheer grit and determination, we keep fighting. As we exhaust one weapon after another, our combat fatigue intensifies, but we still continue to press on…and on…and on. Until one day, we hit a wall, forcing us to stop dead in our tracks. Too weak to get back up, we lie there in a puddle of our own sweat and tears, feeling guilty for not being able to save our self-destructing child from themselves. When we finally have the strength to stand up and assess the collateral damage of a war we never should have been fighting alone, we see the destruction it has taken on our families, friendships, and our lives personally.

Grit is defined as "firmness of mind or spirit: unyielding courage in the face of hardship or danger."[42] One of its synonyms is "fortitude," meaning "a strength of mind that enables a person to encounter or bear pain or adversity with courage."[43] Both grit and fortitude have one thing in common. Each can describe human strength of mind or courage in the face of extreme adversity or danger. When fighting for our children, we have two choices-we can either fight with all **our** strength, or we can fight with **God's** strength. If we fight with our own strength, it will eventually give out. How often I started off fighting for my son and doing everything in my power to save him, only to burn out from sheer exhaustion. I either ended up physically ill or so emotionally depressed and anxious that I felt like calling it quits. Thankfully, just because we are worn out doesn't mean we have to give up. When we are fighting for our children and for our families, it's God's grace that strengthens us and helps us carry on.

> "You then, my son, be strong in the grace that is in Christ Jesus." (2 Timothy 2:1 NIV)

Along with fighting with all our grit, most of us moms will also admit to having feelings of deep grief. For those of us whose children are still alive, our grief differs from those whose child has passed away. Because I have not lost a child, I cannot comprehend the all-consuming sorrow felt by a grieving mother who daily must face life without her son or daughter. If this is you, precious mom, I pray our Lord will comfort you and give you a peace that passes all understanding.

For the rest of us, our grief expresses itself differently. Because our children are still alive, we have hope. But this hope does not negate the intense grief we are living with. When someone we love is physically alive, but no longer emotionally or relationally part of our lives, we suffer a unique type of loss called "ambiguous loss." Dr. Pauline Boss, Ph.D, an educator and researcher who coined the term, wrote that:

> "human relationships are ruptured indefinitely by ambiguous loss, causing trauma and frozen grief." [44]

This is an unresolved grief that occurs when we are stuck in ambiguous loss with no end in sight. As Christian moms whose hope is in the Lord, it's hard to wrap our minds around the idea of being frozen in our grief. Yet that's exactly what we are experiencing: a deep loss and grief that doesn't change while our children remain stuck in their addiction.

Day after day, we face the uncertainty of an unknown future for our children. As their moms, we want to believe if we have enough faith, pray hard enough, and stay in a perpetual state of spiritual warfare, we can guarantee our child will eventually have victory over their addiction. We strive to remain faithful, but when we wake up crying after yet another sleepless night worrying about our child's safety, we truly grasp the depth of our grief. We grieve for every second we've lost with the son or daughter we once had, yet are unsure we will ever have again. How do we get over this paralyzing grief and stay hopeful for our children's lives and futures?

Only by the Grace of God.

On our journey between guilt and grace, it's normal to vacillate between these intense feelings of grit and grief. Depending on what we are facing with our addicted child, we will either stand up and fight or break down and sob. I have done both...many times. I am grateful for God's gift of grace, aren't you? Because of His love for us, we can confidently approach the Lord in our weakest moments, assured He will show us mercy and grace when we need it most.

> "Let us then with confidence draw near to the throne of grace, that we may receive mercy and find grace to help in time of need." (Hebrews 4:16 ESV)

Grace is God showing us His kindness and giving us what we don't deserve. Mercy is God being compassionate towards us and not giving us what we deserve. We need both, don't we? On the days when I accuse Him of not caring about me or my child, I need His mercy. For the times when He pours out His kindness towards me and I don't even acknowledge Him, I need His grace. To receive both, we will need to come out from behind the shadows of our guilt and confidently approach the throne of grace, the throne of Jesus. Are you willing? Can you run to your Father instead of bolting for the door to make another go at trying to fix things yourself? Can you go to Him, kneel at His feet, and admit your powerlessness to save yourself or your child? Can you ask for His mercy? Can you receive His grace? At His throne is where this exchange takes place, our guilt for His grace.

We have reached a crossroads on our journey. May I be direct? You now have a decision to make about where you will go from here. Most likely, you picked up this book because, like me, you've lived with overwhelming feelings of guilt long enough. You may be feeling ready to break free from your guilt and bask in Christ's forgiveness. Exhausted, you no longer have the energy to power through, doing things your own way with grit, sheer will, and determination. You desire to feel the Lord's healing balm of mercy wash away your grief. And you are finally ready to step into His grace.

Or, while you relish the idea of breaking free from guilt, perhaps you are unsure of what these changes will mean to your relationship with your son or daughter. You may be more comfortable keeping things as they are, remaining on the same path you've walked on for years, and waiting for your child to change first. It's not an easy decision, although it is an obvious one. Stepping into grace requires absolute surrender on your part. You will be venturing into uncharted territory. Are you ready to make a fresh start? Are you ready to be a new creation? Are you ready to be transformed from guilt to grace? If your answer is "Yes," let your transformation begin.

TRANSFORMED BY GRACE

Do you remember the hit show from the early 2000s called "Extreme Makeover"?[45] The contestants signed up to appear on the show, hoping to win an extreme body makeover that included plastic surgery, cosmetic dentistry, LASIK eye surgery, radical diets, fitness, a fresh hairstyle and makeup, and a new wardrobe. After months of starvation diets, hours spent in the gym, surgery and recovery, they would step onto the stage a whole new person from head to toe, literally unrecognizable to their family and closest friends. While the show focused on the woman's outward beauty, it did nothing to address her underlying issues, such as a lack of confidence or low self-esteem. What if, instead, they focused on her inner beauty and the transformation of her heart? The show probably would have been canceled in the first season! In a society where our outward appearance is everything, Jesus always looks at our inward beauty from His eternal perspective.

"Do not let your adorning be external—the braiding of hair and the putting on of gold jewelry, or the clothing you wear—but let your adorning be the hidden person of the heart with the imperishable beauty of a gentle and quiet spirit, which in God's sight is very precious." (1 Peter 3:3-4 ESV)

While it's good to care for our outward appearance, these verses encourage us to focus on where our true transformation takes place: the hidden person of the heart. Unlike the women on Extreme Makeover, whose results were only temporary, our heart transformations will last forever. Reflect on what it would look like for you to be truly transformed. What would change about how you think, feel, and live your life? What is something you would release, once and for all? It's hard to imagine how spiritual transformation can produce a lasting change in us, but isn't that what it's all about?

Before addiction ransacked my life, I thought the Lord had already accomplished most of His major reconstruction in my heart and mind years before. I knew I had a few rough edges that needed smoothing out, some personality quirks that required a little refining. But I convinced myself that most of the finishing touches were simply cosmetic.

The belief that God and I were "okay" was not based on my thinking I had life all figured out. I was too insecure to believe that. It's just that for a few years things seemed to go smoothly for me. I was living the status quo and cruising through life without too many obstacles getting in my way. While I was grateful for God's goodness in my life, I started taking my blessings for granted, and my spiritual growth waned because of it.

When our lives are good, we can get a bit too cozy and think we are exactly where God wants us. Because He is blessing us, we must be doing it right. But that's not always the case. When things are going our way and life is easy, we risk falling into spiritual laziness, even apathy. It's tempting to start to think and act independently of God. This shift in our attitudes is most likely unintentional, but it's human nature to become prideful and start doing life our own way.

Enter the suffering. And then the beauty.

As silver is refined in the heat of a fire, so the Lord refines us in the heat of our adversities. Like clay that is formed under the pressure of the potter's hands, Jesus forms us under the pressure of our sufferings. As wood is shaped with each whittle of the sculptor's knife, so the Holy Spirit shapes us in our afflictions.

In the hands of its artist, each piece of raw material is transformed from the ordinary into the extraordinary, resulting in vessels of beauty. And like these works of art, we are being refined and formed and sculpted into something beautiful in our Master's hands. But the truth is, while we long for imperishable beauty, being transformed hurts. In our lives, we will experience times of deep suffering, pain, and sorrow. And sadly, too often, these intense trials enter by way of those we love most, the ones we would sacrifice everything to protect.

It's hard to accept that living in a fallen world brings with it this much hardship and heartbreak. We strain to wrap our heads around the idea that good and evil can coexist on the same planet at the same time. But for Jesus, the world would perish under the weight of its own sin. Because we live in this sin-filled world, we suffer. Thankfully, because of God's grace, as His children, we won't suffer much longer. We carry in our hearts the hope of eternal glory. It is this hope that transforms us from brokenness to beauty.

"And after you have suffered a little while, the God of all grace, who has called you to his eternal glory in Christ, will himself restore, confirm, strengthen, and establish you." (1 Peter 5:10 ESV)

But the question of "how" still lingers in the forefront of our minds. How does the Lord transform us, especially when our child is spinning out of control and self-destructing? What is our part in our transformation? Are we just supposed to sit back, do nothing, and wait? Not at all. We take part in our transformation as we cease striving and start claiming God's promises. This verse reminds us that after we have suffered a little while, Jesus will restore, confirm, strengthen, and establish us. These words are rich in promise. The Lord Himself will complete and perfect us. He will make us strong and able to stand. He will make us mobile and fully functioning. Jesus will establish us, secure us, and keep us grounded. We don't have to fix ourselves. We don't have to try harder. Nor do we need to wait to get to Heaven for Jesus to transform us. He is making us beautiful in the midst of our brokenness right now, today. Our part is to trust Him with the process.

When the Holy Spirit transforms us by His grace, we are no longer the same person. Because of grace, our sins are forgiven, our minds are renewed, our hearts are regenerated, and we are empowered to change. How is that for a transformation?

> "And we all, who with unveiled faces contemplate the Lord's glory, are being transformed into his image with ever-increasing glory, which comes from the Lord, who is the Spirit." (2 Corinthians 3:18 NIV)

When we are transformed by His grace, we are forever changed. We can love freely and deeply even though we risk having our hearts broken. We can hope for a miracle even when it looks like our hopes might be dashed. We can have a faith that moves mountains when unbelief surrounds us. And we can rejoice in hope because Jesus is our hope. That's what God's transforming grace does in our lives. It makes us new. Then, when others look at us and ask how we can be so joyful amidst deeply trying circumstances, we can smile and answer, "Because Jesus has transformed me by His grace."

Mom, as we near the end of our journey together, my prayer for you is that you will know how very loved you are by our Lord and Savior. This is my prayer for your son or daughter as well. May they know the love of Jesus and find healing and freedom in His presence. As we close, my prayer and proclamation over you and your child are found in the book of Psalms.

> "I believe that I shall look upon the goodness of the LORD in the land of the living! Wait for the LORD; be strong and let your heart take courage; wait for the LORD!" (Psalm 27:13-14 ESV)

Reflection Questions

1. Have you struggled with unforgiveness towards your child, others who have hurt you, or yourself? Explain.

2. How has what you've learned about forgiveness in this chapter affected how you will forgive your offenders?

3. Along with feelings of guilt, have you also experienced grit and grief? Explain how you have coped with your child's addiction in both cases.

4. In what ways has God transformed you by His grace? How will this transformation help you in your relationship with your son or daughter?

From One Grace Girl to Another

I am grateful for God's grace towards me. To be honest with you, I still question why He called me to write this book. The words I've penned have been tested in the fire of adversity. At times, I have failed to practice what I preached. There were days I was close to calling it quits, pleading with Him to send someone else, someone better qualified, someone whose faith remained strong as they battled for their child's life. Instead, He strengthened me to persevere and encouraged me to carry on.

While Jesus has blessed me with the gift of endurance, I often grew weary as I wrestled with the words He called me to share and those I would have rather kept to myself. But He reassured me that these are not my words you are reading, anyway. They are His. And His word never returns void. It always accomplishes His purpose (see Isaiah 55:11).

On our journey from guilt to grace, we can have the faith to believe Jesus will accomplish His purpose in our lives even when we feel unworthy or underqualified. Our role is to trust and obey Him in the process. Then, as transformed grace-girls, we can boldly deliver this message of hope and healing to other guilt-ridden moms who need to be transformed.

As you embark on your journey, my prayer is that guilt will no longer have a hold on you. Instead, may you bask in His glorious grace.

"For from his fullness we have all received, grace upon grace." (John 1:16 ESV)

A Prayer for Our Children

*D*ear Lord Jesus,

We pray for our struggling children who are bound by addiction and life-destructive behaviors. They are hurting, confused, and wandering far from You. Some have rejected their faith, while others have never known You as their Lord and Savior. We pray for their salvation and spiritual healing. May they know Your love for them. We pray against the lying words of the enemy as he hisses in their ear that no one, not even God, can love them. May they know Your unconditional love for them as written in John 3:16, *"For God so loved the world, that he gave his only Son, that whoever believes in him should not perish but have eternal life."*

We ask You to set them free from their strong physical desire for drugs. May they find victory and freedom from these strongholds through You, Jesus. May they surround themselves with fellow believers who will encourage them in their faith. We pray that they will be men and women of noble character, honoring You with their thoughts, words, and actions. We pray they will have a hunger for Your Word and will grow in wisdom and understanding as they read it.

May our children understand their identity is found in You. We pray they will embrace the gifts and talents You have given them. May they use their gifts for Your glory as they seek to help others. May they not look to the world to fill the voids in their lives but know that You are the source of everything they want and need.

Lord, we pray our children will see their bodies as temples of the Holy Spirit. May they cherish them and take care of their physical and emotional health. We pray our children will have sound minds and experience healing from any damage that occurred while abusing drugs or other substances. We pray they will not continue to harm their bodies, but will desire to live long and healthy lives.

We pray our children will be strong and able to resist temptation. May they have the power to say "No" to sin as they lean into Your strength. May our children be brave and not fear when trials come their way. We ask You to protect them from the enemy who seeks to kill and destroy their lives. May they be firm in their faith as they put their trust in You. We pray our children will be humble and teachable. May they resist pride and the need to do things their own way. May they always desire to honor You as Lord of their lives.

As their moms, we ask You to give us wisdom to know how to pray for our children. May we have the faith to walk in obedience to Your will and not get in the way of the work You are doing in their lives. May we always look to You as we hope for their freedom, healing, and transformation. Lord, we surrender our beloved children to You, trusting that You have a good plan and purpose for their lives. We receive and believe Philippians 1:6 that says, *"And I am sure of this, that he who began a good work in you will bring it to completion at the day of Jesus Christ."*

In Jesus' name, we pray.

Amen.

Recommended Reading

Addictions: A Banquet in the Grave by Edward T. Welch

Boundaries by Dr. Henry Cloud and Dr. John Townsend

Christian Families in Recovery: A Guide for Addiction, Recovery & Intervention Using God's Tools of Redemption by Robert Tucker and Stephanie Tucker

Counting Spoons: A Memoir of Heroin, Heartache, and Hope by Kathryn Mae Inman

Freedom from Addiction by Neil T. Anderson and Mike & Julia Quarles

Good Boundaries and Goodbyes by Lysa TerKeurst

Jesus and the Addict by Dr. Pam Morrison

Letting Go: Rugged Love for Wayward Souls by Dave Harvey and Paul Gilbert

Moments of Clarity: Wisdom from the Father of a Prodigal by Tom Yohe

Prodigals and Those Who Love Them by Ruth Bell Graham

Setting Boundaries with Your Adult Children by Allison Bottke

Sexpectations: Helping the Next Generation Navigate Healthy Relationships by Barb Winters

Still Standing After All the Tears by Valerie Silveira

Still Standing After All the Tears Workbook: Faith in the Battle Edition by Valerie Silveira and Dawn R. Ward

The Heart of Addiction: A Biblical Perspective by Mark E. Shaw

The Hope of A Homecoming: Entrusting Your Prodigal to a Sovereign God by Brendan O'Rourke, PH.D. and DeEtte Sauer

The Parent's Battle Plan: Warfare Strategies to Win Back Your Prodigal by Laine Lawson Craft

The Power of Praying for Your Adult Children by Stormie Omartian

When You Love a Prodigal: 90 Days of Grace for the Wilderness by Judy Douglass

You Are Not Alone: Hope for Hurting Parents of Troubled Kids by Dena Yohe

Acknowledgments

*T*o my husband and best friend, Steve. Thank you for your support throughout this journey. Seriously, as my biggest cheerleader, you made sure I didn't quit when I felt like giving up. I am grateful for your insight and wisdom as I wrote and rewrote this book. Thank you for believing in this message and for reminding me to trust the Lord with His message. I love you always and forever.

To my sons, Kyle and Matthew. Thank you for trusting me to share your stories. You are amazing men who have fought hard, worked hard, and loved hard during the highs and lows of your lives. I am honored to be your mother and to be on this journey with you. I am in awe of your strength of character and determination to beat the odds and prove that with God all things are possible. Words can not express the love I have for each of you.

To my daughter, Jadyn. You are my silent warrior. Your love for Jesus is reflected in the sweetness of your personality and your devotion to your family. Thank you for reading my words and finding my typos. You are a blessing to me. Love you, my sweet girl.

To my family, my father, brother, and sister, Kenzie, Jamie, and Travis. Thank you for being there for me. We have weathered many storms in this life, but we have always stuck together as a family. Thank you for supporting me as I share pieces of our story, trusting that it will help someone else heal and have hope. I love you all.

To those who have already passed on, my mother, Gloria, and my stepmother, Barbara. Thank you for always loving and standing by our family. You inspire me to do the same. I miss you both more than you know.

To my sister from another mother, Jennifer. Thank you for being my sweet friend since we were eleven years old. You have been a mighty prayer warrior for me and for my family. I am blessed to have you as a friend who daily reminds me I am a daughter of the King. Love you always.

To all the friends and family who have been with me on this journey. Thank you for being the blessings you are to me. You offered support, love, and a shoulder to cry on. I love and appreciate you all.

To the administrators of Christian Moms of Addicted Children. Thank you for your faithfulness to serve Jesus Christ by serving the women of our community. You are all dear friends to me, and I am sincerely grateful for each of you. Our Lord knew what He was doing when he brought us together. I love you all very much.

To the members of Christian Moms of Addicted Children. Thank you for being part of my story. I had no idea when the Holy Spirit nudged me to start our group that we would become a family. You are some of the bravest women I have ever had the honor of knowing. Words are not enough to express how grateful I am for each of you and for your prayers and support throughout the years. God bless you all.

To my friend, Valerie. Thank you for getting me out of my shell and writing again. God brought us together to share hope with the world. What an honor to serve alongside you. Love you, my friend.

To the counselors, therapists, first responders, medical professionals, and total strangers who helped us on our journey. I can't thank you enough for doing what you do. You've been there when our family needed you more often than you can imagine. Thank you for stepping into the Lord's calling for your lives. I am forever grateful to each of you.

To those called to minister and care for our addicted loved ones and their families. Thank you, thank you, thank you! Words are not enough to express my gratitude for what you do. Thank you for helping heal broken hearts and lives as you share the love of Jesus with those who are hurting.

To my November 2022 hope*books cohort buddies. Thank you, friends, for loving my book as much as you loved your own. You each encouraged and supported me (and each other) as we laughed, cried, and prayed together on this exhausting, yet joyous journey. Thank you for celebrating each other the way you do. Your dedication and devotion don't go unnoticed! I love you all.

To the staff of hope*books. Thank you for all you did to make this book possible! How grateful I am for your expertise in the areas of publishing, editing, proofreading, formatting, and moral support! The education and support you provided made me a better writer. Thank you all.

To my book endorsers. Words are not enough to express my gratitude for the support and kindness you have shown me. When I asked for your endorsements, I did so because you each have blessed my life tremendously through your ministries. Thank you for taking the time to read part or all of my manuscript and pen your words with careful thought and consideration. With all my heart, I thank you.

To my beta reader friends. How can I thank you for all you did to make this book better? You were willing to have the hard conversations with me. Because of your sincere desire to help me write a book that will truly change lives, you were willing to be honest with me, even when it was difficult for you. I couldn't have done it without you. Thank you from the bottom of my heart.

To all my sister bloggers and writers and podcasters who became dear friends along the way. Thank you for believing in me and inviting me to share with your readers, listeners, and followers. When I didn't believe my words needed to be shared, you all did. I am forever grateful for each of you.

To Ellie and Callie, my sweet little dogs. Thank you for being my constant companions on this journey. You sat with me as I typed every word. You snuggled with me when I cried. You brought me up when I was feeling down. I am convinced you have little angel wings hidden under all that fur!

To Jesus, my Lord and Savior. I saved the best for last, but You will always be first in my life. Thank You for calling me to follow You and allowing me to serve You. I am forever grateful.

> "He saved us and called us to a holy life—not because of anything we have done but because of his own purpose and grace." 2 Timothy 1:9a (NIV)

Citations

1   https://al-anon.org/blog/al-anons-three-cs/

2   "Blame Game." *Merriam-Webster Dictionary* https://www.
merriam-webster.com/dictionary/blame%20game#:~:text=-
noun,%E2%80%A6. Accessed 10 March 2024.

3   Graham, Billy. "10 Quotes from Billy Graham on Truth."
Billy Graham Library, Accessed 10 Mar. 2021, https://bil-
lygrahamlibrary.org/blog-10-quotes-from-billy-graham-on-
truth/.

4   NIDA. "Drug Misuse and Addiction." *National Institute
on Drug Abuse*, Accessed 5 Jan. 2024, https://nida.nih.
gov/publications/drugs-brains-behavior-science-addiction/
drug-misuse-addiction.

5   Talcherkar, Anjali. "The 5 Reasons Addicts Tend to Lie."
Addictions.com, https://www.addictions.com/blog/the-hon-
est-truth-why-addicts-lie/. Accessed 14 Mar. 2024.

6   Volkow, Nora D., et al. "Neurobiologic Advances from the
Brain Disease Model of Addiction." *New England Journal
of Medicine*, 28 Jan. 2016, https://www.nejm.org/doi/
full/10.1056/nejmra1511480. Accessed 14 Mar. 2024.

7   Maté, Gabor. *The Myth of Normal: Trauma, Illness & Healing in a Toxic Culture*. Avery, 2022.

8   Shaw, M. *The Heart of Addiction: A Biblical Perspective.* Bemidji: Focus Publishing, 2008, 2018.

9   Welch, Edward T. *Addictions: A Banquet in the Grave, Finding Hope in the Power of the Gospel.* Phillipsburg: P&R Publishing, 2001.

10 Keller, T. *Counterfeit Gods: The Empty Promises of Money, Sex, and Power, and the Only Hope that Matters.* New York City: Penguin Books, 2009.

11 "Codependency." *Merriam-Webster Online Dictionary*, https://www.merriam-webster.com/dictionary/codependency Accessed 18 June 2024.

12 Bible Hub, Strong's Concordance #8582. *Bible Hub*, https://biblehub.com/hebrew/8582.htm. Accessed 18 June 2024.

13 "Boundary." *Merriam-Webster Online Dictionary*, Merriam-Webster, https://www.merriam-webster.com/dictionary/boundary/. Accessed 18 June 2024.

14 Cloud, H. and Townsend, J. *Boundaries: When to Say Yes, How to Say No to Take Control of Your Life.* Grand Rapids. Zondervan, 1992

15 Cloud, H. and Townsend, J. *Boundaries: When to Say Yes, How to Say No to Take Control of Your Life.* Grand Rapids. Zondervan, 1992.

16 *Bible Hub*, Strong's Concordance #2256, https://biblehub.com/strongs/hebrew/2256.htm.

17 Terkeurst, L., *Good Boundaries and Goodbyes: Loving Others Without Losing the Best of Who You Are.* Nashville: Nelson Books, 2022.

18 Anderson, N. and Quarles, M. and J. *Freedom from Addiction: Breaking the Bondage of Addiction and Finding Freedom in Christ.* Ventura: Regal Books, 1996.

19 *Bible Hub*, Strong's Concordance #5331, *https://biblehub. com/greek/5331.htm.*

20 Vines, W. E., M. A. Entry for 'Sorcery' Vine's Expository Dictionary of NT Words, https://www.studylight.org/dictionaries/eng/ved/s/sorcery.html

21 Smith, C. *Biblical Counseling: A Topical Index for Christian Living.* Costa Mesa: The Word for Today, 2016.

22 *Bible Hub*, Strong's Concordance #G570, https://biblehub. com/strongs/greek/570.htm.

23 *Bible Hub,* Strong's Concordance #4102, https://biblehub. com/greek/4102.htm.

24 *Bible Hub*, Strong's Concordance #1411, https://biblehub. com/greek/1411.htm.

25 *Bible Hub*, Strong's Concordance #3875, https://biblehub. com/greek/3875.htm

26 Huiskes, Katherine. "*Timeline: The September 11 Terrorist Attacks.*" Miller Center. https://millercenter.org/remembering-september-11/september-11-terrorist-attacks/ Accessed 14 March, 2024.

27 Harvey, D. and Gilbert, P. *Letting Go: Rugged Love for Wayward Souls.* Grand Rapids: Zondervan Publishers, 2016

28 *Bible Hub*, Strong's Concordance #26, https://biblehub. com/greek/26.htm.

29 *Bible Hub*, Strong's Concordance #1680, https://biblehub. com/greek/1680.htm

30 *Bible Hub*, Strong's Concordance #5485, https://biblehub. com/greek/5485.htm.

31 "Conviction." *The Holman Bible Dictionary.* https://www. studylight.org/dictionaries/hbd/c/conviction.html.

32 *Bible Hub*, Strong's Concordance #1651, https://biblehub.com/greek/1651.htm.

33 *Bible Hub*, Strong's Concordance #181, https://biblehub.com/greek/181.htm.

34 *"Trauma."* APA Dictionary of Psychology, American Psychological Association, n.d., *https://dictionary.apa.org/trauma*.

35 Hide-and-Seek

36 Edward Shillito, *"Jesus of the Scars"*; as cited in D. A. Carson, *How Long, O Lord?* Grand Rapids: Baker Books, 1990.

37 *Bible Hub*, Strong's Concordance #1680, https://biblehub.com/greek/1680.htm.

38 *Bible Hub*, Strong's Concordance #2617, https://biblehub.com/greek/2617.htm.

39 *Bible Hub*, Strong's Concordance #5046, https://biblehub.com/greek/5046.htm.

40 *Bible Hub*. Strong's Concordance #4161, Bible Hub, https://biblehub.com/greek/4161.htm

41 "Guilt." *Merriam-Webster.com.* https://www.merriam-webster.com/dictionary/guilt/.

42 "Grit". *Merriam-Webster.com.* https://www.merriam-webster.com/dictionary/grit). Accessed 26 March, 2024.

43 "Fortitude." *Merriam-Webster.com.* https://www.merriam-webster.com/dictionary/fortitude Accessed 26 March, 2024.

44 Boss, Pauline, Dr. *Ambiguous Loss*. Ambiguous Loss, https://www.ambiguousloss.com/, Accessed 26 Mar. 2024.

45 Extreme Makeover. Directed by John Smith, Performances by Actor/Actress Name, ABC Studios, 2002. *IMDb*, https://www.imdb.com/title/tt0364807/.